Soviet Policy
Toward Black Africa

Helen Desfosses Cohn
foreword by
John N. Hazard

The Praeger Special Studies program—utilizing the most modern and efficient book production techniques and a selective worldwide distribution network—makes available to the academic, government, and business communities significant, timely research in U.S. and international economic, social, and political development.

Soviet Policy Toward Black Africa
The Focus on National Integration

PRAEGER SPECIAL STUDIES IN INTERNATIONAL POLITICS AND PUBLIC AFFAIRS

Praeger Publishers New York Washington London

PRAEGER PUBLISHERS
111 Fourth Avenue, New York, N.Y. 10003, U.S.A.
5, Cromwell Place, London S.W.7, England

Published in the United States of America in 1972
by Praeger Publishers, Inc.

© 1972 by Praeger Publishers, Inc.

Library of Congress Catalog Card Number: 72-75686

Printed in the United States of America

Black Africa in the early 1960's looked to
Soviet leaders like the opportunity for which they
had been waiting since the 1920's. At the end of
the 1960's, the dreams had vanished, or almost so.
The hopes of the Communist International expressed
in its program of 1926 had been dashed. A quick
jump from colonial status as tribally oriented communities to a form of social organization inspired
by what Lenin had created in Russia seemed out of
the question. While some of the newly independent
states were moving in a direction that their leaders
described as incorporating socialist elements, none
were following precisely the Soviet model.

To Soviet policy-makers, the role the Soviet
Union could and should play in African development
became a matter of great importance. Lenin had expected that the awakening peoples of Asia and
Africa would become the reserves of his revolutionary movement. Even though many Soviet leaders
reared in his shadow adhered to his long-range program, realism was a part of their training. While
Lenin had dreamed, he had preached also the need to
retreat at times when the dreams were beyond the
possibility of realization. Africa in the late
1960's was clearly out of the question as an arena
for experimentation with Soviet models, but should
Soviet leadership abandon its early expectations
completely?

Helen Desfosses Cohn believes that the answer
to this question is to be found in the minds of the
Soviet Union's Communist Party leadership in view
of their experience. The Soviets had approached
Africa with high hopes, because their experience
was minimal during the colonial period. They knew
little of African reality but theorized a great

deal. They plunged into what had been the Belgian Congo, expecting to be able to find the right men and to shape the future in the Soviet image. Their experience was disappointing.

Nikita Khrushchev began to shift his ground in light of a new appreciation of African reality. He sought to play for time while supporting nationalists regardless of their social orientation. Above all, it seemed desirable to keep the former colonial powers from reasserting their authority and help the new nations develop. Without development, independence of policy and possible support for Soviet policies were out of the question. Yet, development without thought to future political choices was not a part of the Soviet thought process.

While the militant thinking of the days of the Communist International had long since faded away, the Soviets had not become simple pragmatists. They thought of themselves as men of revolutionary principle, forced at times to retreat in the face of reality, but lacking in cynicism. It might take more time than the men of the 1920's had supposed, but the game might still be won. Stalin's policy of building socialism in one country, even if unaccompanied by similar efforts elsewhere, had created an attitude that called for giving primary attention to Soviet development. In short, the hope of expansion of the Soviet system was relegated to the background when it conflicted with the needs at home. Yet, it was never forgotten, for development at home was always linked with the hope, no matter how remote, that a strong Soviet Union would emerge as the motherland of revolutionary socialists, to which they could turn for inspiration, technical advice, financial aid, and perhaps ultimately substantial military support for indigenous movements toward the left. Soviet policy toward black Africa was shaped within the confines of this thinking. It was a combination of hope and growing appreciation of realities.

Dr. Cohn's study has caught the essence of the problem facing the Soviet leaders. She has laid

the groundwork for an understanding of what may be
expected in the future, as the forces of revolutionary idealism and reality play upon each other. She
has traced their interplay over a decade, relating
this interplay not only to what was being learned
in Africa but to what was occurring within the USSR
itself. She finds the leadership of Brezhnev and
Kosygin and their colleagues beset with problems
and lacking unity of purpose. She finds that in
this situation Africa was given a lower position on
the Soviet scale of foreign policy priorities, although it was by no means forgotten.

To those seeking an understanding of Soviet
policy--past, present and future, in a part of the
world that often seems enigmatic to Americans limited to reading the headlines telling of coups and
countercoups, conflicts of left and right and bloc
alignments--Dr. Cohn's analysis will serve as a key
to unlock a continent.

November, 1971   John N. Hazard

This study analyzes Soviet theories regarding the nation-building process in black Africa. This topic received little attention in the USSR until 1962-63, when the Congo problem flared into a serious crisis, again involving United Nations troops supported by the United States and other Western powers. The Katanga secession finally was ended, but thoughts of the example this might set for other regions or ethnic groups, the disruption of African solidarity that the secession entailed, and the opportunity that it provided for expansion of Western influence persisted in Soviet circles. The Congo crisis indicated that black African ethnic conflicts were potentially an interstate problem. Therefore, Soviet Africanists were encouraged to investigate the nature of these problems and possible solutions.

The objectivity of these studies was questionable. Nikita Khrushchev's renewed optimism--in the face of several successes--about the prospects for the diffusion of socialism throughout black Africa persuaded him that the states of national democracy could, by virtue of their noncapitalist orientation, resolve the national question. Soviet research remained colored by these official preconceptions.

In September, 1964, Dr. Ivan Potekhin, the rigid and formalistic Director of the Africa Institute, died. One month later, Khrushchev was deposed. The way was cleared for a new approach to black Africa by scholars and officials. With the 1966 declaration by the Brezhnev-Kosygin regime that domestic development was the primary internationalist duty of the USSR, official interest in black Africa declined. Among scholars, debates on the applicability of the Soviet nation-building model to Africa flourished.

Certain features of the Soviet nation-building
model, such as a dominant nationality group, had
long been recognized as inapplicable to most black
African countries. However, the relevance of major
social, political, and economic aspects has been
the subject of detailed discussion for many years.
On almost all aspects, the progression of Soviet
analysis has been fairly uniform: from a positive
assessment during most of the Khrushchev era to one
characterized by pragmatism and flexibility.

For example, under the category of social measures to promote national integration, the Soviet
model emphasized the development of universal education and a single national language and the eradication of religion and traditional cultural values.
Toward the end of the Khrushchev period, Soviet Africanists began to state that the implementation of
these measures in Africa would produce serious political problems. These analysts now urge the adoption of a gradual approach toward social reform.

The evolution of Soviet views regarding the applicability of political and economic aspects of the
Soviet integration model exhibits a similar trend
toward flexibility. Thus, Africanists now acknowledge the progressiveness of certain military leaders, and state that the vanguard party used as a
governing and integrative mechanism in the USSR
might degenerate under black African conditions
into an institution possessing little contact with
the masses. They continue to urge the replacement
of mass parties with vanguard institutions, as the
latter could better implement a planned industrialized economy. However, they admit that the installation of both a socialist-type economy and political party in black Africa will be a very slow process.

Although traditional ideological tenets have
been retained on certain issues, such as the right
of a nation to self-determination, increased pragmatism and objectivity of Soviet African Studies
have been allowed by the Brezhnev-Kosygin regime
because they conform to certain official policy

objectives. These include reducing the economic
drain represented by Africa, promoting stability in
the sub-Sahara region in order that official attention can be concentrated on the Middle East and
Southeast Asia, and establishing strong government-
to-government relations with the maximum number of
African states.

ACKNOWLEDGMENTS

I should like to thank Professor Alphonso A. Castagno, Director of the Boston University African Studies Center and the first reader of this work, for having stimulated my interest in the study of African integration and for his kind assistance throughout my doctoral training. To Professor Walter Clemens, Jr., who was always willing to discuss the Soviet aspects of the manuscript and who served as its second reader, I also wish to express my gratitude.

I sincerely appreciate the help and friendly encouragement given to me by Susan Jo Gardos, Librarian of the Harvard University Russian Research Center. For financial assistance and kind support, I am particularly grateful to the Coretta Scott King Foundation of the American Association of University Women.

Finally, I owe more than I can express to my husband, Daniel, to whom this book is dedicated. His willingness to set aside his own work to support me throughout the research and writing of this study will always be remembered warmly.

CONTENTS

Chapter   Page

Soviet Policy
Toward Black Africa

There are several themes current in Western literature regarding the nature of African Studies in the USSR. These themes stress the subservience of this discipline to the dictates of an official party, the obligation of Soviet Africanists to determine the applicability of the Soviet model of development, and the lack of objectivity that characterizes Soviet writing on black Africa. It is the purpose of this book to investigate the validity of these assumptions by studying Soviet writings on nation-building efforts[1] in black Africa. This topic is an important one, not only because it has never been thoroughly analyzed, but also because its concerns are mirrored in the extensive corpus of Western writings on African national integration --writings that provide non-Soviet Africanists with a convenient basis for understanding and evaluating the Soviet efforts. Furthermore, because the general theories of national integration have ramifications for Soviet domestic policy and for Moscow's foreign policy goals, a survey of Soviet writings on the African national question provides insights into the objectivity of Soviet African Studies and the relationship of scholarship to policy.

It is my hypothesis that the decade of the 1960's has witnessed an increasing impartiality in the works of Soviet Africanists. Admittedly, these scholars are often charged with developing theoretical justifications for policy lines deemed in the best interests of the Soviet state. However, the role of Soviet African specialists in the formulation of policy is not completely passive. Certain American scholars deny an active policy-making role to Soviet academics or ideologues, stating that

> their prime function is to explore, explain and embroider policies adopted or in preparation. Thus, one is unlikely to arrive at a very satisfactory appreciation of Soviet foreign policy in the Third World from a reading of published sources--if only because these are the work of men who stand on the lower fringes of the decision-making process.[2]

This view is challenged by Sovietologists of the "pressure group" school who "hypothesize that the more problematic and technical the issue, the more dependent on expert judgment elites will be. Consequently, they will be more likely to consult policy groups, who will thereby be more influential on such issues."[3]

The truth undoubtedly lies somewhere between these two positions. Thus, although one cannot credit Soviet Africanists with a major role in policy formulation, one can quite properly speak of their pivotal role in this process. At times, they provide theoretical elaborations for previously adopted policies, while at other times their work may spark a policy reappraisal, for example, regarding the role of the working class in Africa. Thomas Thornton speaks of a "feedback" between policy and scholarship in the Soviet Union,[4] and this term perhaps best captures the essence of the relationship.

This feedback is probably stronger in the field of African Studies than in many other scholarly realms because of the relative newness of both Soviet political involvement in Africa and concentrated academic research on black African problems. It is true that Soviet Africanists have been officially organized as a professional group only since 1959, the year that the Africa Institute was established in Moscow, and that, as a result, they do not represent a strong inbred corps of influential academics able to ensure that their views carry equal weight with those of others involved in the policy-making process. However, because it is really only the decade of the 1960's that has witnessed a major Soviet official interest in Africa, it is probable that the government has not had time to assemble an influential corpus of bureaucratic experts on Africa. Therefore, it still must rely heavily on the scholars.

Indeed, there is a discernible connection between the topics of investigation pursued by Soviet Africanists and the concerns of officialdom. For example, Nikita Khrushchev's statement to the 1959 Twenty-first Congress of the Communist Party of the Soviet Union (hereafter cited as CPSU) that "problems of social development" in underdeveloped countries "must be analyzed more deeply,"[5] signaled the beginning of serious Soviet research into the relatively neglected area of African nationalism. This connection was emphasized by Dr. Ivan Potekhin, then Director of the Africa Institute:

> It is a matter of honor for our orientalists that they should produce works that would promote a further creative elaboration of questions connected with the foreign policy of the Soviet Union in relation to the countries of the East.[6]

Nor has this connection weakened over the years. The years 1965 and 1966 saw the outbreak of serious

tribal dissension in many parts of Africa (most notably in Nigeria) and manifestations of national
communism within the Soviet bloc itself. The stub-
bornness of these problems and the lack of agreement among Soviet officials regarding the correct
policy prompted an appeal at the 1966 Twenty-third
Congress of the CPSU to

> ethnographers and social scientists
> to study processes of social develop-
> ment which hitherto has not been ade-
> quately done. . . . As far as prob-
> lems of multi-national social rela-
> tionships in the various spheres of
> social development are concerned, and
> the process of mutual closer associa-
> tion and merging of nationalities,
> such questions have not had adequate
> attention paid to them. As a result,
> the basic principles of the origins
> and formation of new international
> structures and the distinguishing
> characteristics of overall communist
> culture have not been scientifically
> posited.[7]

This appeal, in turn, evoked a new series of articles in such journals as Voprosy istorii (Problems
of History) on the theory of a nation and a serious
discussion by scholars of the obstacles to national
integration in Africa.

Another indication of the close connection be-
tween African research and African policy in the
USSR is provided by an analysis of the political
backgrounds of prominent Soviet Africanists.
Vasily Solodovnikov, current director of the Africa
Institute, is head of the Soviet-African Friendship
Association and played a major role in Soviet ac-
tivities in the United Nations Trusteeship Council.
B. G. Gafurov, editor-in-chief of Azia i Afrika
Segodnia (Asia and Africa Today) and director of
the Institute of Asian Peoples (until 1960, the
Institute of Oriental Studies), is the Tadzhik

Party Secretary. B. N. Ponomarev, a specialist on
the international communist movement and a frequent
contributor to Africanist journals, has been a Secretary of the Central Committee of the CPSU since
1961.

Ponomarev represents a tradition in Soviet
historical writing increasingly found in African
Studies: collective scholarship. This tradition
is important in establishing the relationship between official Soviet views and the work of academics. For, as Lowell Tillett has observed:

> Ordinarily one would not look for of-
> ficially sancioned interpretations in
> textbooks and survey histories, but
> the Soviet practice is unusual in this
> respect. Since the middle 1930's
> textbooks and survey histories have
> been prepared by whole brigades of
> historians who have worked together
> to produce acceptable interpretations.
> Preliminary drafts have been widely
> read and criticized, sometimes by
> party officials themselves. These
> general works, therefore, can be said
> to be the historians' best estimate
> of the favored interpretation.[8]

Solodovnikov has edited several volumes on Africa,
and in view of his political links, it is probable
that the opinions expressed in these works corre-
spond very closely to official persuasions.

However, this analysis of the connection between policy and scholarship in Soviet African
Studies should not lead one to conclude that little
impartial research is being conducted. Five factors have aided Soviet Africanists in maintaining
relatively higher levels of objectivity than scholars in other social science disciplines: (1) lack
of agreement among Soviet officials regarding bloc
nationality policy: (2) Moscow's relatively late
start in its involvement in African politics;

(3) its desire to impress African leaders and to attain a prominent position in international Africanist forums; (4) collective leadership; and (5) the downgrading of Africa on the Soviet scale of foreign policy priorities under Leonid Brezhnev and Aleksei Kosygin.

The different views held by Soviet leaders on the correct course of bloc nationality policy means that scholars have been able, if not encouraged, to explore the many facets of the national question at home and abroad. Because no clear formulations have been released regarding the development of the nation or the role of nationalism within the Communist system, Africanists have been freed somewhat from the typical constraints of adapting their views to the single body of ideas normally associated with Marxist-Leninist ideology.

A second factor involved in a discussion of the objectivity of Soviet African Studies is the Soviet Union's belated recognition of the importance of Africa to the government's quest for an expanded world role. After a short period (1955-59) of believing that their experience elsewhere was sufficient to enable them to cope with African realities, Soviet leaders placed an urgent emphasis on developing major institutes for African research. Africa was moved out of its subordinate slot as a division of Oriental Studies and accorded an important position as an independent area of concentration. The events of 1960, "Africa Independence Year" (so named because so many countries achieved their independence then), served only to intensify this new Soviet dedication.

The Soviet Union began its involvement in Africa with the same air of exaggerated optimism that characterized early attitudes in the United States. Soviet authorities were no less certain of the possibilities of creating socialist societies there than their American counterparts were of creating models of Western-style democracy. In fact, both great pow-

ers cited Nigeria as the potentially most rewarding
area of concentration. The 1960 Soviet statement
that "independent Nigeria may well contribute
greatly to the cause of universal peace and to the
liberation of the whole of Africa from the colonial
yoke"[9] has more than one parallel in U.S. literature on Africa.

This optimism naturally affected the attitude
of Soviet Africanists. This influence was especially pronounced in discussions of African nation-
building. The view of Potekhin that national consolidation was inevitable in Africa dominated the
few articles that were written on the topic in this
early period.

However, neither the paucity of literature nor
the optimistic aura were to remain characteristic
of Soviet scholarship on African integration. The
crisis in the Congo impressed upon Soviet authorities the tenuousness of national unity in many
African countries and the extreme volatility of
intertribal relations. It also demonstrated the
ramifications of African nation-building problems
for Soviet foreign policy. For, if one of the primary aims of this policy was to increase Soviet influence in Africa, any conditions that caused an
increase of Western involvement and, potentially,
influence could not be tolerated. Furthermore, the
Congo crisis led to a deep fissure in African anti-
imperialist unity, a fissure that the Soviet authorities feared could become permanent if subjected to continued stress.

A consequence of this Soviet assessment of the
implications of the Congo events was that Soviet
Africanists began intensive research into the problems of national integration in Africa. However,
although the influence of Potekhin's view of the
"inevitability" of African success in nation-
building was diminished, the fact that Khrushchev
continued to proclaim that Soviet prospects in
Africa were excellent (his persistence in this

attitude was partly attributable to the ideological
challenge posed by the Communist Chinese) meant
that African Studies would continue to reflect the
optimistic view. It was not until the advent of
Brezhnev and Kosygin that Soviet African Studies
attained a higher degree of impartiality.

Nevertheless, the Khrushchev regime was concerned that Soviet Africanists attain a respected
position in international circles. Just as it is
important to the prestige of the Soviet Union to be
well represented at science conferences and col-
loquies around the world, so it is important that
Soviet African scholars be elevated to key positions in the various international conferences and
associations. In fact, African Studies symposiums
have an added dimension in that they are usually
well-attended by African governmental personnel.
This often provides Soviet scholars with an opportunity to expound ideas that could be used for
propaganda purposes later.

Initially, this concern with propaganda value
was quite strong. However, Soviet authorities soon
realized that although the polemical, anti-Western
tone of the work might be momentarily appealing to
the Africans, it would not serve to divert their
attention permanently to the so-called Soviet model
of development. Potekhin acknowledged this in 1962:

> If previously Soviet scholars have
> studied the economics of the enslaved
> African nations with the aim of dis-
> crediting the colonial system, nowa-
> days this on its own is not sufficient.
> Of course, the discrediting of colo-
> nialism will continue to be important,
> inasmuch as there remain colonial
> countries in Africa, and inasmuch as
> colonial exploitation remains in a
> new guise in many countries which
> have gained political independence.
> But the discrediting of colonialism
> must be supplemented by the study of

> the prospects of developing the na-
> tional economies of the African
> countries.[10]

This statement heralded a new emphasis on field research, and a drive to reduce Soviet dependence on
Western data. More importantly, the ratio of po-
lemics to analyses steadily decreased.

That the quality of Soviet analysis has greatly increased since the mid-1960's is attributable,
directly or indirectly, to the collective leadership ushered in by Brezhnev and Kosygin in October,
1964. Collective leadership implied that the facade of monolithism would remain but that those in
power would be more accessible to different groups.
Because the two leaders (as well as a number of
their more influential colleagues, such as N. V.
Podgorny and A. P. Kirilenko) have different outlooks on foreign policy matters and priorities,
they would not only be receptive to persuasive arguments from like-minded scholars but, in some
cases, may seek them out. Each scholar can lend
his views on the aura of dogma, for, as one Third
World specialist frankly admitted, "In Lenin's
works there is such a wealth of wisdom that each
new epoch will find something new in them."[11]

Because collective leadership spawns a situation in which different politicians, jockeying for
power, are seeking bases of support and legitimization for their own particular views, scholars are
free to tailor the theories of Marxism-Leninism to
fit a variety of purposes. They can develop a
theory to explain a phenomenon, embellish it with
appropriate quotes from Marx or Lenin, and present
it with an authoritativeness equaling that of
scholars with completely contradictory opinions.[12]

The field of African Studies is especially
open to such manipulation, as there are certain
topics on which official pronouncements have never
been made. Thus, Vladimir Kudriavtsev, a political
commentator for _Izvestia_ and a credible exponent of

the official Soviet view on many issues of contemporary African politics, often refers to the arguments of well-meaning, "progressive" (that is, Soviet) scholars--arguments that he then proceeds to
refute.[13] The fact that reference to these clashes
of opinion is made in the pages of the official Soviet government organ implies that they are taking
place at a high level and/or that they have come to
the attention of top government figures.

In recent years, fewer and fewer topics of
African affairs have been the focus of official Soviet pronouncements--evidence of a downgrading of
Africa on the scale of Soviet foreign policy priorities. The current leadership has been too preoccupied with the Middle East, Southeast Asia, Communist China, and internal problems to be able to
expend time and money on black Africa. In addition, the "low profile" accorded Africa by the administration of Richard Nixon increases the proba-
bility that this situation will continue--barring,
of course, another crisis on the scale of the Congolese civil war. (In fact, a crisis could result
from the increased East-West involvement in Somalia,
an involvement that can be traced partly to the
country's strategic importance vis-à-vis the Middle
East.)

The significance of the apparent diminished
Soviet official interest in Africa for this study
is two-fold. First, it implies that Soviet academic literature must be relied on increasingly. Second, it implies that these academic works can be
expected to be more objective, because official
interest in African Studies--and, accordingly, official control--has declined.

Thus, the writings of Soviet Africanists and
my interviews with Soviet scholars have been the
main source of material for this study, because
both their reliability and significance have been
steadily increasing and because "policy only appears in its proper dimensions when the thinking
behind it is understood."[14] It is the purpose of

this volume to analyze the ideas of Soviet academic
specialists regarding the problems and prospects of
national integration in contemporary black Africa
and to relate these theories to the policies adopted by the Soviet government toward the many concrete aspects of this issue. Such an examination
and comparison, it is hoped, will prove to be a
contribution to African Studies in the West by providing the necessary material for understanding the
Soviet Union's approach to the problems of African
national development. Perhaps with this knowledge,
the reader may gain a better perspective on the Soviet Union in world affairs.

The book is divided into eight chapters. Chapter 2 treats early Soviet views* regarding black
Africa, views mainly related to the role that this
area could play in the anti-imperialist struggle.
Chapter 3 analyzes the progression in Soviet official thinking from an almost total concern with the
ramifications of black African developments for Soviet foreign policy to a realization of the necessity to understand the nature of African domestic
problems. The more immediate solutions to African
centrifugalism proposed by Soviet authorities (fo-
cusing on their educational, social, and cultural
suggestions) are studied in Chapter 4, while Chapter 5 discusses the Soviet evaluation of the political obstacles and incentives to African nation-
building efforts. Chapter 6 is concerned with economic development, deemed by Soviet Africanists the
ultimate long-range solution to national disintegration. Chapter 7 analyzes the increasing Soviet
realism regarding the potential role of various social strata in accelerating the nation-building

---

*When the term "Soviet views" is used, it could
refer to the opinions of the government, the party,
the scholars--or all three--unless otherwise specified. Furthermore, it must be recognized that,
among Soviet scholars, there is often no consensus
or unanimity.

process. Finally, Chapter 8, the conclusion, sum-
marizes the results of this study, and analyzes the
reasons for, and implications of, increasing Soviet
pessimism regarding the prospects for rapid national development in black Africa.

NOTES

1.   There are no exact translations in Soviet
social science terminology for the English terms
"nation-building" and "national integration."
However, phrases such as <u>splochenie natsii</u> (the
consolidation of the nation), <u>formirovanie natsii</u>
(the formation of the nation), and <u>razreshenie
natsional'nogo voprosa</u> (the resolution of the national question) appear to be synonymous with the
English expressions. Although a noted American political scientist recently proposed that the more
accurate terms "state-building" and "state integration" be substituted for "nation-building" and "national integration," the latter will be retained
here for purposes of correspondence with the terminology employed by both Soviet and Western Africanists. Cf. Walker Connor, "Ethnic Nationalism as a
Political Force," <u>World Affairs</u>, CXXXIII, 2 (September, 1970), 91-93.

2.   John Keep, "The Soviet Union and the Third
World," <u>Survey</u>, 72 (Summer, 1969), 29.

3.   J. Schwartz and W. Keech, "Group Influence
and the Policy Process in the Soviet Union," <u>Amer-
ican Political Science Review</u>, LXII, 3 (September,
1968), 848.

4.   Thomas Thornton, ed., <u>The Third World in
Soviet Perspective</u> (Princeton, N.J.: Princeton
University Press, 1964), p. x.

5.   "Khrushchev's Report to the Congress," in
Leo Gruliow, ed., <u>Current Soviet Policies III: The
Documentary Record of the Extraordinary Twenty-first</u>

Communist Party Congress (New York: Columbia University Press, 1960), p. 60.

6. I. I. Potekhin, "XXI S"ezd KPSS i zadachi vostokovedeniia" ("The 21st CPSU Congress and the Tasks of Oriental Studies"), _Problemy vostokovedeniia_, 1 (1959), 22.   (Italics mine.)

7. Speech by I. I. Bodiul, First Secretary of the Communist Party of Moldavia, _Shorthand Report of the XXIIIrd CPSU Congress_, Vol. I; cited in Mary Holdsworth, "Current Soviet Theories on State Integration in Africa and in the Homeland," in Kenneth Kirkwood, ed., _African Affairs_, No. 3 (London: Oxford University Press, 1969), p. 51.

8. Lowell Tillett, _The Great Friendship: Soviet Historians on the Non-Russian Nationalities_ (Chapel Hill: University of North Carolina Press, 1969), p. ix.

9. O. Orestov, "Vseobshchie vybory v Nigerii" ("General Elections in Nigeria"), _Sovremennyi vostok_, 4 (1960), 54.

10. I. I. Potekhin, "Report on the Third Coordinating Conference of Soviet Africanists," _Vestnik Akademii Nauk SSSR_, 7 (1962), 110; quoted in "Some Features of Soviet African Studies," _The Mizan Newsletter_ (hereafter, _Mizan_), IV, 9 (October, 1962), 2-3.

11. K. Ivanov, "The National-Liberation Movement and the Non-Capitalist Path of Development," _International Affairs_, 9 (September, 1964), 35.

12. William Zimmerman, _Soviet Perspective on International Relations 1957-1967_ (Princeton, N.J.: Princeton University Press, 1969), p. 287; also pp. 9-16.

13. See, for example, V. Kudriavtsev, "Unity and Separatism," _Izvestia_, November 17, 1967, p. 2; trans., _Current Digest of the Soviet Press_ (hereafter, _CDSP_), XIX, 46 (December 6, 1967), 16-17.

14. "Editorial," <u>Mizan</u>, VIII, 1 (January-February, 1966), 1.

2

AFRICAN NATIONALISM
AS A WEAPON IN
THE ANTI-IMPERIALIST STRUGGLE:
A SURVEY
OF SOVIET ATTITUDES

TWO ASPECTS OF AFRICAN NATIONALISM

Nationalism has both an internal and an external connotation: Internally, it applies to the
feeling of involvement and attachment to a particular state; externally, it involves the ideology of
a political movement dedicated to the establishment
of an independent and sovereign state. Soviet ideologues have only recently come to appreciate the internal ramifications of African nationalism. However, they have long supported it in its external
aspects, because they sensed that it could be a
valuable weapon in the anti-imperialist struggle. It
is important that their views on this be analyzed,
for such an analysis reveals the way in which their
initial narrow perspective widened only gradually
to disclose the necessity of understanding the many
facets of African domestic politics.

SOVIET EMPHASIS ON THE EXTERNAL
ASPECT OF NATIONALISM, 1917-63

Despite increasingly heated debate in Soviet
official and academic circles regarding the definition of a nation and the related right of a polity

to claim independent state existence, the formulation proclaimed by Stalin in 1913 still obtains.
Thus, in the absence of any official agreement on a
revised version, the nation is characterized as "an
historically evolved, stable community of people
formed on the basis of a common language, territory,
economic life, and psychological makeup manifested
in a common culture."[1] Because Soviet ideology is
viewed as a unified whole, this definition should,
in theory, be applied to African as well as Soviet
national groups. However, since only a few African
states could satisfy this Stalinist formulation, it
has often been overlooked. When it is deemed in
the best interests of the Soviet state to champion
the cause of an African country, whether a country
has had a national (that is, anti-imperialist) movement becomes more important than objective characteristics in establishing its right to be called a
nation.[2]

Such circumvention of ideology stems primarily
from the Soviet wish to undermine Western power in
a certain area as a prelude to the establishment of
its own influence. The countries of black Africa
have provided Moscow with this opportunity in two
forms: (1) the independence movements; and (2) the
struggles for territorial unification. Regarding
the former, nationalism as a manifestation of the
desire to be free from imperialist domination was
appraised positively by Soviet ideologues because
it could assist in effecting the downfall of the
world capitalist system. Thus, in Lenin's view,
the national independence movements would compel
the imperialist powers to expend energy and resources
to combat them; more importantly, if these uprisings
were successful, the Western countries would be denied a major source of raw material and an important
market for manufactured goods. The profits of monopoly capitalist firms would fall, with the result
that they could no longer seduce the workers with
high wages and benefits. The level of class consciousness of the proletariat would rise, increasing the likelihood that this all-important class
would join in the struggle for a worldwide socialist victory.

Thus, although Lenin perhaps never fully understood the complexity of the nationalism issue in its
ramifications for Soviet domestic policy, he had a
clear appreciation of the way it could be manipulated to advance Communist power at home and abroad.
In fact, he later shifted the emphasis of communism
from concentration on the political potential of the
industrial proletariat to the role that national
self-determination could play in hastening the col-
lapse of the capitalist system--a shift that several
Western Sovietologists see as one of the prime indicators of Lenin's political genius:

> He wove the twin themes of national
> self-determination and internation-
> alism into a common policy fabric.
> . . . He predicted that all nations
> would in time be united in a common
> bond of brotherhood--communism. How-
> ever, since they first had to be free
> from the domination of "imperialist"
> powers, national self-determination
> for all nations had to be supported.[3]

It was hoped that any measure which weakened
the power of the capitalist nations would redound
to the benefit of the socialist system. Thus, in
the early years of Bolshevik power (1917-21), when
the exigencies of the war-communism period demanded
that the Soviet government secure the support of
their national minorities--especially the Muslims,
who occupied a pivotal geographical position--the
famous "Appeal to All the Toiling Muslims of Russia
and the Far East" was issued. This "Appeal" had a
two-fold purpose: (1) It was designed to assure
the key minorities within the Soviet Union that the
Bolsheviks were proponents of the free development
of all nationality groups; and (2) it was aimed at
the worldwide extension of the revolution in order
to reduce the threat to the Soviet government posed
by the imperialist powers.

Similarly, in the early 1920's, the Kremlin
supported Kemal Ataturk's campaign against Britain,
France, and Greece. This policy was motivated by

security concerns but was "rationalized as support
of a nationalist, anti-imperialist regime which
could be transformed into a socialist government at
a later stage."[4] That the reasons given were truly
a rationalization can be seen from the fact that
Moscow supported the Kemalist government even though
it stringently suppressed the activities of the
Turkish Communist Party. In spite of this contra-
indication, Moscow continued to strive for friendly
relations with Turkey, as well as with other Eastern
governments, such as Persia and Afghanistan. The
level of their revolutionary potential was irrelevant; Moscow needed "pawns" in its diplomatic struggles with the West.

Lenin was aware, however, that Communist support of nationalist movements in the East might have
consequences similar to those that occurred in the
Soviet Union. In other words, he feared that these
nationalist movements might become ends in themselves, eluding Communist domination completely, or
that manifestations of national communism might ensue. Therefore, he warned repeatedly that nationalist movements should be supported only in so far as
they were a means to effecting the triumph of socialism.[5] He opposed any attempts to present nationalism as a vehicle for setting forth the tenets
of Marxism, or worse, to unite Marxism with nationalism. For, although Lenin was not averse to using
nationalism as a stepping-stone to the consolidation of Communist power, he insisted that, in the
final analysis, "Marxism is irreconcilable with
nationalism, be this the most 'just,' 'pure,' subtle
and civilized. Marxism puts forward in place of any
form of nationalism--internationalism."[6]

In the early years of his rule, it appeared
that Stalin would continue this opportunistic,
though wary, approach toward Third World nationalism. In 1924, for example, he declared that, although national movements must be examined "not
from the formal point of view, not from the point
of view of abstract rights," he would continue to
evaluate their contribution to "the interests of

the World revolutionary movement."[7] After establishing this premise, Stalin proceeded to apply it
to the Egyptian independence struggle, performing
one of the few analyses of African politics to be
found in Soviet literature before 1955. He insisted
that

> the struggle that the Egyptian mer-
> chants and bourgeois intellectuals
> are waging for the independence of
> Egypt is objectively a <u>revolutionary</u>
> struggle, despite the bourgeois ori-
> gin and bourgeois title of the lead-
> ers of the Egyptian national movement
> and despite the fact that they are
> opposed to socialism; whereas the
> struggle that the British "Labour"
> Government is waging to preserve
> Egypt's dependent position is for
> the same reason a <u>reactionary</u> strug-
> gle, despite the proletarian origin
> and the proletarian title of the mem-
> bers of the government, despite the
> fact that they are "for" socialism.[8]

The Egyptian liberation movement, which began in
1918, would cause Great Britain to divert its attention from the Russian borderlands to Africa, while
a nationalist victory would deprive her of one of
her main colonial dependencies. In other words,
the struggle would aid the Soviet Union both directly and indirectly; therefore, its revolutionary
character was assured.

However, 1928--the year that the Sixth Comintern Congress was convened to examine the prospects
for world revolution--also marked the beginning of
Stalin's collectivization campaign. The two events
were closely related, for the new emphasis on the
industrial development of the Soviet Union necessitated a shift in the international policy priorities
of the Soviet government and its foreign policy arm,
the Communist International. The overriding goal of
both became the development of the Soviet Union, the

construction of "socialism in one country." Of
course, there were strong objections, notably by
Maurice Thorez, spokesman for the French Communist
Party, and Palmiro Togliatti, founder of the Communist Party in Italy, who felt that the Comintern
should recognize the Soviet Union as the platform
of world revolution, but not as its center. These
concerns about the fate of Communist parties in
other countries were overridden, however. The Program of the 1928 Comintern Congress declared, without any evidence of compromise, that

> the Soviet Union is the true father-
> land of the proletariat, the strongest
> pillar of its achievements, and the
> principal factor in its emancipation
> throughout the world. This obliges
> the international proletariat to for-
> ward the success of socialist construc-
> tion in the Soviet Union and to defend
> the country of proletarian dictator-
> ship by every means against the at-
> tacks of the capitalist powers.[9]

World revolution was of secondary importance; the
primary task now was the defense of the Soviet
Union--a country ravaged by economic dislocations
and completely disillusioned by the failure of the
Chinese revolution and the rupture in diplomatic relations with China and Great Britain.[10] The Soviet
government felt threatened both from the East and
the West--a feeling that was intensified by knowledge of its own internal weakness and by expectations of Western hostility. Moscow's response to
this situation was a two-sided one. First, on the
level of diplomatic relations, it appealed for
"peaceful coexistence of the two social systems" in
order to secure "conditions of peace and freedom
from external disturbances for our socialist construction," and in order to expand trade relations
with the West.[11] Second, the Comintern, meanwhile,
was instructed to emphasize the inevitable clash between the two systems. Stalin had to justify the
need for sacrifices at home and his decision to

subordinate the goal of world revolution to the development of the power of the USSR; for these purposes, the theory of capitalist encirclement was
ideal. Furthermore, Stalin did not trust the bourgeois leaders in the capitalist world or the underdeveloped countries. He urged the adoption of a
"class against class" approach according to which
the local Communist parties would no longer cooperate with bourgeois leaders, but rather, would attempt to discredit them. They were instructed to
pass to "independent leadership . . . along the entire front against social-democracy," including
Africa, which Molotov specifically mentioned.[12]

During the 1928-to-mid-1930 period, the Communists were hampered in their efforts to manipulate
the national-colonial question in Africa by two related propositions: (1) that the national bourgeois leaders could direct the liberation movements
only along the path of national reformism--an ideology that would redound to the benefit of the imperialists; and (2) that the national question for blacks
throughout the world was, and must be, subordinate to
the class issue. Thus, they tried to unite the
blacks of Africa with those in the United States in
one proletarian movement. This effort, concretized
in such manifestations as the International Conference of Negro Workers, convened by the Comintern
Executive Committee in Hamburg in July, 1930, reflected a deep lack of knowledge of conditions in
the underdeveloped areas. The Comintern was aware
of the popularity of Marcus Garvey's "Back to Africa" movement among certain American blacks and of
the number of adherents to George Padmore's Pan-
Africanist teachings that could be found on both the
American and African continents; therefore, it was
assumed that this ideological kinship reflected a
more basic similarity of political conditions and political attitudes. For Garveyism and Pan-Africanism
were both separatist movements of sorts; both looked
to a special and unique role for the Negro state in
world politics. The Soviet Communists felt that the
success of either movement would cost them the allegiance of the blacks to the revolutionary struggle:

Garveyism would pursue the "political aim of divert-
ing the Negro masses from the real liberation struggle against American imperialism," while Pan-
Africanism might render the entire African continent
impervious to Communist penetration. Therefore, the
Comintern reminded its members that "a clear distinction" must be made between "the demand for
'right of self-determination' and the demand for
governmental separation." Furthermore,

> Negro Communists must <u>clearly dis-
> sociate</u> themselves from all bourgeois
> currents in the Negro movement, must
> indefatigably oppose the spread of
> the influence of the bourgeois groups
> on the working Negroes, . . . in or-
> der to guarantee the <u>hegemony of the
> Negro proletariat</u> in the national
> liberation movement of the Negro popu-
> lation, and to coordinate wide masses
> of the Negro peasantry in a steady
> fighting alliance with the proletar-
> iat.[13]

Early in 1931, Stalin set the International
Communist Movement on a zigzag course regarding national liberation revolutions that was to last
throughout the postwar period and was to result in
the loss by the Communists of any real influence in
the colonies. In 1931, Communist parties in the
colonies were ordered to disregard the national liberation cause in order to spotlight German and Japa-
nese aggression. From 1934 through World War II
(except during the Molotov-Ribbentrop Pact, 1939-41),
the Communist parties in the West aligned themselves
with bourgeois parties of the left and right to combat the threat of Fascism. The exigencies of the
struggle meant that the Third World was all but ignored. The Soviets did rouse themselves to protest
Mussolini's invasion of Ethiopia in 1935. That this
move was not motivated by any real respect for the
right of that country to independence, however, was
revealed by Stalin's apparent willingness during the
years 1939-41 to assign Ethiopia to Italy's sphere

of influence.[14] In 1947, the Cominform (Communist
Information Bureau) was established to replace the
Comintern, which had been abolished in 1943 in order to placate the Allies, among other reasons.
Its establishment heralded the adoption of a new
attitude toward international relations: The world
was divided into two hostile camps, and no nation
could claim to stand neutral in the struggle. The
Communist parties in the Third World were ordered
to sever all relations with bourgeois leaders and
to engage in an armed struggle to oust them from
power--a policy that alienated the masses, to say
nothing of their leaders. The Communists entered
the decade of the 1950's bereft of any influence
in the underdeveloped areas, their movement a vic-
tim of Stalin's concern to use colonial revolutions
to divert Western attention from his empire-building
objectives in Eastern Europe.[15] The national concerns of the colonial peoples had again been subordinated to the needs of Soviet power. The evidence
does suggest that, by 1952, Stalin realized that
communism had to devise a new approach toward nationalism if it were to gain any influence over the
developing nations; however, his old thought patterns resisted any sudden change. "Ignorance, ob-
stinacy, and an unrealistic reliance on the threat
of force [remained] Stalin's major failings"[16] regarding the role of nationalism in the international arena.

    Nikita Khrushchev, however, inaugurated a pol-
icy toward Third World nationalism based on a pragmatic assessment of the power of this movement.
The relative ease with which Moscow was able to use
the sale of arms to Egypt to thwart the consolidation of the Baghdad Pact indicated to Khrushchev
that a power vacuum existed in the Third World--one
that he might be able to exploit in the interests
of expanding Soviet power. Furthermore, the success of the 1955 Bandung Conference of Non-Aligned
Nations and the events of 1960--Africa Independence
Year--indicated the ability of Third World nationalism not only to diminish the power of the West but
also to affect the course of world politics through

its foreign policy variant, neutralism or nonalign-
ment.

    This very posture implied that the chances for
Soviet influence in the underdeveloped areas were
as good or better than those of the West, because
presumably these countries would welcome a force
that could balance the previously overwhelming power
of the capitalist states. However, neutralism also
implied a wariness lest any major power or ideology
assume undue influence. Because nascent local Communist parties would be immediately suspect and were
significantly weaker than the domestic nationalist
movements, Khrushchev resolved to use the latter as
a vehicle for Soviet expansion. Of course, he continued to proclaim the establishment of strong Communist parties as his ultimate goal. Nevertheless,
that he was more interested in Soviet than Communist
expansion can be deduced from his attitude toward
Nasser's imprisonment of the Egyptian Communist
leaders in 1958. He expressed his displeasure ver-
bally, but the fact that he took no reprisal steps
such as arms or aid limitation indicates his willingness to sacrifice the local Communist Party to
the diplomatic interests of the Soviet Union.

    This altered view of the impact of underdevel-
oped areas on international politics had great ramifications for the Soviet attitude toward the struggle of the African nations for independence. Whereas Stalin had mainly denied the validity of this
struggle, considering that, in a two-camp world, the
small nations could not really function as free
agents, the post-Stalinist leadership decided "that
the nationalist movements of Africa were essentially progressive and deserved support."[17] Indeed,
soon after Khrushchev assumed power, Potekhin (ap-
pointed Director of the Africa Institute in 1959)
used a statement attributed to Stalin to justify an
approach toward African politics basically antithet-
ical to that of the Stalinist era. He claimed that
Stalin's observation that, in the epoch of imperialism, the national question "has been turned into an
interstate matter, instead of just an intrastate

affair" meant that the (new) Soviet policy of regarding national movements as progressive was a
correct one.[18]

Of course, Khrushchev did follow Stalin's lead
in subordinating the interests of the colonial peoples to those of the Soviet Union; the essential
difference was that Khrushchev was alert to the opportunities presented by the African nationalist
movement, whereas Stalin's "two-camp" approach allowed for no such appreciation. Khrushchev was
ready to support African nationalism to the extent
that it hastened the downfall of imperialism; if,
on the other hand, the drive for self-determination
aided the imperialist cause, then it was strongly
rejected. R. Tuzmukhamedov explained this apparent
dualism in a 1963 book on the concept of national
sovereignty in international law:

> the right to self-determination is
> unconditional, but it is not ab-
> stract: Its sociopolitical and legal
> essence is the strengthening of peace
> on the basis of the sovereign equal-
> ity of all peoples. Therefore, any
> attempt to use this right to further
> nonpeaceful, aggressive, or reaction-
> ary goals is juridically and socio-
> politically inconsistent, as this in-
> evitably means the violation and per-
> version of the principle of self-
> determination.[19]

This dualism differs little from that discernible
in the writings of Marx. However, it is interesting to see Tuzmukhamedov's acknowledgment that it
was 1960 (to which the Soviets also refer as "Africa Independence Year"), which signaled the beginning of a completely new program in Soviet international law aimed at "the clarification and deepening of the understanding of national sovereignty."[20]

The need for this clarification--and the ambivalent purposes that it would serve--was underscored

by two prominent events of 1959-60: the drive for
the unification of British and French Cameroon and
the Katanga secession. Toward the former case, Soviet ideologues demonstrated great flexibility;
since the right to self-determination had traditionally been predicated upon a people's compliance with
the precepts of the Stalinist definition of a nation,
this definition was all but jettisoned completely.
For, although Soviet authorities acknowledged that
the two territories were populated by different
tribes and had never existed as a unified entity,
they proclaimed their support in the United Nations
for unification. Potekhin was called upon to justify this ideological departure, a task he fulfilled
by implying that it was "the will of the people"[21]
that was the dominant consideration in determining
the validity of a claim to national sovereignty.
In reality, Moscow's primary concern was whether a
national movement would further Soviet objectives
in West Africa. The Cameroon unification drive sat-
isfied this precondition in two ways: (1) It was
possible that the extremist Union des Populations
du Cameroun would be strengthened by merging with
the Cameroon Party, thereby making the new state
susceptible to Soviet influence;[22] and (2) in the
unified--and presumably, stronger--state, the power
of the British and/or the French might be diminished.

     In the case of the bid of the Congo's Katanga
Province to form a separate state, it was apparent
to the Kremlin leaders that such a turn of events
would not advance the cause of socialism. First of
all, it could be manipulated by the imperialist powers to reconsolidate their influence in South-
Central Africa. Secondly, it could lead to a situation of extreme political instability on the continent, one that could only disturb the delicate
balance of East-West power. Third, the issue of
"imperialist intervention" in the Congo only served
to intensify the split between the Brazzaville and
Casablanca countries, thereby decreasing the USSR's
chances of extending its influence over the continent as a whole. In view of these considerations,
Potekhin abandoned the flexible interpretation

devised to cover the Cameroon case; in fact, he now
declared that

> our understanding of the national ques-
> tion is that a nation has definite at-
> tributes, which are the result of its
> historical development and <u>cannot be
> created or destroyed by people's will</u>.
> Stalin defined these attributes as
> community of territory, of economic
> life, of language, and of culture.[23]

Of course, the possibility exists that the Russians
might have welcomed the Congolese crisis, if the
USSR could have profited from it. However, they
supported Patrice Lumumba. When he was assassinated
in February, 1961, they lost all hope of turning the
crisis to their advantage. They increased their efforts to defeat Moise Tshombe's movement--efforts
prompted by their realization that not all slogans
regarding the right to self-determination were directed against imperialism. Furthermore, the danger existed--especially in Africa--that these slogans could be used in the interests of tribalism,
thereby thwarting any real national movement.[24]

Tuzmukhamedov later expressed this in more formal terminology, declaring that, in a state that has
already won its independence, the sovereignty of national groups "comes out not as the right to national statehood but as the whole aggregate of popular-
legal means to guarantee real independence and national renaissance."[25] These groups could never
attain this "renaissance" in a country colonized by
the imperialists, but they could realize it in a
newly independent African state, irrespective of
the heterogeneity of its population or the artifi-
ciality of its boundaries. Soviet authorities typically lost no opportunity to attack the Western powers for their arbitrary partition of Africa. However, when they realized that any attempts at revision might produce chaos, they limited their dis-
approval of the Western actions to criticism rather
than counterproposals.

For Moscow, as always, was interested in the
African nationalist movement mainly as a wedge for
the expansion of Soviet influence. Nor did the Soviet Union hesitate to turn against this movement
when its actions might contradict Soviet interests.
In 1960, Khrushchev made it clear to the United Nations General Assembly that the Soviet Union would
not support the expansion of the U.N. Councils to
admit more African members, unless Communist China
were represented. Furthermore, he demanded that the
"universal" issue of disarmament take precedence
over the "local" issue of colonialism.[26] Then, in
September, 1961, Moscow announced its intention to
resume atmospheric nuclear testing on the eve of
the Belgrade Conference of Non-Aligned Nations, indi-
cating that the views of Third World nations were
secondary to the concerns of the Big Power struggle.
Finally, the Soviet refusal to offer any but the
most indirect support to colonial revolutions
against the Great Powers--for example, the Franco-
Algerian conflict--indicated that self-determination
was not a primary Soviet concern.

Nevertheless, Moscow would continue to lend
verbal support to the tenets of African nationalism
because of the devotion to this ideology evidenced
by the continent's statesmen and leaders. Thus, although Potekhin warned as late as 1962 that the African leaders might be "treacherous" enough to
equate their own interests with those of the nation
and then present the nation as a higher loyalty
than class,[27] this admonition was apparently an example of the lag time that often exists in the USSR
between diplomatic and party recognition, on the
one hand, and scholarly compliance, on the other.
For, in fact, Soviet diplomacy had been allying itself with the native African bourgeoisie since 1954--
an alliance whose importance was acknowledged by the
1959 Twenty-first Party Congress.[28] By early 1963,
Potekhin had revised his earlier remarks about the
counterrevolutionary potential of the African leaders. He now acknowledged the existence of a group
of leaders "which has mastered the scientific prin-
ciples of Socialism and is ready to devote all its
strength and knowledge for the good of its people."[29]

The modification of Potekhin's views mirrored, albeit belatedly, Khrushchev's departure from the negative tenets of the Stalinist era. He realized that the bourgeois leaders were the only group that had the support of the peasant masses and could "infuse the raw social materials of agrarian discontent, etc., with the organization and leadership necessary for their success."[30] He further acknowledged that, if the goal of expanding Soviet influence were to be fulfilled, the bourgeoisie--the ruling group in most countries on the African continent--would have to be courted assiduously.

The courtship had to be justified in ideological terms, especially because of the increasingly strident claims of the Communist Chinese to represent the true revolutionary interests of the Third World peasant masses. However, the results of these Soviet efforts at rationalization were rather convoluted. The first step was to stress the anti-imperialist aspect of African nationalism; the second was to identify the national bourgeoisie as the carrier of this tradition and, therefore, as the representative of the revolutionary (anti-imperialist) aspirations of the masses; the third and final step was to stress the socialist aspect of nationalism, thereby rendering it eminently worthy of Soviet support. Thus, in May, 1964, in a no less authoritative vehicle than an editorial in Kommunist, it was proclaimed that nationalism, if it is truly based upon patriotism, "must inevitably develop on the side of socialism."[31]

In sum, during most of the Khrushchev era, Soviet authorities stressed the "positive" or anti-imperialist aspect of African nationalism and modified their ideological views to include a more favorable evaluation of the role of the national bourgeoisie--the "vanguard" of the national liberation struggle. The effect of this new evaluation of African nationalism was also obvious in the policy sphere. The Soviet authorities, in an effort to take advantage of this new force, seemed to disregard their observations regarding its "negative" or national chauvinism aspect; they appeared

heedless of the fact that African nationalism could
represent an obstacle to the diffusion of communism
throughout the continent. As indicated above, their
short-range goal was to displace the Western powers
and spread Soviet influence in Africa. Therefore,
their policies apparently were directed at intensifying African nationalism, because this was the
most available vehicle for ousting the West. Also,
in line with Khrushchev's stress on "peaceful coexistence," this seemed the safest policy; the Soviet
Union could not be accused of openly inciting or
sponsoring these anti-Western manifestations, because it was, of course, only "indirectly" involved.

As a result of this assessment, Soviet historians were urged to help the Africans to discover
their glorious past and to investigate the distinc-
tively African aspects of their history and culture.
Soviet authorities were to denounce the results of
these efforts in later years as "manifestations of
national exclusiveness" and efforts to present a
"uniquely African path to socialism." However, during this period it was proclaimed that

> the task of Marxist Historians [is]
> to root out each and every falsifi-
> cation of African history, to help in
> the development of feelings of na-
> tional consciousness among the Afri-
> can peoples--that important factor in
> the struggle for independence and
> freedom.[32]

This emphasis extended through 1963, when Tuzmukhamedov, a specialist on the role of the nation in international law, declared that "this nationalism of sub-
jugated nations during the struggle against imperialism, for national independence, and a national
Renaissance has the support of all democrats and is
historically justified."[33]

1963--YEAR OF REAPPRAISAL

1963 signaled a shift in Soviet views regarding
the extent to which African nationalism could serve

as a vehicle for Soviet expansion. The intensification of the Congo crisis and the renewed U.N. involvement were instrumental in sparking this reappraisal. Yet, perhaps the dominant influence was
the increasing virulence of the Sino-Soviet con-
flict--a conflict that had two major ramifications
for Soviet African policy. The first was that
Khrushchev had to divert his attentions from Africa
to reconciling the problems within the Soviet bloc
itself. Another result was that Chinese charges of
Soviet revisionism regarding the role of the national bourgeoisie in the underdeveloped countries
forced Soviet ideologues to modify their views on
the entire national question in order to justify
their claims of continued ideological orthodoxy.

Therefore, the official Soviet view of the potential role of African nationalism underwent considerable modification. The appraisal of nationalism that appeared in the 1963 edition of Fundamen-
tals of Marxism-Leninism was appreciably more cautious than that which appeared in the 1960 edition;
furthermore, the later edition listed many negative
aspects not mentioned in 1960.[34] Even Tuzmukhamedov, who earlier proclaimed that Third World nationalism should be supported by all democrats, now
warned that the "class character" of the national
liberation movements must not be overlooked. He
stated that working-class leadership was preferable,
because the nationalism of even the most anti-
imperialist bourgeois governments could "intensify
the contradictions within the new state" and lead
to the "widening of agreement between the local
bourgeoisie and imperialism." If these were the
effects of nationalism, then it must be recognized
as "incompatible with democracy and with the principle of equality of rights of states, peoples, and
nations."[35]

The regime of Leonid Brezhnev and Aleksei
Kosygin continued this rather negative appraisal of
the role of African nationalism in international
affairs--that is, its potential as an instrument
for the advancement of Soviet state interests was
downgraded. For example, ideological efforts to

present the bourgeoisie as a possible vehicle for ushering in the noncapitalist era were considerably curtailed; also, the ideological position that support of Third World nationalism would accelerate the development of proletarian internationalism was abandoned. Thus, in 1965, it was predicted that

> if in modern conditions nationalism . . . is a uniting element in the national-liberation anti-imperialist movement, then by force of the frontal character of the opposition of all colonial peoples and young states, as well as all socialist countries, to imperialism, such "nationalism" cannot but become international. Moreover, the apparent paradox of such international "nationalism" is that not bourgeois or petty-bourgeois national egoism, but rather proletarian internationalism, will become more and more the factual ideological base of relations between peoples in the process of the struggle for a real guarantee of their national independence.[36]

However, by early 1966, the Soviets were stressing the "tendencies of national superiority and egoism" that were appearing not only within individual African nations, but that were leading to declarations of a "special" role for the whole continent. It was noted in Kommunist that

> these tendencies not only do not aid the interests of the future rapprochement of the national-liberation movement with other contemporary revolutionary forces, but also do not aid the strengthening of the anti-imperialist solidarity of the peoples of Asia and Africa. . . . Besides this, reactionary nationalism, as a rule, is inextricably connected with anticommunism.[37]

Thus, whereas their earlier view was that African
nationalism could be a stage in the development of
proletarian internationalism, Soviet authorities
now deemed it an obstacle to the creation of proletarian unity.

Brezhnev and Kosygin have continued to examine
the struggles of African national groups for self-
determination on the basis of their ramifications
for the power position of the Soviet Union.   In
fact, Soviet theorists now link the fate of these
struggles to the fortunes of the USSR.[38]   An obvious corollary to this "link" theory is that, if a
nationalist struggle strengthens the Soviet position, it is a positive phenomenon; if not, it must
be combated. The Biafran conflict has provided
Brezhnev and Kosygin with the most significant test
case for this proposition; the policy course they
adopted indicates their decision to maximize their
influence in Africa first and worry about the coin-
cidence of policy and self-determination theory
later. To support Biafra would have secured for
the USSR the allegiance of dissatisfied minority
groups on the African continent; however, the power
of most of these groups was even less than that of
the Ibos. On the other hand, aiding the Federal
Government would help the USSR to secure access to
the Nigerian market, to displace the British from
their dominant position in Nigerian politics, to ensure the identification of France with a losing
cause--a cause that was condemned by the Organization of African Unity, to impress governments
throughout black Africa, several of which are
threatened by secessionist tendencies similar to
those that devastated Nigeria, and, finally, to
gain some influence among the many military regimes
that today are such a persistent feature of African
politics. Furthermore, by aiding Nigeria in sub-
duing the Ibo rebellion, the USSR would increase
the chances of stability prevailing on the African
continent. The Soviet leaders are interested in
providing both theoretical and practical help to
the Africans to maintain this stability; their conflicts with Communist bloc countries, their involvement in the Middle East, and rising consumer demands

at home have persuaded them that their power resources cannot undergo further serious challenges
or strains.

NOTES

1.   Joseph Stalin, <u>Marxism and the National
and Colonial Question</u>, Marxist Library, Works of
Marxism-Leninism (New York: International Publishers, 1934), XXXVIII, pp. 5-8.   For a comprehensive
analysis of the current definitional debate, see
Grey Hodnett, "What's in a Nation?" <u>Problems of Com-
munism</u>, XVI, 5 (September-October, 1967), 2-15.

2.   Iu. Semenov, "Iz istorii teoreticheskoi
razrabotki V. I. Leninym natsional'nogo voprosa"
("From the History of the Theoretical Work of V. I.
Lenin on the National Question"), <u>Narody Azii i
Afriki</u>, 4 (1966), 128.

3.   Alvin Rubinstein, ed., <u>The Foreign Policy
of the Soviet Union</u> (New York: Random House, 1960),
pp. 342-43.   See also Cyril Black and Thomas Thornton, eds., <u>Communism and Revolution</u> (Princeton, N.J.:
Princeton University Press, 1964), pp. 417-48.

4.   Walter C. Clemens, Jr., "Soviet Policy in
the Third World: Five Alternative Futures," <u>Orbis</u>,
XIII, 2 (Summer, 1969), 478.

5.   See, for example, his speech to the Baku
Congress of Peoples of the East on November 22,
1919, V. I. Lenin, <u>Sochineniia</u> (30 vols; 3d ed.;
Moscow: Gospolotizdat, 1928-37), XXIV, p. 551;
cited in Alfred Meyer, <u>Leninism</u> (Cambridge, Mass.:
Harvard University Press, 1957), p. 154.

6.   V. I. Lenin, <u>Sochineniia</u>, XXIV, p. 131.
For a recent exposition of this thesis, see E.
Bagramov, <u>Natsional'nyi vopros i burzhuaznaia
ideologiia</u> (<u>The National Question and Bourgeois
Ideology</u>) (Moscow: Mysl, 1966).

7. Joseph Stalin, "Foundations of Leninism,"
Works (13 vols.; Moscow: Foreign Language Publishing
House, 1953-55), VI, p. 148.

8. Ibid., p. 149. (Italics in the original.)

9. Jane Degras, ed., The Communist International, 1919-1943, Documents (3 vols.; London: Oxford University Press, 1956-65), II, pp. 512-13.

10. Xenia Eudin and Robert North, eds., Soviet
Russia and the East, 1920-1927 (Stanford, Calif.:
Stanford University Press, 1957), p. vii.

11. "Press Statement by M. M. Litvinov on His
Appointment as Commissar for Foreign Affairs," re-
printed in Jane Degras, ed., Soviet Documents on
Foreign Policy (3 vols.; London: Oxford University
Press, 1951-53), II, pp. 449-50.

12. Address by V. M. Molotov to the Sixteenth
Party Congress (July 5, 1930), quoted in Xenia
Eudin and Robert Slusser, Soviet Foreign Policy,
1928-1934 (University Park: Pennsylvania State University Press, 1966), I, p. 63.

13. "Extracts from a Resolution of the ECCI
[Executive Committee of the Communist International]
Political Secretariat on the Negro Question in the
United States," October 26, 1930; reprinted in
Degras, ed., The Communist International, III, pp.
133-34. (Italics in the original.)

14. See Robert Legvold, Soviet Policy in West
Africa: 1957-1968 (Cambridge, Mass.: Harvard University Press, 1970), pp. 16-17.

15. Rubinstein, op. cit., p. 377.

16. J. M. MacKintosh, Strategy and Tactics of
Soviet Foreign Policy (London: Oxford University
Press, 1962), p. 71.

17. Legvold, op. cit., p. 19. See also, Walter Laqueur, The Soviet Union and the Middle East (London: Routledge and Kegan Paul, 1959), pp. 136-37.

18. I. I. Potekhin, "Zadachi izucheniia etnicheskogo sostava Afriki v sviazi s raspadom kolonial'noi sistemy" ("Tasks of Studying the Ethnic Base of Africa in Connection with the Fall of the Colonial System"), Sovetskaia etnografiia, 4 (July-August, 1957), 105.

19. R. Tuzmukhamedov, Natsional'nyi suverenitet (National Sovereignty) (Moscow: Izd'vo Mezhdunarodnik Otnoshenii, 1963), p. 17.

20. Ibid., p. 54.

21. I. I. Potekhin, "Bor"ba za vossoedinenie Kameruna" ("The Struggle for the Unification of the Cameroon"), Sovetskaia etnografiia, 5 (September-October, 1959), 63, quoted in George von Stackelberg, "Soviet African Studies as a Weapon of Soviet Policy," Bulletin of the Institute for the Study of the USSR, VII, 9 (September, 1960), 6.

22. Fritz Schatten, Communism in Africa (London: George Allen and Unwin, 1966), p. 110.

23. I. I. Potekhin, Africa's Future: The Soviet View, an abridgement of Afrika smotrit v budushschee (Moscow: Izd'zo Zostochnoi literatury, 1960), printed as a supplement of Mizan, III, 4 (April, 1961), 15.

24. These admissions by Potekhin are quoted in a transcription by R. Ismagilova entitled "Zasedanie uchenogo soveta instituta Afriki AN SSSR posviashchennoe problemam Kongo" ("A Meeting of the Scientific Council of the Africa Institute of the USSR Academy of Sciences Concerning the Problems in the Congo"), Sovetskaia etnografiia, 3 (May-June, 1961), 93.

25. Tuzmukhamedov, op. cit., p. 54; also G. Starushenko, Natsiia i gosudarstvo v osvobodaiu-shchikhsia stranakh (Nation and State in the Liberated Countries) (Moscow: Mezhdunarodnye Otnosheniia, 1967), p. 118.

26. S. Yakobson, "Russia and Africa," in Ivo Lederer, ed., Russian Foreign Policy (New Haven, Conn.: Yale University Press, 1962), pp. 486-87.

27. I. I. Potekhin, "Nekotorye problemy Afrikanistiki v svete reshenii XXII S"ezda KPSS" ("Certain Problems of African Studies in Light of the Resolutions of the 22d Party Congress of the CPSU"), Narody Azii i Afriki, 1 (1962), 10. See also "Nationalism: A New Soviet Appraisal," Mizan, IV, 3 (March, 1962), 5-12.

28. Leo Gruliow, ed., Current Soviet Policies III: The Documentary Record of the Extraordinary Twenty-first Communist Party Congress (New York: Columbia University Press, 1960), p. 201.

29. I. I. Potekhin, "On 'African Socialism,'" International Affairs, 1 (January, 1963), 75.

30. M. Watnik, "The Appeal of Communism to the Underdeveloped Peoples," in Berthold Hoselitz, ed., The Progress of Underdeveloped Areas (Chicago: University of Chicago Press, 1952), p. 162.

31. "Soiuz sil sotsializma i natsional'no-osvoboditel'nogo dvizheniia" ("The Union of Forces of Socialism and the National-Liberation Revolution"), Kommunist, 8 (May, 1964), 9, cited by Arthur Klinghoffer, Soviet Perspectives on African Socialism (Rutherford, N.J.: Fairleigh Dickinson University Press, 1969), p. 156.

32. G. A. Nabokov, "Bol'she vnimaniia voprosam istorii Afriki" ("Greater Attention to Questions of African History"), Voprosy istorii, 11 (November, 1961), 137.

33.　Tuzmukhamedov, op. cit., p. 9.　(Italics mine.)

34.　Klinghoffer, op. cit., pp. 176-79.

35.　Tuzmukhamedov, op. cit., p. 68.

36.　R. A. Tuzmukhamedov, ed., Organizatsiia Afrikanskogo edinstva (The Organization of African Unity) (Moscow:　Mezhdunarodnye Otnosheniia, 1965), p. 17.

37.　K. Brutents, "Voprosy ideologii v natsional'no-osvoboditel'nom dvizhenii" ("Questions of Ideology in the National-Liberation Movement"), Kommunist, 18 (December, 1966), 40.　See also Lev Stepanov, "The Future of Afro-Asia," New Times, 51 (December 22, 1965), 6-8; and "British Imperialism Sours Nigerian Conflict," TASS, June 7, 1969.

38.　Starushenko, op. cit., p. 52.

3

THE ROLE
OF NATIONALISM
IN THE AFRICAN
INTEGRATION
PROCESS

Whereas the concern of Khrushchev and his predecessors with advancing the interests of the Soviet state impelled them to concentrate mainly on
outward-directed nationalism in Africa--that is,
the drive for independence and sovereignty in the
international system--this same concern has prompted the Brezhnev-Kosygin regime to investigate the
impact of nationalist manifestations on Africa itself. For, if this impact should be a negative one
--that is, if it should lead to centrifugalism and
instability on the scale of the Congolese and Nigerian crises--it might involve the USSR in a military effort that its strained power and financial
resources could not tolerate.

NATIONAL INTEGRATION STUDIES DURING
THE KHRUSHCHEV ERA

During the Khrushchev era, the national integration question was not ignored entirely, although
awareness of its importance did develop rather
slowly. This halting progression is attributable
to three interrelated factors: (1) the Soviet
Union's lack of familiarity with African realities;

(2) its desire to counter the objections of certain
Western countries to African independence; and (3)
its hopes that its influence could easily supplant
that of the West. These factors were so influential that, in the pre-1960 period, Soviet African
Studies were characterized by a tendency to see national unity where, in fact, it did not exist.

The strength of tribal consciousness was denied. Potekhin signaled the inauguration of this
era of optimism in 1954: "The feeling of attachment to one's tribe, developed over the centuries,
the sense of blood kinship with one's fellow
tribesmen, tribal solidarity--although still alive,
have lost their force."[1] His colleague, R. N.
Ismagilova, took this argument one step further by
claiming that there never had been a serious tribal
problem in Africa. She claimed that allegations of
tribalism had been trumped up by the colonial powers in order to dissuade the United Nations Trusteeship Council from recommending that independence
be granted:

> In the [1955] report of the English
> authorities to the Trusteeship Council,
> it was stated that there are 120
> tribes in Tanganyika. A census was
> given of none of these groupings,
> therefore one gets an impression of
> an enormous ethnic splitting of the
> population. In reality, things are
> otherwise. Ninety-six percent of
> the people belong to one language
> group--the Bantu.[2]

Ismagilova obviously was doing the same juggling with the concept of "ethnic splitting" that
the British allegedly were doing, albeit for contrary purposes. Thus, as an ethnographer, she undoubtedly was aware that people could belong to the
same language group but still speak mutually incom-
prehensible dialects and consider themselves members of distinct ethnic units. However, because
the Soviet government was striving to represent the

African nations as ready for independence--and to
present itself as champion of the African cause in
the Trusteeship Council debates--the science of
ethnography had to bow to the needs of policy.
Ismagilova did acknowledge that, "in some colonies,"
the process of national consolidation "had gone
further than in others"; nevertheless, she continued to claim that the significant growth of national consciousness, the establishment of national organizations, and detribalization were hallmarks of
all the tropical African countries.[3]

Although most of the early Soviet Africanists
were well trained in their disciplines (ethnography,
linguistics, and so on), it is questionable whether
their knowledge of Africa was extensive or, more
importantly, whether there was any awareness--on
the academic or official level--of the need to investigate specifically African conditions. The
Central Committee Report to the 1956 CPSU Congress
made no reference to the internal conditions in the
African countries, and confined its remarks regarding the domestic situation of underdeveloped nations in general to the broad statement that

> the liberated Asian countries are
> building up their own industry,
> training their own technicians, rais-
> ing the people's living standards,
> and developing their age-old national
> cultures. Historic prospects for a
> better future are opening up.[4]

It is clear from the Central Committee report that
the exclusion of the Soviet Union from the 1955
Bandung Conference had made it appreciative of the
importance of the external orientation of the Third
World countries; ironically, however, the traditional Marxist exhortation to examine the class
(that is, internal) situation of the outside world
seems to have been temporarily disregarded.[5]

The pressure of events did not allow this situation to continue. In 1957, Ghana became the

first black African colony to obtain its independence--an event that prompted Potekhin to spend two months in the Gold Coast observing African "realities." He concluded that "the ethnic composition of Ghana is complicated. There is not one nation of Ghanaians and there are no grounds for such a nation to form in the future."[6]

In December, 1958, the Accra Conference of African Peoples was attended by many Soviet Africanists. The conference debates regarding the proper method of dealing with traditional institutions persuaded Potekhin that tribalism was not dead. Consequently, he proclaimed that liquidating these institutions would "entail great difficulties and a fierce struggle."[7] In the fall of 1959, the Chinese Communists were quite openly engaged in arms shipments to the Algerian Front de Liberation Nationale (FLN) and to the rebel movement in the Cameroon--an indication that, if African instability continued, they would not hesitate to exploit it to improve their own international position. Then, in August, 1960, serious tribal disturbances broke out in the Middle Belt of Nigeria; they were acknowledged by Soviet authorities to be a result of a combination of "class contradictions" and "national contradictions." The disturbances convinced them of the explosiveness of this particular combination.[8] Finally, the failure of the much touted Mali Federation to bridge the widely varying political views of the leaders of Dahomey, Upper Volta, Senegal, and Sudan illustrated to the Soviet authorities that their earlier idea that "the idea of union is a living, progressive idea, and therefore will triumph sooner or later"[9] was politically naive. Soviet leaders now believed that they would have to help the Africans to overcome these differences--a task that could not be undertaken unless the distinctive national cultures and problems of the new African states were understood.

Soviet appreciation of the importance of the nationalist leaders to the success of the African liberation movement (that is, progression toward

socialism) was another factor in their search for
more detailed knowledge of the national integration
process. For national integration was obviously a
primary goal of these leaders: Tribal conflicts
could be exploited by both domestic and foreign
elements to oust them from power. Furthermore, as
a result of their Western education and service in
the colonial administration, this elite possessed
"a sense of supratribal identity and a desire for
political authority and autonomy coextensive with
the territorial boundaries drawn by the Euro-
peans."[10] And many of the African leaders--men
like Leopold Senghor, Kwame Nkrumah, and Mamadou
Dia--had become strong proponents of the Pan-
African cause during their sojourns in Europe. At
first, they had considered African unity the solution to national integration problems. By the
1960's, however, all but Nkrumah realized that continental unity could not be attained until the
intra- and inter-state conflicts caused by ethnic
particularism were resolved. Soviet authorities
moved to respond to this reassessment by attempting
to show that they shared the elite's goal of national integration and that, in contradistinction
to the "splitting tactics" of the West, their intentions included a thorough study of African tribalism in order to accelerate the unification
process.

However, this declared Soviet desire to investigate African conditions objectively[11] was somewhat negated by the air of optimism that permeated
Soviet African Studies during the pre-1962 period.
Chinese ideological criticism and the recentness
of Moscow's political and financial involvement in
Africa made the Soviet leaders especially anxious
that their efforts produce an early triumph of the
noncapitalist factions; this anxiety, not unexpect-
edly, was stronger than their search for objectivity in certain instances. Thus, they spoke of a
rapid process of urbanization that was effecting a
"definite" and permanent detribalization of the
townspeople, making no reference to the voluntary
associations and tribal settlement patterns that

were working to maintain tribal distinctiveness.[12]
They mentioned the "half worker, half peasant" mentality of migrant workers, but went on to insist
that "this cannot serve as a basis for the impossi-
bility of setting up trade union organizations"[13]
of these laborers. Finally, they made an assertion
counter to all Marxist tenets that, "under certain
conditions, the labor unions, led by men trained in
theory, may assume the role of leadership over the
working class and represent the latter in its relationship with the broad masses."[14] The working
classes, of course, according to the Report of the
1961 Twenty-second CPSU Congress, would be very receptive to socialist direction, as would the peasants whose traditional communal society was a possible "starting point for the noncapitalist development of a country and for the building of socialism."[15] The Russians, spurred by their optimism
and desire to win over the African elite, were thus
accepting one of the major tenets of African socialism.

At this 1961 CPSU Congress, the Soviet leaders
also officially expressed their hope that no redrawing of national boundaries would be necessary
in order to produce viable nation-states in black
Africa. The Draft Report of the Congress attributed demands for revision to the imperialist tactic
of "using the poisonous weapon of national and
tribal discord . . . to split the ranks of the national liberation movement."[16] Of course, Soviet
authorities had supported the cause of Ewe reunifi-
cation and Cameroon amalgamation in the United Nations for several years, envisioning that the
change in national frontiers that these projects
entailed would be instrumental in reducing the power of the imperialists. In 1961, however, they began to disregard similar causes in their urge to
establish stable diplomatic relations with the new
African states. Because any revision of borders
might produce domestic unrest and international
conflict, distracting the African governments from
the cause of sociopolitical transformations, such
revision must be denounced.

In contrast to the pre-1962 period, a period characterized by optimism, the years 1962-64 witnessed a pronounced change from optimism to realism in Soviet African Studies. The Congo crisis, the apparent receptivity of many African states to associate with the European Economic Community, the barriers to African unity and Soviet influence that this association would entail, and the lack of progress toward worker states[17] served to modify the hopes that Khrushchev had for Africa. Furthermore, he began to worry that the military and economic aid might be used to further causes that were not in the best interests of the Soviet Union.

For, as Adam Ulam has indicated, Soviet leaders saw Africa as providing the perfect opportunity for "harassment of the West without the risk of precipitating a major war, and of showing to their own peoples the allegedly free world to be everywhere in retreat and confusion."[18] When it became clear to them that the independent actions of the African leaders might shift the level of superpower interaction from indirect harassment to direct East-West confrontation, Khrushchev launched a grandstand play that would allow Moscow to eschew its involvement under international pressure. On December 31, 1963, he proposed an international agreement rejecting the use of force to resolve territorial disputes. Khrushchev was careful to say that "the demands of the liberated states for the handing over of territories that still remain under the colonial yoke or under foreign occupation are absolutely justified"; not to have excluded these conflicts from his proposal would have severely strained Soviet-Third World relations. However, he did warn that

> in our time, when the development of
> international relations has led to a
> close intertwining of the interests
> of states . . . and when ramified
> systems of alliances exist, in these
> conditions a conflict that occurs in
> any one place and that seemingly

> involves a purely local character,
> could very quickly involve other
> states. . . . At the same time we
> must not fail to take into account
> that wars that begin with the use of
> simple weapons could at the present
> time grow into a world war with the
> use of thermonuclear weapons.[19]

Khrushchev's attempt to secure a global agreement
faltered on the skepticism of the world powers and
the tendency of the underdeveloped nations to include all their disputes in the "justifiable" category. Nevertheless, the fact that he undertook
this internationalization effort indicates the extent of his worries regarding the ramifications of
any Third World national conflicts.

Regarding the impact of nationalism on domestic African politics, Khrushchev adopted a very
ambivalent attitude. Thus, on the one hand, he was
prompted, by the realization that the USSR was not
consolidating its influence over Africa as rapidly
as expected, to decry the nationalist concerns of
the African leaders. He claimed that these concerns
caused them to pursue a "fence-sitting policy" regarding the choice between the capitalist and noncapitalist paths; furthermore, the leaders' preoccupations with developing national consciousness in
their people led them to ignore the class struggle,
which was a "matter of fact" in their countries.[20]

On the other hand, however, Soviet authorities
exhibited a growing concern during this 1962-64 period that, regarding the African masses, the lack
of national consciousness was a definite problem.
Thus, a conference devoted to an analysis of the
Third World was convened by the Soviet Institute of
World Economics and International Relations in the
spring of 1962. P. Avakov and G. Mirskii, scholars
who are particularly involved in the analysis of
class consciousness, noted that its development was
impeded by the localism and particularistic orientation of the bulk of the population.

> A significant segment of the working
> class of these countries is composed
> of yesterday's peasants, who have not
> fully severed their ties with the
> land and return to the village peri-
> odically. This is the reason for the
> rather wide incursion of petty-
> bourgeois ideology into the ranks of
> the workers.[21]

They went on to explain that in black Africa, the
workers might still play an important role because
the more reactionary classes, such as the bourgeoisie and feudalists, were also underdeveloped. However, other writers were not convinced. K. Ivanov
reminded his readers that

> there is no jumping out of this phase
> when the country concerned is to a
> certain extent backward and the masses
> are not organized. One may do so in
> one's imagination, but the phase will
> remain there just the same.[22]

The traces of optimism that remained in the
Soviet writings on the African proletariat were not
at all visible in their treatment of the peasantry.
Soviet Africanists complained that not only could
they not discern any class consciousness among this
stratum but that even their national consciousness
was still at an extremely rudimentary level. This
lack of political awareness was attributed to the
persistence of tribalism, which even Potekhin admitted could no longer be described as "simply the
intrigues of the imperialists." He now defined it
(somewhat redundantly) as "an ideology of tribal
particularism, of exclusiveness, of tribal 'patriotism,'" and called for extensive research into the
reasons for its persistence.[23] The impetus toward
objective research was still weakened by the Kremlin's interest in trying to discern positive revolutionary trends. Nevertheless, the fact that the
existence of tribalism was no longer ignored, and
its grip on the masses no longer denied, provided

ample indication of the relative realism that per-
vaded Soviet African Studies during the 1962-64
period.

The year 1964, however, ushered in a period of
neo-optimism. In July, 1963, a Soviet-Nigerian
trade agreement was signed providing for an exchange of goods worth $2.5 million, there was a no-
ticeable cooling in U.S.-Guinea relations, and
China was criticized by the African delegates to
the sixth session of the Afro-Asian Peoples Solidarity Organization (Algeria, March, 1964) for its
condemnation of Soviet African policies. Furthermore,

> the devotion of certain African lead-
> ers to scientific socialism, their
> efforts to transform single, mass
> parties into close-knit ideologically
> well-heeled cadre parties, and the
> growing convergence of their foreign
> policies with Soviet policy, had per-
> suaded Khrushchev that these coun-
> tries might soon make the transition
> to socialism.[24]

There was increasing reference to the "national
democratic path," which, according to Soviet analysts, would enable many liberated countries to
solve those problems that had previously nurtured
reactionary tendencies. States of national democracy would grant "wide democratic rights and free-
doms" to the masses, thereby paving the way for an
increase in class consciousness and the realization
of a workers' state.[25]

Great progress toward resolving the national
question was also seen in these special, transi-
tional states. In Ghana, Guinea, and Mali, for
example, the governments were credited with consistently applying the principle of equality of
different ethnic groups, thereby increasing the
sense of loyalty and allegiance to the national regime. Neocolonialist regimes, by contrast, were

criticized for making certain ethnic groups the
centers of emerging nations. Soviet Africanists
admitted that, in Mali, Bambara culture was becoming dominant; they insisted, however, that this was
happening "spontaneously" as a result of the progressive policies of the government.[26] This dual-
ity in Soviet attitudes is not atypical; throughout
their writings on Africa, there is a tendency to
condemn the actions of hostile governments and to
support the policies of regimes with which they en-
joy good relations. The latter group is seen to
consist not only of states on the noncapitalist
path but also of states whose strategic importance
outweighs the significance of any reactionary political ideology. Thus, in 1964, Soviet Africanists were even praising the nationality policies of
the Kenya African National Union, the ruling party
of Kenya,[27] and they have adopted a similar attitude toward the policies of Haile Selassie.

THE BREZHNEV-KOSYGIN TAKEOVER:
CATALYST FOR NEW APPROACHES
TO AFRICAN INTEGRATION

In September, 1964, Potekhin died, and, in
October of that year, Nikita Khrushchev was deposed.
The way was cleared for an entirely new approach to
Africa by theorists and politicians, and, by 1966,
this approach was in sharp focus. The views of
scholars and policy-makers were infused with a
realism that would allow only one conclusion: Africa's development would be a long and tortuous
one, promising no quick or easy opportunities for
a consolidation of Soviet influence. This realism/
pessimism was summarized in an authoritative article in Izvestia:

> The mixed economies of most of the
> countries, . . . the complex pattern
> of different forms of property—from
> primitive communal to capitalist
> property—the great political, trib-
> al and religious diversity of the

> populations of these countries make
> for a prolonged transitional period
> that could occupy an entire histori-
> cal epoch charged with acute class
> conflicts.[28]

The overthrow of Nkrumah of Ghana in 1966 and Keita
of Mali in 1968 were indications that the class
struggle might not result in the installation of
"progressive" governments; Moscow's problems with
Peking, Havana, and Hanoi persuaded the Soviet
leaders that even "progressive" governments could
constitute a serious drain on their economic resources and a challenge to their political authority. It would be very difficult for Moscow to dis-
engage itself from existing commitments--both because of Communist bloc and international pressures.
However, the Soviet regime could be very cautious
regarding new involvements, judging any new opportunity for influence according to the strategic importance of the area in question and the ease with
which any gains might be realized. Viewed in this
perspective, Africa was less important than certain
other underdeveloped areas, namely the Middle and
Far East, and, within Africa, only a few countries
were significant enough to warrant any serious Soviet involvement. Nigeria, the largest, most pop-
ulous, and wealthiest state in black Africa, was
obviously one of them. Furthermore, there was little chance that Nigeria might become an African
Cuba, thereby forcing the Soviets to assume responsibility for its economy and political actions.
This meant that Moscow could justify any support of
the Nigerian Federal Government on the basis of the
trade opportunities and benefits to Soviet (not
Communist) interests that would ensue. Such considerations were paramount to the new regime. As
Mikhail Suslov, the ranking party ideologist,
stated shortly after Brezhnev and Kosygin assumed
power, "Our contribution to the cause of the international struggle of the working people of the entire world is expressed above all in the building
of Communism in the USSR."[29] Brezhnev echoed these
sentiments at the Twenty-third CPSU Congress, thus

enshrining them as the keynote of Soviet foreign
policy.

Soviet Africanists continued to examine African political problems, but the solutions they proposed were directed more toward ensuring stability
than promoting the noncapitalist path. V. Shelepin
warned African leaders against "ultra-revolutionary
hastiness," claiming that "nothing could be more
damaging to them." He referred to a left-wing approach to agriculture, industrialization, and Western aid as a petty-bourgeois failing, claiming that
the young governments must proceed cautiously if
they would establish "deep roots among the masses"
--the only way they could remain in power. However,
he was forced to admit that the governments would
have to learn to cope with tribalism, a problem he
frankly termed "the scourge of Africa."[30] Region-
alism and the once highly touted Organization of
African Unity (OAU) could not be expected to solve
the national integration problem, nor could the
Africans rely on the Soviet Union to provide the
economic aid necessary to promote the equal development of all tribes and regions. The Soviet Union
would be willing to help the Africans to develop
the correct domestic policy, but guidance rather
than unilaterally beneficial aid would receive the
major emphasis.[31] As Brezhnev stated in his speech
to the International Communist Conference (Moscow,
1969),

> the masses of working people in the
> developing areas are more and more
> vigorously demanding the implementa-
> tion of profound transformations ca-
> pable of actually solving the fundamen-
> tal problems that trouble them. . . .
> The responsibility that rests with us
> Communists in the matter is large.
> What is required of the Communist
> movement is an enormous amount of at-
> tention to the peasant allies of the
> proletariat and the additional elab-
> oration of certain aspects and tactics

to conform to the specific conditions
of the former colonial countries.[32]

NATIONALISM AND SYMBOLIC CAPABILITIES
IN BLACK AFRICA

One of the tactics called for by the specific
problems of black Africa was the manipulation of
nationalism to promote the integration process.
For, although Brezhnev and Kosygin have expressed
disillusionment about the potential role of African
nationalism in world affairs--that is, they have
realized that attempts to exploit it in order to
extend Soviet influence could well be counterpro-
ductive--they have attempted to evaluate the role it
might play in African domestic politics. Alarmed
by the opportunity that national conflicts provide
for an extension of Western power in Africa and by
the disruption in continental unity that these conflicts inevitably entail, Soviet authorities have
devoted increasing attention to the role of nationalism in building viable African nations. They
have not abandoned the position that socialism is
the only system that "leads to the full liquidation
of national antagonisms"; however, they now admit
that there may be another approach to resolving the
national question; "the all-democratic, which allows a significant weakening of national contradictions even under conditions of presocialist society."[33]

"All-democratic" is, of course, an accolade
similar to "state of national democracy"; the criteria for its bestowal are never fully elucidated,
so that Soviet ideologues are able to label as
"all-democratic" the policies of any state they regard favorably. Thus, if the nationalism propounded by a certain African state leads to opposition
to the presence of foreign monopolies, to the na-
tionalization of certain industries (primarily
banks and other lending institutions), and to the
replacement of tribal consciousness by the national,
then it is evaluated positively.[34] If, on the

contrary, the nationalism of a certain African
state is detrimental to the cause of continental
unity or assumes such policies as the curtailment
of Soviet activities, then it can hardly be labeled
"all-democratic."

Whatever the motivations behind these recent
Soviet analytical efforts, it is impressive that
they are finally examining domestic nationalism
carefully, rather than praising or criticizing the
national-liberation movement in general--a process
typical of the Stalin and Khrushchev eras. Such
sweeping generalizations were damaging to Soviet
prospects in Africa; they blinded Stalin to the potential for influence that certain national movements provided, while the positive nature of the
assessment after 1955 caused Khrushchev to underestimate the obstacle nationalism might present to an
expansion of Soviet activity. Also, throughout
most of the Khrushchev period, official notice was
focused on the international role of African nationalism. A closer look would have revealed that
the domestic or continental role had several ramifications for Soviet foreign policy concerns--a
lesson the Katanga secession crisis eventually made
clear.[35]

Another impressive aspect of this post-1965
Soviet analysis of African nationalism is that the
authorities have not allowed their ideological
aversion to nationalism to blind them to the positive role it may play under contemporary African
conditions, or to push them into urging African
leaders to eradicate it as soon as possible. For
example, they have actually encouraged Sekou Toure
in his stress on African nationalism and culture,
viewing this as a possible solution to the Soussou-
Malinke-Foulah rivalry that is plaguing Guinea.[36]
Furthermore, they have extracted an appropriate
quote from Lenin to justify this new tolerance.
According to Evgenii Zhukov, a member of the Presidium of the USSR Academy of Sciences, Lenin
pointed out in his "Initial Draft of the Theses on
the National and Colonial Questions" (1919) that

the more backward a country is, the
stronger small-scale agricultural
production, patriarchal nature, and
provincialism are; and these inevitably lead to the special strength
and stability of petty-bourgeois
prejudices, namely, the prejudices of
national egoism, national narrowness.
Eradication of these prejudices cannot fail to be very slow, since they
can disappear only following the disappearance of imperialism and capitalism in the advanced countries and following the radical alteration of the
entire basis of the backward countries'
economic life. Hence, the obligation
for the conscious communist proletariat of all countries to adopt an attitude of unusual caution and special
attention regarding vestiges of national feelings among the longest-oppressed
countries and nationalities, and equally, the obligation to make certain
concessions to more swiftly overcome
the distrust and prejudices mentioned.[37]

The tolerance of nationalism in African states
and the appreciation of its role in the integration
process evidenced in Soviet writings since the
Brezhnev-Kosygin takeover are quite appropriately
justified by a quotation from Lenin. For they
represent an interesting application of Lenin's
"one step forward, two steps back" approach to politics. Internationalism--that is, the development
of proletarian unity across national lines--will
falter if the level of consciousness of the African
proletariat remains at the stage of tribal loyalties; because neither communism nor Communist parties have registered any concrete or rapid successes
in Africa, perhaps the ideology of nationalism could
be used to advance the level of consciousness of
African workers beyond this tribal stage. Secondly,
until there is national integration in Africa,
there will be conflicts among various tribes within

a given state and also among states because of the
division of tribal groups that resulted from the
colonial partition. Such conflicts divert the attention of the African worker from class to tribal
interests and also hinder the development of proletarian solidarity within the African continent.
Thirdly, conflicts within African states (for example, Nigeria) or between them (for example, Morocco
and Tunisia or Somalia, Kenya, and Ethiopia) frequently involve the Western powers, causing the
proletariat of these advanced states to be divided
by the varying positions adopted by their governments. Finally, situations of national, and therefore political, instability in Africa encourage increasingly restive socialist governments to see
Africa as an arena for developing their own foreign
policy approach and for securing "allies" to increase their freedom of maneuver vis-à-vis the Soviet Union. Communist China and Yugoslavia have
taken full advantage of this opportunity, thus
erecting a further obstacle to internationalism.

        Furthermore, on the more positive side, Soviet
authorities can cite several reasons for responding
favorably to the domestic impact of African nationalism. First, this nationalism spurs the African
people to oppose monopolies and other extensions
of Western influence. Second, in the process of
the nationalist struggle in several countries, more
leftist elements have acceded to the leadership of
nationalist parties.[38] Third, nationalism might
motivate the people to reject their leaders' efforts to adhere too closely to Western political
concepts and to the Western camp, in general.[39]
Fourth, because any attempt to redraw the existing
territorial boundaries in Africa would result in
great political instability and might involve the
Great Powers, nationalism directed toward the creation of nation-states within the present boundaries is a positive phenomenon. Fifth, nationalism
hastens the disintegration of the communal structure of African society, thereby increasing the potential receptivity of the masses to socialism.
Finally, Soviet appreciation of the dual nature of

African nationalism--that is, as a force of anti-
imperialism and as an expression of a desire for
national integration and prestige--allows Moscow
to present the Soviet Union both as a fortress of
resistance to the West and as a model of internal
development and nation-building.

In view of these considerations, Soviet authorities have embarked on a course of encouraging
the growth of nationalism <u>as a means of nation-
building</u> in Africa. They have moved away from
their earlier conceptions of African nationalism as
only a weapon in the anti-imperialist struggle,
charging now that "it is absolutely incorrect to
explain the ideology of African nationalism only as
a reaction to racism during the colonialist period
and to rebellion against suppressed dignity, as it
is often being done in the West."[40] Instead, they
now define nationalism as

> the complex of political tendencies di-
> rected toward the creation of nation-
> states within the limits of existing
> territorial boundaries. This type of
> nationalism can be one of the impor-
> tant weapons in the fight against
> tribal conflicts, against tribal con-
> sciousness, which work against the
> social and economic progress of the
> various countries.[41]

Moscow is aware that the building of strong
states in Africa, a process essential to making the
African countries strong allies in international
relations, is impossible without the prior formation of viable nations. The nation-building process, in turn, is heavily dependent on the development of the emotional and symbolic spurs to integration: nationalism and cultural pride. For, if
the government can effectively manipulate the symbolic outputs--for example, an emphasis on the
glories of African history, the richness of African
culture, a commitment to a distinctive "African
path of development," and the use of anthems, flags,

and official ceremony--they might engage the emo-
tions of the populace and divert their attention
(at least temporarily) from expectations of more
concrete governmental performance. In other words,
manipulation of the symbolic capability might work
to bind loyalties to the nation until the government could develop the more functional and long-
range methods of national integration (for example,
urbanization, economic development, social welfare,
and so on).[42]

As L. O. Iablochkov explained to the delegates
at the 1967 International Congress of Africanists,
although the ideology of nationalism can be used
for reactionary purposes,

> at the same time, even in its local
> variety, it cannot be denied the role
> of a consolidating factor. The na-
> tional idea can serve as an impetus
> in each country. . . . It helps to
> solve some state problems by formulat-
> ing them in a comprehensive form, by
> focussing attention on common needs,
> by mobilizing the will and energy of
> the people.[43]

Iablochkov appeared to be urging the African governments to make better use of nationalism as a symbolic output in order that they might proceed with
their development programs. In fact, the suggestion is implicit that promotion of the "national
idea" might provide a better tool for problem-
resolution than certain concrete programs.[44]

G. Starushenko, Deputy Director of the African
Institute, while not admitting that emphasis on the
symbolic aspects of nationalism could replace definite policies as a solution to African integration
problems, states that this avenue should not be ignored. He writes of certain African leaders who
"mistakenly" felt that the national problem could
be abolished by laws and that the creation of a
unified nation was simply a matter of decree. He

reminds the reader somewhat ruefully that

> nationalism was called into existence
> by the _necessity_ of resolving the
> national-colonial question at the
> same time that Marxism had postulated
> as its goal the liberation of peoples
> from all types of oppression, not
> only the national.[45]

Soviet authorities, of course, are not unmind-
ful of the dangers that the unrestricted development
of African nationalism could represent. They continue to warn that it might be manipulated by the
bourgeoisie to mask its own interests and goals or
that it might develop such a particularistic taint
that the entire movement toward African unity would
be destroyed. They are also aware that it could be
an obstacle to the diffusion of socialism. In the
last analysis, then, their attitude toward African
nationalism could be termed one of cautious optimism. They are hopeful that it will boost the integration process and, eventually, the consolidation of the revolution. However, they are also
aware that expectations that this process will be
rapid are illusory. For, as E. Zhukov wrote,

> Apart from the chief, determining
> socioeconomic differences of the so-
> called Third World countries, not in-
> considerable influence is exerted on
> the nature of the national liberation
> struggle by ideological, historical,
> cultural and everyday peculiarities.
> Their role is neither identical nor
> constant: in some cases they promote
> the development of the popular masses'
> anti-imperialist activity; in others,
> they represent a braking factor. But
> in one way or another these peculiar-
> ities leave a considerabl imprint on
> the forms of the national liberation
> struggle. Any failure to consider
> them can only hinder the correct

          understanding of the extremely com-
          plex processes taking place in the
          "Third World" countries.[46]

     Thus, Soviet authorities have acknowledged
with increasing frankness that there are several
factors peculiar to black Africa that not only in-
terfere with the use of nationalism as an integrating factor but also render the entire African
nation-building process distinctive. Soviet analysis of these peculiarities falls into five catego-
ries: (1) the role of colonialism in retarding national development; (2) the limited power and resources of the state; (3) the absence of a class
structure; (4) the artificial basis of self-
determination; and (5) the impermanence of the independence struggle as a spur to unity.

                PECULIARITIES OF THE AFRICAN
                  NATION-BUILDING PROCESS

     Soviet efforts to present colonialism as re-
sponsible for Africa's late start and continuing
difficulties in realizing true national integration
are not unexpected or surprising; indeed, early Soviet research on African development problems cen-
tered almost wholly on the colonial heritage.
Potekhin was the primary representative of this approach, although even he was impelled to note that,
"by the beginning of the imperialist partition of
Africa, its peoples still had not embarked on the
path of capitalist development and as a result did
not succeed in forming nations and establishing national states."[47] He attributed this to the slave
trade, which pitted one village against another and
instigated a series of wars so that a people might
have prisoners to trade on the slave market. This
period left Africa "atomized," precluding the possibility of tribes merging into nationalities and
nations and forming large centralized states. Of
course, he then proceeded to add that, when certain
African peoples, such as the Zulus and the Ashanti,
began to form nation-states in the period 1820-40,

their efforts were completely nullified by the
European invasions. In conclusion, he notes that

> the peoples of Africa were going
> through the same processes of over-
> coming tribal and feudal divisions
> and the establishment of large cen-
> tralized states, but these were taking
> place later than similar processes in
> Europe. This natural historical de-
> velopment was violently disrupted by
> colonialist intervention.[48]

More recent Soviet authors have adopted a more
moderate approach to the role of colonialism in
hampering African integration. Admittedly, they
would not confirm the views of such Western scholars
as Ernest Lefever, who attributes a "unifying"
rather than "Balkanizing" effect to European colonialism.[49] However, they now admit that colonial-
ization only served to accentuate certain separatist
tendencies that were occurring in black Africa even
in the precolonial period.[50]

The Soviet experts deem the limited power and
resources of the state another obstacle to national
consolidation in Africa. Because the level of economic development is low, there is no functional
impetus to the creation of a unified nation; similarly, there is no highly developed bourgeoisie
whose economic interests compel it, as in Western
Europe, to push for national integration. Furthermore, in most cases there is no single ethnic group
that represents a majority of the population and
could provide a nucleus and force for an integrated
nation. In the absence of these factors, the role
of the state is especially significant. In contrast to Western Europe, where the formation of
government was a result of the growth of the nation,
the state in Africa is the instrument of the nation's creation.[51]

However, the very obstacles to national integration for which the state is supposed to compensate

prevent it from fulfilling this task. The state
often cannot move decisively against a rebeliious
ethnic or religious group because that group forms
part of its power base; this hesitation, in turn,
angers other groups, which therefore become disaf-
fected from the system. In the economic sphere,
the lack of resources prevents the state from promoting the equal development of all regions, thereby depriving it of the ability to consolidate the
nation through economic inducements. Finally, the
small, but pivotal nature of the African bourgeoisie means that the regime must be careful to retain
its loyalty; as a result, it is often driven to
neglect the economic and political requirements of
the country as a whole. These negative factors
have been noted by Starushenko, Sobolev, Frenkel',
and Kozlov; they are also cited by Western scholars.
Arnold Rivkin, for example, writes that this con-
stellation of disintegrative forces

> has made it all but impossible for
> truly national institutions represen-
> tative of and responsive to the total
> nation to develop and grow. It has
> also made the formal constitutional
> structure meaningless. . . . When
> the uncertainties of geography are
> added, the result has been a facade
> of institutions which have not been
> able to command support or to induce
> participation by an ever-increasing
> part of the public.[52]

The lack of a well-developed class structure
is another drawback that Soviet ideologues feel the
Africans must face in their nation-building efforts.
This factor is significant, for in the absence of
class interests that can absorb the energies and
loyalties of the Africans, their attachment to
their ethnic group and to its advancement remains
strong. This, in turn, impedes the growth of class
consciousness. For example, the workers in Sierra
Leone see themselves as Mende or Temne and not as
miners who should join together to secure greater

economic and social benefits vis-à-vis their capitalist employers. There is, of course, an element
of self-interest in the Soviet concern for this
lack of development, as they view the proletariat,
in union with the working peasantry, as the prime
mover in the development of a socialist nation.[53]

Ideological considerations aside, Soviet authorities acknowledge that the absence of a strong
bourgeoisie has serious ramifications for nation-
building. This class played the predominant role
in the nations of the West; it cultivated the
spread of national consciousness and culture, as
well as the establishment of a strong unified state,
in order to secure political protection for its
economic market. The African bourgeoisie, on the
other hand, is not primarily interested in invest-
ing in productive enterprises that would necessitate an expansionist outlook, but rather in more
static areas such as real estate.[54] Without the
economic motivation to secure a larger market, it
is unlikely that the bourgeoisie would be interested in furthering the political expansion of the
state.

Furthermore, although the bourgeoisie that
held sway in Africa in the early years of independence was highly Westernized through foreign education and service in the colonial civil service, the
new group can be termed, very aptly, a national
bourgeoisie. These are men who, for the most part,
have served in African armies and have been educated in African universities. To be sure, this
gives them a greater sense of identification with
the mores and problems of the African masses; however, both Western and Soviet authors worry that
this identification might be too strong. Lefever,
for example, describes the corruption that may result from bureaucrats' exhibiting special prefer-
ences for their fellow-tribesmen and the resistance
to change that may be a result of their traditional
cultural orientation.[55] Iordanskii borrows the
Western term "supertribalization" to characterize
the attitude of this partially modernized elite,

explaining that this is facilitated by "the practice of the bourgeoisie of this or that ethnic
group of maintaining for itself a monopoly of trade.
'Ethnic' monopolies are one of the characteristic
peculiarities of trade in several African countries."[56] If enterprises are established on an
ethnic basis and cater to a certain ethnic group,
it is difficult to see how economic development and
the expansion of a trading class will lead to the
rapid detribalization of African society.

The weakly developed class structure is also
evidenced by the lack of a strong African peasantry,
a class whose growth is impeded by "economic and
social backwardness, . . . the predominance of
feudal and strong pre-capitalist social relations,
. . . the tremendous influence on the consciousness
of the very widest sectors of the masses of the
1000-year-old burden of patriarchal, national, racial, religious, and communal prejudices and survivals. . . ."[57] Soviet Communists, unlike the
Chinese, do not expect the peasantry of any country
to be the vanguard of the socialist revolution;
however, they do speak of the "working peasantry"
as the allies of the workers in this movement.
However, regarding the peasants, Africa is caught
in a vicious circle: Tribalism impedes economic
development, while the lack of economic growth, in
turn, leads to the "supertribalization" of those
peasants who cut themselves off--at least nominally
--from village society. These migrants find themselves in the cities with no opportunity for employment; in order to survive, they depend on the
tribal associations, thus continuing the pattern of
ethnicity that so hampers African nation-building.

Another inhibiting factor is the artificial
basis of self-determination in Africa.   Self-
determination did not take place on a national
basis, as in Western Europe, but on a territorial
one set up by alien powers. As a result, the
states have no natural-geographic, economic, or
ethnic justification, as Potekhin noted;[58] they are
multilingual, multitribal, and in some cases,

multinational units. The Africans embarked on the
course of independence with a difficult complex of
problems with which to cope; they intensified their
problems by refusing to abandon the previously de-
marcated territory as a focus for their nation-
building efforts. In certain English-speaking territories, there at least occurred an independence
struggle that could rally the people around the
existing political unit; however, whereas in states
such as Ghana, "there was nationalism without a nation, in the ex-French territories they have to
build nations without nationalism."[59]

Thus, either the African states had no national liberation struggle to act as a spur to unity or
the influence of the movement was very short-lived.
There are countries, such as the Somali Republic,
which have been able to maintain this "unity-above-
all" feeling, but this has been largely a result of
the threat that Kenya and Ethiopia have posed to
the cause of further Somali unification.[60] In
other words, the sense of unity has been strengthened by the fear of an outside enemy. However,
most African states do not have serious border conflicts, and the danger of neocolonialism is too
diffuse and abstract to serve as an integrating in-
centive.[61]

In view of the growing Soviet awareness of the
peculiarities of African nation-building problems--
peculiarities that prevent the wholesale adoption
of the Soviet model--it is important to examine
what alternatives to, or variants of, this model
are recommended. At least one American Sovietologist has claimed that the Soviet interest in this
issue is purely negative--that is, that the primary
aim is to criticize the colonialist legacy. However, it will be shown in the following chapters
that the Soviet interest has been more than a passing one and has revolved around several concrete
proposals. Admittedly, in the early years of their
African involvement, Soviet authorities would write
about the centrifugal tendencies plaguing black Africa, only to remark that "African peoples will

find their own solution to this problem," "Life
will show how this is to be done," and "Great political tact and wisdom is required of the African
leaders."[62] The Soviet authorities were disinter-
ested in national integration during this period
because it was the potential international impact
of the African states that concerned them; events
had not yet shown that internal crises could nulli-
fy or complicate this impact. Once this was made
clear by the Congo crisis (and later, by the
Biafran situation, which provided Moscow with the
opportunity to increase its influence in Nigeria,
but at the price of a high level of political, economic, and diplomatic involvement that it was no
longer prepared to accord to Africa), Soviet investigations of possible integration solutions for
Africa began in earnest.

NOTES

1. I. I. Potekhin and Dmitri Ol'derogge, eds.,
Narody Afriki (Peoples of Africa) (Moscow: Institut
Etnografii AN SSSR, 1954), p. 445.

2. R. N. Ismagilova, "Etnicheskii sostav
naseleniia Tanganiki" ("The Ethnic Makeup of the
Population of Tanganyika"), Sovetskaia etnografiia,
3 (May-June, 1956), 98-99.

3. Ibid., pp. 96, 102.

4. Leo Gruliow, ed., Current Soviet Policies
II: The Documentary Record of the Twentieth Commu-
nist Party Congress and Its Aftermath (New York:
Praeger, 1957), p. 34; cited in R. A. Yellon, "The
Winds of Change," Mizan, IX, 2 (March-April, 1967),
54.

5. Note Mikoyan's criticism of Soviet specialists for not "elucidating the peculiarities of
development of individual countries." He concluded
that "the Academy of Sciences does have an Institute

that studies the problems of the East, but all that can be said of it is that although in our day the whole East has awakened, this Institute is still dozing." Gruliow, op. cit., p. 87.

6. I. I. Potekhin, Gana seqodnia (Ghana Today) (Moscow: Izdatel'stvo geograficheskoi literatury, 1959); quoted in "Soviet Writing on Ghana: An Introduction," Mizan, II, 11 (December, 1960), 18.

7. I. I. Potekhin, "O nekotorikh zadachakh afrikanisitiki v sviazi c konferentsiei naradov Afriki" ("On Certain Tasks of African Studies in Connection with the Conference of African Peoples"), Sovetskaia etnografiia, 2 (March–April, 1959), 13.

8. L. Kim, "Pervyi god nezavisimosti Nigerii" ("Nigeria's First Year of Independence"), Mirovaia ekonomika i mezhdunarodnye otnosheniia, 8 (August, 1961), 99.

9. I. I. Potekhin, "God borby za edinstvo" ("The Year of the Fight for Unity"), Sovremennyi Vostok, 12 (1959), 46; Robert Legvold, Soviet Policy in West Africa: 1957–1968 (Cambridge, Mass.: Harvard University Press, 1970), pp. 90–91.

10. Ernest Lefever, "State-Building in Tropical Africa," Orbis, XII, 4 (Winter, 1969), 987.

11. B. G. Gafurov, "Mezhdunarodnyi forum orientalistov (k itogam XXV mezhdunarodnogo kongressa vostokovedov)" ("The International Forum of Orientalists [On the Results of the XXV International Congress of Orientalists]"), Voprosy istorii, 11 (November, 1960), 9.

12. M. I. Braginskii, "Sotsial'nye sdvigi v Tropicheskoi Afrike posle vtoroi mirovoi voiny" ("Social Trends in Tropical Africa After the Second World War"), Sovetskaia etnografiia, 6 (November–December, 1960), 31–42.

13. N. Gavrilov, "O migratsii rabochei sily v zapadnoi Afrike" ("Labor Migration in West Africa"), Problemy vostokovedeniia, 3 (1959), 89.

14. I. I. Potekhin, "Kharakternye cherty raspada kolonial'noi sistemy imperializma v Afrike" ("Characteristics of the Fall of the Colonial System of Imperialism in Africa"), Problemy vostokovedeniia, 1 (1960), 19; quoted in Kurt Muller, The Foreign Aid Programs of the Soviet Bloc and Communist China (New York: Walker, 1967), pp. 102-3.

15. I. I. Potekhin, Africa's Future: The Soviet View, an abridgement of Afrika smotrit v budushschee (Moscow: Izd'zo Zostochnoi literatury, 1960), printed as a supplement of Mizan, III, 4 (April, 1961), 15. See also Philip E. Moseley, "Soviet Policy in the Developing Countries," Foreign Affairs, XLIII, 1 (October, 1964), 92-93.

16. Fritz Schatten, Communism in Africa (London: George Allen and Unwin, 1966), p. 110; George von Stackelberg, "Soviet African Studies as a Weapon of Soviet Policy," Bulletin of the Institute for the Study of the USSR, VII, 9 (September, 1960), 6; Curt Gasteyger, "The Soviet Union and the Tiers Monde," Survey, 43 (August, 1962), 20.

17. This lack of progress was illustrated by Guinea's rapprochement (albeit temporary) with the United States and by Communist China's partial success in rallying the Afro-Asian Solidarity Movement against the Soviet Union. Legvold, op. cit., pp. 147-48.

18. Adam Ulam, "Nationalism, Panslavism, Communism," in Ivo Lederer, ed., Russian Foreign Policy (New Haven, Conn.: Yale University Press, 1962), p. 59.

19. "Message from N. S. Khrushchev, Chairman of the USSR Council of Ministers, to Heads of State

of Countries of the World," Pravda and Izvestia, January 4, 1964, p. 1; trans., CDSP, XVI, 1 (January 29, 1964), 4. See also Uri Ra'anan, "Soviet Tactics in the Third World," Survey, 57 (October, 1965), 31-33.

20. N. S. Khrushchev, "Speech in Sofia," Pravda, May 20, 1962, pp. 1-3; trans., CDSP, XIV, 20 (June 13, 1962), 7.

21. P. Avakov and G. Mirskii, "O klassovoi strukture v slaborazvitikh stranakh" ("On the Class Structure in Underdeveloped Countries"), Mirovaia ekonomika i mezhdunarodnye otnosheniia, 4 (April, 1962), 73.

22. K. Ivanov, "The National and Colonial Question Today," International Affairs, 5 (May, 1963), 4.

23. I. I. Potekhin, "Nekotorye problemy Afrikanistiki v svete reshenii XXII s"ezda KPSS" ("Certain Problems of African Studies in Light of the Resolutions of the 22d Party Congress of the CPSU"), Narody Azii i Afriki, 1 (1962), 14. See also, V. P. Verin, Prezidentskie respubliki v Afrike (Presidential Republics in Africa) (Moscow: Mezhdunarodnye Otnosheniia, 1963).

24. Legvold, op. cit., p. 209.

25. K. Brutents, "Nekotorye osobennosti natsional'no-osvoboditel'nogo dvizheniia" ("Certain Peculiarities of the National-Liberation Movement"), Voprosy filosofii, 6 (1965), 33-34; also N. I. Gavrilov, ed., Nezavisimye strany Afriki (The Independent Countries of Africa) (Moscow: Nauka, 1965), pp. 289-90.

26. A. B. Letnev, "Novoe v Maliiskoi derevne" ("New Developments in the Malian Village"), Sovetskaia etnografiia, 1 (January-February, 1964), 87.

27. V. Kudriavtsev, "Kenya: African Problems in Sharp Focus," International Affairs, 2 (February, 1964), 67.

28. A. Iskenderov, "The Army, Politics, and the People," Izvestia, January 17, 1967, p. 2; trans., CDSP, XIX, 3 (February 8, 1967), 9-10.

29. Pravda, October 5, 1965; quoted in Legvold, op. cit., p. 234.

30. V. Shelepin, "Africa: Why the Instability," New Times, 52 (December 30, 1968), 21-24. See also A. Iskenderov and G. Starushenko, "Intrigues of Imperialism in Africa," Pravda, August 14, 1966, p. 4; trans., CDSP, XVIII, 33 (September 7, 1966), 19-20.

31. Interview with V. Vigant, Economist, Africa Institute, Moscow, October, 1969.

32. L. I. Brezhnev, "For Strengthening the Solidarity of Communists, For a New Upswing in the Anti-Imperialist Struggle," Pravda and Izvestia, July 8, 1969, pp. 1-4; trans., CDSP, XXI, 23 (July 2, 1969), 9.

33. G. Starushenko, Natsiia i gosudarstvo v osvobodaiushchikhsia stranakh (Nation and State in the Liberated Countries) (Moscow: Mezhdunarodnye Otnosheniia, 1967), p. 248.

34. See R. A. Ul'ianovskii, "Aktual'nye problemy natsional'no-osvoboditel'nogo dvizheniia (po itogovomu dokumentu mezhdunarodnogo soveshchaniia kommunisticheskikh i rabochikh partii, 1969)" ("Actual Problems of the National-Liberation Movement [according to the Final Document of the International Conference of Communist and Workers' Parties, 1969]"), Narody Azii i Afriki, 4 (1969), 1-14.

35. Yellon, op. cit., pp. 55-57.

36. Interview with R. Benneville, Economic Officer, United States Embassy, Dakar, Fall, 1969. Mr. Benneville was formerly attached to the U.S. Embassy in Conakry.

37. E. Zhukov, "Natsional'no-osvoboditel'noe dvizhenie narodov Azii i Afriki" ("The National-Liberation Movement of the Peoples of Asia and Africa"), Kommunist, 4 (March, 1969), 32. (Italics mine.)

38. Ul'ianovskii, op. cit., p. 8. Note that such optimism is politically naive, as nationalism is often exploited more skillfully by rightist elements than by groups on the left.

39. Interview with M. Bourdakin, First Secretary, Soviet Embassy, Accra. Bourdakin was especially desirous that nationalism should restrain the Westernism of Dr. Busia.

40. E. A. Veselkin, "The African Personality," in M. A. Korostovtsev, ed., Essays on African Culture (Moscow: Nauka, 1966), p. 72.

41. Ia. Ia. Etinger, Politicheskie problemy Afrikanskogo edinstva (Political Problems of African Unity) (Moscow: Nauka, 1967), p. 106.

42. L. O. Iablochkov, "Evolution of African Nationalism as a Political Ideology," Papers Presented by the USSR Delegation to the Second International Congress of Africanists, Dakar, 1967, p. 13. (Mimeographed.)

43. Ibid., p. 13.

44. Cf. Gabriel Almond and C. Bingham Powell, Jr., Comparative Politics: A Developmental Approach (Boston: Little, Brown, 1966), p. 215. The authors warn that "one of the common patterns of political instability has been to shift from a capability pattern to one emphasizing regulation and symbolic satisfaction. The political changes which

took place in Ghana in the last years before Nkrumah's overthrow can be viewed from this perspective."

45. Starushenko, op. cit., pp. 243, 246.
(Italics mine.)

46. E. Zhukov, op. cit., p. 33.

47. I. I. Potekhin, "Zadachi izucheniia
etnicheskogo sostava Afriki v sviazi s raspadom
Kolonial'noi sistemy" ("Tasks of Studying the Ethnic Makeup of Africa in Connection with the Fall of
the Colonial System"), Sovetskaia etnografiia, 4
(July-August, 1957), 103.

48. I. I. Potekhin, "Legacy of Colonialism in
Africa," International Affairs, 3 (March, 1964),
15-16.

49. Lefever, op. cit., p. 987.

50. V. Iordanskii, "Tropicheskaia Afrika: o
prirode mezhetnicheskikh konfliktov" ("Tropical
Africa: On the Nature of Interethnic Conflicts"),
Mirovaia ekonomika i mezhdunarodnye otnosheniia, 1
(January, 1967), 48.

51. B. V. Andrianov, "Problemy formirovaniia
narodnostei i natsii v stranakh Afriki" ("Problems
of Forming Nationalities and Nations in the Countries of Africa"), Voprosy istorii, 9 (September,
1967), 112.

52. Arnold Rivkin, ed., Nations by Design
(New York: Anchor, 1967), p. 17; also V. I. Kozlov,
"O razrabotke teoreticheskikh osnov natsional'nogo
voprosa" ("Elaboration of the Theoretical Founda-
tions of the National Question"); Narody Azii i
Afriki, 4 (1967), 84; Starushenko, op. cit., p. 239;
A. Sobolev, "Some Problems of Social Progress,"
World Marxist Review, X, 1 (January, 1967), 28;
M. Frenkel', "Plemena--partii--biurokratiia"
("Tribes--Parties--Bureaucracies"), Mirovaia

ekonomika i mezhdunarodnye otnosheniia, 11 (November, 1968), 110.

53. S. Bruk and N. Cheboksarov, "Sovremennyi etap natsional'nogo razvitiia narodov Azii i Afriki" ("The Current Stage of National Development of the Peoples of Asia and Africa"), Sovetskaia etnografiia, 4 (July-August, 1961), 77; also D. Zarine, "Classes and Class Struggle in Developing Countries," International Affairs, 4 (April, 1968), 47-48.

54. G. Mirskii and T. Pokataeva, "Klassy i klassovaia bor"ba v razvivaiushchikhsia stranakh" ("Classes and Class Struggle in Developing Countries"), Mirovaia ekonomika i mezhdunarodnye otnosheniia, 2 (February, 1966), 40.

55. Lefever, op. cit., p. 994.

56. Iordanskii, op. cit., p. 52. It is interesting that all of the footnotes in this article on ethnicity are from Western sources.

57. B. G. Gafurov, G. F. Kim, et al., Natsional'no-osboboditel'noe dvizhenie v Azii i Afrike, Vol. III (Na Novom Puti) (The National Liberation Movement in Asia and Africa [On a New Path] (Moscow: Nauka, 1968), p. 152; also Iordanskii, op. cit., p. 52; Gavrilov, op. cit., p. 48.

58. Potekhin, "Legacy of Colonialism in Africa," p. 17.

59. David Williams, "How Deep the Split in West Africa?" Foreign Affairs, XL, 1 (October, 1961), 125.

60. I. M. Lewis, "Integration in the Somali Republic," in Arthur Hazlewood, ed., African Integration and Disintegration (New York: Oxford University Press, 1967), p. 281.

61. S. T. Kaltakhchian, "On National Unity, Real and Imagined," Pravda, November 26, 1968,

pp. 3-4; trans., <u>CDSP</u>, XX, 48 (December 18, 1968),
4.

62.   I. I. Potekhin, <u>Africa's Future: The
Soviet View</u>, <u>op. cit.</u>, p. 17; "Zadachi izucheniia
. . . ," p. 104; "Bor"ba za vossoedinenie Kameruna"
("The Struggle for Unification of the Cameroon"),
<u>Sovetskaia etnographiia</u>, 5 (September-October,
1959), 63.

4

SHORT-TERM SOLUTIONS TO AFRICAN CENTRIFUGALISM: THE SOCIAL SPHERE

The possible solutions to African centrifugalism that Soviet scholars have investigated include both long-term and short-range answers. The long-term, viewed by these writers as the only definitive approaches, stress a program of economic development (preferably along the noncapitalist path) and the elevation of the progressive sectors to dominance in the political system. The short-term proposals, which this chapter will examine, center on educational, religious, and cultural measures that might accelerate the nation-building process in black Africa.

EDUCATION

The educational procedures suggested by the Soviet authorities include a re-evaluation of the role of the school in the integrative process and the adoption of the "correct" approach to the question of a national language. The correlation between these areas is obvious. The new state must depend on the educational system to inculcate a national consciousness in its citizens. Because language is one of the prime indexes--and perpetuators--

of ethnic exclusiveness, this education must be presented through the vehicle of a single national language.

Soviet Africanists no longer devote much attention to the school *per se* in the integrative program. In the early 1960's, they were very concerned with developing formal education systems in Africa--a concern that found its parallel in the West. Thus, prior to 1965, they envisioned an extensive school network that could overcome the effects of the traditional education most children were receiving from tribal elders and religious leaders (especially the Muslim clergy). V. Kudriavtsev deemed this new system essential, as "there could be no advance to socialism without a simultaneous attainment of general literacy and higher cultural standards."[1] He and other Soviet analysts admitted during this period that it would take a long time before a level of universal education could be attained; however, this was deemed a realizable and positive goal. N. I. Gavrilov, for example, wrote in 1965 of the time when African youths could learn their native language in primary school, study a second language in middle school, and proceed to foreign languages at the university level. He recommended, of course, that the African countries try to use the experience of the Soviet Union, where, during the 1929-30 period, over 40,000 teachers were working for free (while 51,000 were paid).[2] He made no reference to the fact that the African governments might not have the "persuasive" powers possessed by Stalin during this period.

The tenor of later Soviet writings on African education was more realistic. The participation of unemployed or underemployed school graduates in antigovernment activities in Ghana, Ethiopia, Burundi, and Senegal demonstrated that educational policy could not be developed in a vacuum; it had to be coordinated with the economic capacity and psychological orientation of the nation. Thus, whereas a policy of substantially increasing the influx of the local rural population into the towns

might be appropriate for the USSR,[3] where the urban
economy could absorb these people, it was not necessarily the best solution for Africa. Most graduates
could not find jobs in the cities, and it was both
economically irrational and politically dangerous to
educate them for white-collar jobs and then attempt
to return them to the villages.[4]

The Soviet Communists have long been aware of
the revolutionary potential of young people in developing countries, but as the Theses of the 1928
Sixth Comintern Congress showed, they viewed imperialist exploitation as its only catalyst. The youth
would tire of the "unbearably burdensome" labor conditions and the "inhuman conduct" of the capitalist
employers and become front-workers in the anti-
imperialist cause.[5] The Communists could not fore-
see that the young people could become dissatisfied
with their lot under an allegedly noncapitalist
regime (for example, Ghana) or one with which the
USSR maintained good relations (for example, Ethiopia). Influenced by the 1928 theses and their traditional views on the necessity for rapid industrialization and its concomitant, urbanization, Soviet
analysts were ideologically unequipped to appreciate the negative potential of the semirural, semi-
detribalized African youth.

Admittedly, Soviet authorities, as early as
1965, were concerned with the economic wastefulness
resulting from a quantity-oriented African education program; this is evidenced by the report by
Babintseva, delivered at a Conference of the Leningrad University Department of Contemporary Capitalist Economics in October, 1965. However, there apparently were no in-depth studies of the possible
political ramifications prior to the publication of
a major article in October, 1967, in the journal
Mirovaia ekonomika i mezhdunarodnye otnosheniia.
In this article on "Social Shifts in the Towns of
Tropical Africa," Iordanskii warns that the urban
economies are not sufficiently developed to provide
jobs for the peasants leaving the villages and for
the young people. "These two groups largely go by

the board of society and are becoming a powerful re-
serve for the social forces desiring to change the
existing system in one way or another."[6] His analysis of the role of the unemployed in the coup against
Nkrumah in February, 1966, indicates that he feared
this change would proceed in a reactionary direction.

Subsequent analysts used these examinations of
the political tendencies of the "declassed" young
people in the urban areas to call for a major shift
in the policies of the young African states. They
urged that the program of "microindustrialization"
be de-emphasized in favor of a concentration on agricultural development. Kudriavtsev declared that
"the noncapitalist path of development, which pre-
pares the country for socialist reconstruction,
cannot develop the city at the expense of the countryside or the area of the capital city at the expense of the remote areas."[7] However, such a re-
structuring of priorities would not take place without difficulty. The leaders and elites of the developing areas have long considered the development
of heavy industry the most rapid means of attaining
economic independence and securing a prestigious
position in the hierarchy of nations; urbanization
has carried similar symbolic connotations. In the
face of such value systems and the supporting recommendations long given by both the United States and
the Soviet Union, it is understandably difficult
for African leaders to effect a major policy change.
Fidel Castro was able to accomplish this as a result of the totalitarian nature of his regime; also
the trade embargo imposed by many Western countries
meant that he did not have to contend with the
vested interests of foreign companies and their native employees. African leaders, on the other hand,
do not possess similar power resources, nor do they
have the same freedom to manipulate the levers of
economic activity.

As a result of these obstacles, the concentra-
tion on agricultural development advocated by the
Soviet Union (and, coincidentally, the United
States) has not been realized. Ghana and Mali, the

two erstwhile "states of national democracy" in
black Africa, never were able to effect this new
policy, while it remains doubtful whether Guinea
has the power or economic capacity to achieve even
moderate success in this effort. Soviet authorities continue to recommend that this policy be
adopted, but, in late 1969, they were still com-
plaining in the Africa Institute annual about "the
disproportion of attention" being paid to African
urbanization.[8]

    Their awareness that no rapid change is likely
in the sphere of economic policy has motivated them
to advocate that a greater pragmatism should at
least be practiced in the area of education. Their
first suggestion is that the African countries
should abandon at least temporarily their goal of
providing everyone with some degree of high school
education. Instead, they should concentrate on a
program similar to that of socialist Cuba. Here,
the "battle of the sixth grade" is being waged--an
effort to increase the literacy level of workers
and farmers to a middle-elementary range.[9] The results of this modified program would be two-fold:
(1) The educational system would no longer be turning out white-collar workers whom the economy could
not absorb; and (2) the increased literacy of the
general population would make even outlying areas
susceptible to the political and nationalistic
propaganda of the government. This would do more
to eliminate the obstacles to integration and development posed by tribalism than any political assault
or ill-funded economic program.[10]

    The second suggestion advanced by Soviet ana-
lysts is that more emphasis be placed on the development of agricultural schools and on inducing students to enter these institutions. Efforts such as
those made by Guinea in 1966 to expand the curricula
of agricultural schools and to double the enrollment
by 1967 are to be applauded. For, "although agriculture is clearly making headway, the difficulties
ahead are still formidable, not the least of which
are inertia and lack of experience on the part of

the local party and administrative workers."[11] Soviet authorities envision these schools as the
spark that will turn the tide in the ability--and
desire--of the Africans to effect extensive agricultural development. They do not mention that they
have been attempting to spur interest in agricultural education in the USSR for several years and
that the program has been quite unsuccessful.[12]

LANGUAGE

Of course, whether the school is an agricultural or academic institution, the question of language will have to be resolved. For, as Richard
Pipes warns, "mass education and mass literacy also
promote national [or ethnic] distinctions by insti-
tutionalizing local languages, histories, literature, etc."[13] In other words, to attempt to in-
struct people in their native languages in order to
communicate national ideas might have the unintended
effect of intensifying their particularistic feelings. On the other hand, the opposite approach of
teaching all groups the same language could also
have negative consequences: Certain groups may rebel against the national regime that is imposing
this alien tongue, or dissatisfied groups, hitherto
separated by their inability to communicate with
each other, would now be able to form a more cohesive opposition. This latter effect has been particularly noticeable among the Muslims of the USSR;
their own languages are mutually unintelligible,
but this obstacle to the development of a Pan-
Islamic orientation has been nullified by the education of all Soviet groups in the Russian language.[14] Thus, the fact that people speak Russian
is not always a sign that they have become assimi-
lated into the dominant cultural network, as Soviet
sources have alleged.

It is apparent that Soviet analysts are aware
of the potential dangers for Africa of both the
assimilationist and moderate approaches to language
policy; however, the lack of clarity in their own

approach to this question at home has made it very
difficult for them to elaborate any concrete suggestions for Africa. For example, Soviet domestic
policy has gone through three distinct phases:
(1) 1917-30, which stressed the development of the
native languages of the larger ethnic groups; (2)
1931 to the present, which emphasized the establishment of Russian as the lingua franca, and (3) an im-
pending phase that would bring "sharp emphasis on
the sblizhenie or rapprochement of the various nationalities and languages with a view to their eventual sliianie or complete fusion."[15] At first
glance, it seems that the trend toward assimilation
is quite clear. The picture is complicated, however,
by the criticism of this trend by the moderates
(criticism that has so far impeded the adoption of
any definite policy by the Brezhnev-Kosygin regime),
by the Soviet refusal to abandon the famous Stalinist precept that culture should be "national in
form, socialist in content," and, finally, by the
continued teaching of minority languages throughout
the Soviet Union. In sum, if the Soviet leaders
have been unable and/or unwilling to impose the Russian language on all groups to the exclusion of
minority dialects, it is questionable whether they
can urge such a policy on the less powerful and ethnically more complicated states of Africa.

The Soviet leaders have moved relatively slowly for a totalitarian government in developing a
single national language; in fact, it would seem
that they have relied as much on functional impetuses to Russification as on specific governmental
policies. They have counted on the exigencies of
urbanization, economic development, industrialization, and extensive migration to force people to
adopt a common language in the interest of communication and self-advancement. Meanwhile, on the policy level, they first imposed the Latin alphabet on
the written languages of many peoples, moving only
later to the Cyrillic, a two-step policy that was
useful to the Bolsheviks in persuading the minorities that they were not going to continue the coercive policies of Tsarism.[16] More recently, they

have relied on such administrative devices as the
amalgamation of several smaller nationalities and a
larger one into a single Republic to bring about
the abandonment of the lesser languages (this has
happened in Tadzhikistan). They have also established suprarepublican institutions such as the Economic Councils of Khrushchev's day, which joined
peoples of different languages into a single functional unit. This arrangement, of course, made the
use of Russian essential; it had the added advantage of appearing to be dictated by the needs of
economic development and not by any repressive tendencies of the Soviet leadership. This front was
important to the Soviets, because, echoing the
views of such Western experts on nationalism as
Carl Friedrich, they have resolved that,

> in the development of relationships
> among nationalities, such factors as
> psychology and human sentiment play
> a role. Any use of compulsion with
> respect to nationalities not only
> does not break down their structure,
> their social life, but, on the con-
> trary, promotes the strengthening of
> their decision to preserve their na-
> tionality and all its attributes,
> and to preserve their language.[17]

This view was quite firmly adhered to by Lenin;
since Stalin, however, compulsion has not been abjured. It is often important only that the appearances of catering to "psychology and human sentiment" be maintained.

In the realm of theory, Soviet linguistic
views have also been clouded. Soviet authorities
have claimed since prerevolutionary days that their
objective was to ensure the flourishing of every
nationality in the USSR. Since Lenin repeatedly
stated that unity of language was one of the basic
features of a nation and Stalin declared languages
to be one of its four essential indicators, it
might have been presumed that the Kremlin would

help every group to develop its national language.
In the 1920's, when it was important to the Bolsheviks to retain the loyalty of the minorities, this
policy was followed; later, however, when the external threat had diminished, they began to concentrate on the potential threat that might be posed
by several cohesive national groups existing within
the confines of the Soviet state. A unite-and-rule
policy seemed the best way to obviate the danger of
certain small groups' escaping the control of the
central system.   Therefore,

> it now seems to be the policy of the
> Soviet Government to sponsor the na-
> tional development only of those
> major units which are large enough to
> merit an organized State structure.
> This in practice means those groups
> which form Union or autonomous re-
> publics.[18]

The theoretical injunction to develop a nation's
unity of language is now applied to the <u>Soviet</u> nation, not to the minority groups.   In fact, the
Soviet government has often separated peoples speaking similar languages by placing them in different
republican units; this tactic has been employed to
divide the Kazakh and Kirghiz people, the Tatar and
Bashkir, and several Caucasian groups.[19]

Of course, this does not prevent Soviet authorities from criticizing the colonial powers for di-
viding linguistically similar African peoples, thus
allegedly torpedoing their chances for national
unity and development. Potekhin, for example,
charged that

> imperialist ethnographers and lin-
> guists try to justify this colonial
> brigandage by claiming that ethnic
> chaos reigned in Africa prior to the
> advent of colonialism and that the
> colonialists introduced some sem-
> blance of order in this respect. In

> reality, however, it was the colo-
> nialists who created ethnic chaos
> by arbitrarily dividing up the con-
> tinent into a host of political
> units.[20]

Post-Potekhin Africanists, interestingly enough,
have continued this polemical approach regarding
the colonial effect on African linguistics--an approach that they have largely abandoned in other
areas of African research. Thus, N. I. Gavrilov,
author of a 1965 study of independent black Africa,
charged not only that the foreign powers imposed
their languages on the colonial peoples but also
that they forbade them to speak their own dialects
at any time in the classroom.[21] The one explanation for this continued negativism that suggests itself is that Soviet analysts are uncertain of the
effectiveness of any solution they propose.

Recently, a few Soviet Africanists have begun
to admit that perhaps the only solution to the language problem in certain countries is the adoption
of the former metropolitan language as the national
one. Grafskii and Strashun, for example, have
stated that, although Akan is so widespread in
Ghana that it might be developed as a national language, perhaps English should continue to be the
official language in Sierra Leone.[22] Other authorities of similar persuasion have not been quite as
frank. Starushenko, for one, admits that, since
European languages will exist in Africa for a long
time, perhaps the best that the African governments
can do is to attempt to develop their local languages simultaneously. Another author, speaking of
the Cameroon, states that none of the country's one
hundred dialects is sufficiently strong to become a
standard national language.[23]

Although no author writing before 1967--and
only a few after that date--would declare openly
that the elevation of a native dialect into a national language might be impossible for most African countries (except, of course, for Tanzania,

where Swahili is so widespread, and for Ethiopia,
where Haile Selassie's regime has been fairly successful in imposing Amharic on some of the smaller
tribes), a chronological survey of Soviet literature reveals an increasing realism. Indeed, one
can even notice a rather significant modification
of the views of Potekhin--a confirmed Stalinist in
his political orientation--on the subject of European versus African language.

In 1957, Potekhin criticized Nkrumah for his
refusal to abandon English as Ghana's national language.[24] The implication of this criticism was
that the Soviet Union then viewed governmental action as the decisive element in the language-
unification process. Presumably, the promulgation
of an official decree would be sufficient to motivate scholars, educators, and the general public to
work toward the diffusion of the new tongue. "In
the opinion of all progressive circles, in each
African country, one can pick one of the languages
(in certain cases, two or three), which can become
the national language." To effect this policy
would only require creating a written language and
literature, and the expansion of the vocabulary of
the chosen dialect, a task that certainly could be
accomplished by "many trained people."[25]

In these recommendations, Soviet analysts were
concentrating on only one aspect of the typical
action-reaction pattern of governmental policy;
even then, their evaluation of the African regime's
capabilities was hardly realistic. In other words,
they failed to consider that the populace might respond negatively to any attempt to impose an alien
language (for even the language of one tribe could
be alien to a neighboring tribe). And they seemed
to have minimized the possibility that the government might lack sufficient resources of power and
talent to effect new language policies. A further
complication that was ignored prior to late 1961
was that the granting of independence hurled the African countries into the international arena, an arena dominated by the Big Powers and their languages.

To reduce instruction in these languages would only
intensify the adaptation problems of the new states.

Soviet specialists never did acknowledge the
obstacle to linguistic unity posed by the low level
of governmental capabilities. They did admit, however, that there were other serious problems.
Potekhin declared that any resolution would "not be
a matter of eliminating the study of foreign languages altogether--that would be a step back." Nor
would it be a matter of governmental decree, since

> the question of a national language
> must be approached with extreme cau-
> tion. The history of multinational
> states shows that every nationality
> cherishes the right freely to use its
> own language and any restriction of
> this right is bound to lead to na-
> tional conflicts.[26]

Thus, between 1957 and 1961, Soviet views on the
African language question became much more realistic and objective.

However, while the assessment of the nature of
the problem had progressed from the purely negative
one of attributing the blame to the colonialists to
a more reasoned account of the ramifications of
tribal chauvinism, the matter of a solution was
still to be resolved. For, by this time, Soviet
analysts had rejected the two most often advanced
proposals: They had turned down the idea of change
by governmental proclamation because of the national
discord that it might provoke, and they had rejected
the suggestion that only the adoption of a metropolitan language could avoid alienating any tribe, claiming that these European languages could hardly provide "the linguistic foundation for the formation of
African nations."[27] Their new recommendation was
that the African governments should allow the language processes to proceed "spontaneously"--a
laissez-faire approach that supposedly would result
in the establishment of a dominant African dialect
in each state.

It must be acknowledged that this new Soviet
position may have been motivated partly by the reluctance of Soviet scholars to corroborate any Western suggestions, by a fear that the consolidation
of a Western language might aid the extension of
Western influence, and by the inability of Soviet
authorities to advance any positive alternative
measures. However, this "spontaneity" theory of
linguistics was also based on empirical observations made by Potekhin and A. B. Letnev in Ghana
and Mali, respectively. Thus, in January, 1964,
Letnev reported on an intensification of the cultural influence of the Bambara, Mali's largest ethnic group and the continued dissemination of their
language throughout the country. In his report, he
was adamant about the spontaneity of this development.

> It was earlier brought about by his-
> torical causes, but now an even
> greater role is played by the estab-
> lishment of new economic relations
> between the various regions of the
> country. . . . Undoubtedly, the ful-
> fillment of the first Five Year Plan
> of economic and social development
> will create that form of economic
> community which was not and could not
> be formed in Mali under colonialism,
> and without which the idea of a na-
> tion is unthinkable.

Letnev admitted that the government was working
hard to "assist" this process by developing a single Latin-based alphabet for the country's four
principal languages (Bambara, Fulfulde, Tamashek,
and Songhai). However, he concluded that the primary impetus to linguistic unification was provided
by the needs and pressures of economic growth.[28]

Potekhin upheld this view in his book on "the
new Ghana" published posthumously in Moscow in 1965.
He explained that linguistic community was an "in-
dispensable indicator" of a national community:

> If there is no common language, there
> is no nation. The formation of a lan-
> guage of a people [narodnost'] or na-
> tion proceeds this way: one of the
> group of tribal languages becomes for
> a variety of reasons a more wide-
> spread, intertribal language, sup-
> planting the others and at the same
> time being enriched by these other
> languages.[29]

Chief among the "variety of reasons" was industrial
development; as a result of the intermingling of
people from different tribes, which the formation
of large enterprises would necessitate, certain languages would become dominant. Akan was already
more widespread and developed than other Ghanian
languages; with the impetus provided by economic
development, "turning Akan into the national language could be accomplished completely spontaneously, without any special steps by the government."[30]

    This faith in spontaneity was a not unexpected
characteristic of the 1963-64 period--a period which
has been analyzed above as Khrushchev's period of
neo-optimism. Politically, the prospects for Soviet
success in Africa seemed quite good: Ghana, Guinea,
and Mali were continuing in their progression along
the noncapitalist path, and, if Moscow was aware of
any political instability in these countries, little
official mention of it was made. Political optimism
regarding these budding socialist states carried
over to the economic sphere, for, surely, if they
embarked on the noncapitalist path, thus extricating
themselves from the web of capitalist exploitation,
developmental plans would be confirmed.

    Soviet expectations regarding the progress of
these states and the possibility that they might
provide an enticing model for other African governments were, of course, not fulfilled. Soviet dis-
appointments in Africa, combined with the more realistic attitude of the new Brezhnev-Kosygin leadership, led to a re-evaluation not only of policies,

but also of the suggestions they advanced to the
African leaders.

This new realism was especially evident in
their proposals regarding the African language problem. Soviet authorities could no longer adhere to
the claim that economic growth would solve the problem, since economic plans were not being fulfilled
(this was noticeably true of the national democratic
states). Furthermore, the sociopolitical dislocations resulting from the economic growth that had
been achieved could no longer be ignored. Thus, it
was evident that efforts such as those of Nkrumah
to increase the profits accruing to the state from
primary products--for example, cocoa--had the effect of uniting the people, but in a very dangerous
and negative direction. The transfer of cocoa marketing from the long-established boards to the state
alienated the middle men, thus uniting them in
grievance with the small producers and peasants, already angered at the falling price of cocoa.

Furthermore, the industrial plants that were
constructed often did not produce the desired integrative effects; in fact, in many cases, their operation actually intensified ethnic conflicts in
several ways. First, industrial plants were few in
number and small in size; therefore, there was often
great competition among members of different ethnic
groups for jobs (for instance, between the Mende and
Temne in Sierra Leone). Second, governments usually
paid lip service to the idea of constructing these
plants in scattered locations throughout the country. In reality, either the political support of
certain ethnic and regional groups was being re-
warded, or else limited port and transportation
facilities dictated that the plants be constructed
in an already developed area (for example, in the
industrial park of Tema, outside of Accra). Such
moves were often construed by certain tribes as
preferential treatment for a rival group, thereby
rekindling ethnic antipathies and suspicion of the
government. Finally, actual contact--in an industrial or any other setting--with people against

whom one has held long-standing prejudices may only
intensify these hostilities. Industrial workers
may learn to cooperate with each other to perform
certain tasks essential to the plant's functioning;
however, there is very little evidence that such
on-the-job collaboration will lead to any rapid
abatement of intergroup hostilities.[31] Thus, although the Fanti have been working with people of
other tribes in Takoradi industry since the early
days of Ghanaian independence, they are still re-
sented as the largest single group in many firms,
and their hesitancy to engage in extensive social
communication with the other tribes is still very
apparent.

The effects of these negative consequences of
economic growth on linguistic unification are obvious. If interethnic hostility and resentment of
dominant tribes still prevail, smaller groups will
not willingly assume the language of the larger
ones. In addition, it seems that, if industrialization proceeds slowly, the positive effects that
will eventually accrue to the national integration
effort will be moved further into the future. In
the meantime, plants and enterprises apparently
will be prizes to be fought over, rather than units
in a vast economic web designed to pull the country
together.

There have been numerous signs in the post-
Khrushchev era that Soviet authorities are aware
that economic development is not proceeding as
planned in many African states and that it cannot
be relied on spontaneously to produce the desired
results in language unification. Thus, they first
began to comment on the "insufficiencies" of the
economics-linguistics relationship and then moved
on to a discussion of specific governmental measures
that would be necessary to effect what Potekhin had
termed a "natural" process. Starushenko's frank
assessment of these insufficiencies in his 1967
book on the role of the state in the new countries
epitomized this new approach:

> In the countries of Tropical Africa,
> where the processes of national con-
> solidation <u>are just beginning</u>, where
> countries have a very complex ethnic
> base, and where <u>often there are no</u>
> <u>ethnic groups forming a majority of</u>
> <u>the population</u>, the influence of the
> statehood factor on the process of
> developing new nations is especially
> strong. The concrete paths of this
> process, especially the choice of a
> single language and its diffusion
> among the population, have not been
> worked out everywhere.[32]

The implication is very clear in this statement
that, in the first decade of independence, allowing
natural processes to go on (that is, the laissez-
faire approach) had had little effect on national
unification. The conclusion was inescapable that
the state, which Mnatsakanian terms Africa's "active organizing force," had to step in to "actively promote the process of developing national languages,"[33] thus becoming the prime mover in the
nation-building program.

Another indication of the growing realism of
Soviet authorities on the question of a national
language for the African states is provided by the
reversal in their theoretical views on the relationship between language and economic growth. Thus,
whereas they had previously considered the fusion
of dialects into one national language to be the result of economic concentration, they now claimed
that the reverse was true. V. I. Kozlov, in an
article billed by the journal <u>Narody Azii i Afriki</u>
(<u>Peoples of Asia and Africa</u>) as an "Elaboration of
the Theoretical Bases of the National Question"
(1967), declared that

> one language and its unimpeded growth
> is one of the most important condi-
> tions of the free and wide trade

circulation corresponding to contemporary capitalism, of the free
and wide grouping of the population
into separate classes, and finally,
of the firm link of the marketplace
with every seller and buyer.[34]

A unified language was now deemed the prerequisite
for economic growth, rather than its by-product.
The significance of this correlation was not lost
on the Soviet leaders: Since they considered Africa's economic development to be in their best interest (and, coincidentally, in the best interest of
Africa), they felt impelled to urge the African
states to adopt concrete measures to accelerate
linguistic unification.

Recently, Soviet authorities have proposed several measures that could lead to the development of
a national language. First, they suggest the establishment of a native vernacular literacy program--a
program they deem so important that they have actually contributed to its support in Guinea. This
program centers on the creation of a written language to express oral dialects and on the publication of national and local works in this language.
These steps, it is hoped, will enrich the national
culture, thereby facilitating the development of a
sense of national belonging, and will pave the way
for the abolition of illiteracy. This second measure, a general literacy drive, would promote linguistic unification because dictionaries could be
published defining phrases from the local dialect
in terms of the more developed languages. These
languages, in turn, would become more widespread,
thus reversing the present situation where "the foreign language, whether it be French or English, is
the possession of the small educated elite and not
of the masses."[35]

Soviet authorities, however, acknowledge that
the replacement of the European languages will be a
lengthy process. Therefore, they advise the young
African states to adopt the policy of "linguistic

pluralism," which has been so successful in the Soviet Union.[36] By recommending this path, they are,
in effect, telling the Africans that a moderate,
gradual program would be the wisest choice. Such a
program would not require a substantial outlay of
funds and, therefore, would free the Soviet leaders
from a potentially embarrassing political situation--
a situation where they would have to deny yet another African request for financial aid.

The third Soviet proposal, that any language
unification program should proceed on a voluntary
basis, is an offshoot of this more realistic and
moderate approach. Soviet authorities recommend
that the radio be used more efficiently to educate
people in the more developed languages, and they
note that perhaps these languages could be used
more extensively in the administration, the legal
system, and in the schools. However, the idea that
an official decree should be promulgated is explic-
itly rejected. For, as Iordanskii wisely notes,

> as soon as suspicion spreads, then the
> power of the resolve to create favor-
> able conditions for [the elevation of]
> one of the local languages immediately
> encounters sharp resistance. In the
> current epoch of awakening national
> consciousness, such protests are very
> strong.[37]

When this statement in 1967 is compared with Potekhin's 1957 recommendation that the government
resolve the language problem by fiat, as it were,
the strides toward realism made by Soviet analysts
in a single decade become very clear.

RELIGION

A third category of short-term integrative measures suggested by Soviet Africanists concerns re-
ligion--a category that is inextricably connected
with the problems of traditions, idealization of

the past, and also cultural heterogeneity. The issue of religion has received both the greatest attention and the most tortuous treatment, for it is
one that involves Soviet theorists in discussions
of ideology, defense of their domestic policies,
and disputes about the political potential of one
of Africa's strongest religions, Islam.

Ideologically, of course, communism has always
been opposed to religion. Marx's famous reference
to religion as the opiate of the masses--that is,
as a force retarding the development of class con-
sciousness--was retained and amplified by the Bolsheviks. As Lenin expressed it,

> God is (from the historical and prac-
> tical standpoint) primarily a complex
> of ideas begotten by the crass sub-
> missiveness of man, by external nature
> and by class oppression--ideas which
> tend to perpetuate this submissive-
> ness, to deaden the force of the class
> struggle.[38]

The deadening effect of Christianity was bad enough,
but it was something the Bolsheviks were relatively
confident that they could overcome; even Lenin had
to admit, however, that the influence of Islam
would be extremely difficult to eradicate.

For there were several key differences in the
nature of the two religions. First, whereas the
idea of Christian brotherhood has always been com-
paratively vague, the concept of the Umma, or Community of Believers, was very strong among the Muslims, thereby perpetuating their sense of separate-
ness from the other Soviet peoples.[39] Second, the
wrongdoings and opulent living of certain members
of the Russian Orthodox clergy were notorious and
could be used to turn people against all organized
religion. In Islam, however, the clergy occupied
no position of comparable relevance; its deeds,
therefore, could not be easily exploited for anti-
religious purposes. Third, for Russian Christians,

the separation of church and state was a relatively well-established principle; as a result, their
religious beliefs presented a distinct and well-
defined target for the activists of the atheism
campaign. Islam, on the other hand, "confronted
the regime not only as a religion but also as a
legal framework, a way of life, and as a whole network of institutions."[40]   These elements were all
intertwined and mutually reinforcing. Since the
regime did not have the power resources to attack
the entire system of religion, land endowments,
courts, and schools, it had to settle for dismant-
ling the institutions one by one. This process was
largely accomplished by 1930, but, even without its
institutional supports and manifestations, Islam as
a belief system remained strong.

        This persistence, of course, is characteristic
of many religions in the Soviet Union; however, the
virulence of Islam is also attributable to geopoliti-
cal factors. Most of the Soviet Union's Muslims are
concentrated in Central Asia, an area characterized
by a relatively low index of economic development.
The nomadic and subsistence farming life-style precluded the formation of a strong proletariat--the
group traditionally relied on by Communists to be
the vanguard of any atheism program. Lenin expected
economic development to bring about "that differen-
tiation of the proletariat from the bourgeois elements which is inescapable"[41] and which would accelerate the demise of organized religion. However,
although Moscow has poured tremendous financial resources into Central Asia, Islam is still widespread. Economic development has not worked to
eradicate Islam. Since World War II, outright suppression has been deemed inadvisable. Geopolitics
continues to render Islam immune to any final solu-
tion--a fact the Soviet government can deplore only
in verbal terms. For, as the editors of _Mizan_ have
pointed out, Soviet policy toward Islam has always
been characterized by two "frequently conflicting"
preoccupations. On the one hand, they distrust it
"as a force capable of mobilizing not only anti-
Communist but also anti-Russian sentiment." However,

they still deem it essential to secure "the good
will and support of Muslims both inside and outside
the U.S.S.R."[42]

Thus, just as in the early years of the Revolution, when the Bolsheviks were willing to downplay
ideology to secure an alliance with the Muslim nationalists, so the CPSU continued to make concessions to the Muslim clergy in order that their
mosques might be showcases to impress visitors from
the Arab and African world. The Soviets are con-
summately skilled in manipulating (or sacrificing)
ideology to serve the needs of policy--a skill they
have demonstrated increasingly in their relations
with the Muslims of Africa.

Admittedly, it took Soviet authorities several
years to recognize the need for a more pragmatic
outlook vis-à-vis Africa's Muslim peoples. In the
early years of their contact with the African nationalist movement, they were strongly influenced
by the views propounded by Lenin at the Second Comintern Congress in July, 1920. He declared that
for all Communist parties,

> it is essential to struggle against
> the reactionary and medieval influ-
> ence of the priesthood, the Christian
> missions, and similar elements. It
> is necessary to struggle against the
> pan-Islamic and pan-Asiatic movements
> and similar tendencies, which are
> trying to combine the liberation
> struggle against European and Ameri-
> can imperialism with the strengthen-
> ing of the power of Turkish and Jap-
> anese imperialism and of the nobil-
> ity, the large landlords, the
> priests, etc.[43]

The implication here was twofold: first, that religion in the colonies served no other purpose than
to mask the "reactionary" intentions of certain
feudal and bourgeois elements; second, that Muslim

groups that joined in the fight against Western imperialism were only trying to remove another obstacle to the consolidation of their own reactionary rule.

A chronological examination of Soviet writing
on religion since the 1950's reveals no easily
determined or radical shifts in attitudes, or any
relaxation of the general suspicion and hostility
toward religion evident in the earliest Marxist
theories. What is discernible, however, is a growing tendency to examine specific nationalist movements in order to determine the actual role of religious groups, to study the influence of religion
on the integrative or nation-building process, and
to suggest more moderate methods of "modernizing"
the masses' world outlook.

In other words, the Western analyst can make
no claim to have discovered, for example, that
whereas in the 1950's, Soviet views on the role of
religion were uniformly negative, the following
decade brought forth an abundance of positive as-
sessments. The trend toward a more objective appraisal is undoubtedly noticeable, but the past
twenty years have been characterized by one con-
tinuous debate. As a result, several more positive
characteristics have been attributed to religion,
but few negative ones have been renounced.

Soviet analysts are critical of the role of religion in Africa for several reasons. First, they
fear that it will retard the development of class
consciousness and, as a result, the deterioration
of the anti-imperialistic ethic. This concern applies particularly to Islam, for the strong concept
of Umma--the idea that "All Muslims are brothers"--
can render the Muslims impervious to Communist
teachings that the basic world conflict is between
classes, not religions. This notion of community
"in reality masks the calls for the division of
workers according to religion, the denial of socialist internationalism and the friendship of peoples
of the USSR, the call for Muslim exclusiveness."[44]

If the followers of Islam are not aware of class
differences, they may fall prey to the machinations
of the imperialists and their bourgeois agents.
This danger is especially real, since, in many African countries, "religion became one of the forms of
nationalistic reaction against colonial enslave-
ment." This support for the liberation cause was,
of course, a positive phenomenon, regardless of the
underlying motivation. However, large segments of
the masses still believe that religion should be
the basis for any "opposition mentality." This retards the development of the liberation movement,
since the imperialist enemy long ago dropped his
Christianizing mission in favor of more subtle
forms of oppression.[45]

A corollary to this Soviet criticism is the
claim that the absence of class consciousness that
religion perpetuates may help to consolidate the
position of the feudal--and bourgeois--reactionaries
in African society. Soviet theorists believe that
all religions can be manipulated for these counterrevolutionary purposes. For example, traditional
animist creeds can be used to bolster the power of
tribal chiefs, men described by Potekhin as "theocratic rulers who rely on the ancient religious beliefs of the people, on the still considerable survivals of the primitive communal structure."[46] Potekhin's theory here is that, if the hold of religion over the masses could be broken, the power of
the chiefs would be correspondingly diminished;
other analysts, meanwhile, present religion as the
basis of support for reactionaries of every type.
Thus, R. A. Ul'ianovskii credits religion with maintaining bourgeois nationalists, landlords, and money-
lenders, claiming that their efforts to develop
"illusions of class peace" work at convincing the
peasants that land reform can be realized without
any "revolutionary action" against these oppressive
groups.[47] The repetition of these charges in 1967
by V. G. Solodovnikov, Director of the Africa Institute, makes it apparent that Soviet analysts still
see religion as a major obstacle to the success of
the anti-imperialist revolution in Africa.[48]

A third Soviet fear regarding the continued
strength of religion in Africa is that it might
thwart communism in its drive to become the basis
for the development of a new African culture and,
coincidentally, of a new Africa. For the past several years, there has been a determined effort by
certain world Muslim leaders to "modernize" Islam,
to make it a suitable vehicle for expressing ideas
essential to the political and economic development
of Asia and Africa. This reform movement is welcomed by the Communists in that it might break down
certain barriers to the consolidation of their own
ideology. However, they cannot be sure that Islam
itself will not become the dominant political ethic
in several African countries.[49]

This would adversely affect Soviet plans in
several ways. First, it might hamper the extension
of Soviet influence over specific governments.
Second, it might provide the foundation for a type
of West African "Muslim League"--a league that
might look to the countries of North Africa and the
Middle East for guidance, rather than to the Soviet
Union. This, of course, approximates Pan-Islam, a
movement that Soviet authorities fear even more
than Pan-Africanism because of its long historical
roots and the basis for unity that religion can provide. Finally, even if Islam did not become the
basis of an independent continent-wide movement, it
could be useful in securing adherents to African
socialism. Mamadou Dia has skillfully exploited it
for this purpose, while Senghor has used Christianity in the same way. Such uses of religion can
only increase Soviet anxieties that any African socialist movement might be more African than socialist.

Of course, religion can also be criticized as a
disintegrative factor--both on the continental and
national level. Interestingly enough, Soviet analysts have paid little attention to the role religion might play in torpedoing any chance for a
United Africa--an indication, perhaps, that they do
not deem the success of African unity to be in
their best interests, or that the prospect is so

remote that they feel religion should be criticized
on other, more relevant grounds.[50] Thus, many analysts have concentrated on the role of religion in
the nation-building process.

For example, Potekhin described religion as an
"obstacle to creating a united national front"--an
obstacle even more difficult than tribalism to overcome. He went on to refer to Ghana's experience,
claiming that Islam "supported the most reactionary
forces during the intense political fight over problems connected with Ghana's constitution."[51] In
more recent articles, Soviet writers have analyzed
the polarization evident in many West African countries between the Muslim North and the animist-
Christian South, especially in Chad, the Cameroon,
and Nigeria. They decry this division not only because it prevents national consolidation, but, more
importantly, because it provides fuel for the separatist tactics of the "forces of local reaction"
and the neocolonialist powers. In Chad, for example, such forces reportedly have prevented "progressive elements from both religious groups" from
uniting "in a single patriotic front."[52]

This admission that religious groups can include progressive elements who would be willing to
cooperate in a single-party system (considered essential to any revolutionary program) is an indication that Soviet analysts have adapted their views
on religion to African conditions. They have realized that religion is a strong force in many African countries and, furthermore, that many African
leaders are determined to retain it as an integral
part of their development ethic. Therefore, "in
order to make the Soviet model more palatable to
religious African nations" and to their leaders who
are among the most charismatic on the continent,
Soviet criticisms of religion have been toned down
significantly. Their approach since 1962 has been
to "couple attacks upon religion with statements to
the effect that even though religion has many negative aspects, it may nevertheless exist in a socialist society."[53]

Soviet authorities have adopted a more realistic attitude toward the problem of religion in Africa for three reasons: first, as noted, to ensure that communism would not be rejected simply because of its atheistic corollaries; second, to bring their theoretical position more in line with the data compiled by their own researchers on the tenacity of religion in Africa; and third, to forestall the West from presenting religion as a basis for continuing rapport with the black African region. The first and last points are closely related, for, if the Communists did not learn to downplay the importance of scientific atheism to their over-all model of development, the West could add to its propaganda arsenal a weapon that the Communists themselves provided. According to certain Soviet analysts, this danger is a real one:

> . . . the imperialists try to use the
> religious question to further their
> own interests and goals. They want
> to find a common language with the
> people of the liberated Afro-Asian
> countries on the following basis:
> "You believe in God, we also believe.
> The Communists do not, therefore
> they are our common enemy. Religion
> can unite us in the struggle against
> the Communist-atheists."[54]

If the nature of the epoch is such that religion could aid the forces of counterrevolution, then the "concrete-historical approach" dictated by Marxist dialectics demands that Marxist-Leninists "find a common language with religious-minded people . . . and work for unity with them."[55]

This same concrete-historical approach has been used by Soviet Africanists in describing the persistence of religion as an element of the African sociopsychological arena. Investigations of specific countries such as Mali, Guinea, and Senegal have provided the factual material for some rather broad and, for Soviet analysts, sober

conclusions. Thus, they have deduced that socialists of every variety will have to take religion
into consideration in formulating their appeals and
programs for a long time to come.

> Religious ideas have been sustained
> for centuries by the whole tenor of
> life. They have been strengthened
> by common customs, family usages, and
> the system of social institutions,
> such as the caste system or village
> communes, whose foundations have
> their reflection in religious no-
> tions. Naturally, these notions
> cannot disappear within a few de-
> cades, all the more so since the
> social conditions of life which gave
> rise to them have changed little.[56]

That the factors influencing the growth of religion
have not yet been eliminated and that the relationship between social structures and religions continues to be a symbiotic one have persuaded the Soviet authorities that neither their atheism nor
their methods of realizing it can quickly be realized in Africa.

The Soviet leaders had the power, resources,
and cadres, for example, to eliminate any threat to
their regime emanating from the Muslim peoples;
furthermore, they were aided in their determination
by the fact that the Muslims were a minority, and a
geographically compact and relatively isolated people. The Soviet leaders could round up certain Muslim nomadic peoples into supervised collectives, impose a unified educational system, and manipulate
the governmental structures of the area to accelerate the assimilation-secularization process. The
fact that their power base was actually the Great
Russian, non-Muslim majority meant that the Communists could even be discriminatory in this process;
they could form six Central Asian republics out of
peoples who could ethnically and culturally have
been grouped into three, thus allowing the Muslims

much less national and cultural homogeneity than exists in the other federal units.[57]

The assimilation of the Soviet Muslims has not been complete, nor has the regime been free of challenges from other religious groups; in fact, as noted previously, the Soviet leaders have had to temper their antireligious efforts at various times during their fifty-year tenure. Nevertheless, the assertion can still be made that, as a result of their unique system capabilities, including a very efficient political socialization network and the material and symbolic resources to reward (or elicit) supportive behavior, their achievements in secularizing the Soviet population have been significant. The system capabilities of the African states, by contrast, are extremely weak. They cannot, as Zotov urges, follow the Soviet example in "resolutely suppressing" any religious activity they deem counterrevolutionary, nor do they have the resources to launch a "cultural revolution" in the form of a crash literacy program to remove the "ignorance of the elementary questions of the universe."[58] Furthermore, an African regime must tread softly lest it lose the support of even the smallest element in its power base; under such conditions, any measures against religious groups often would be extremely ill-advised.

Soviet analysts have acknowledged the significance of religious tolerance to the continued existence of contemporary African regimes. In fact, in an article on socialist regimes in the Third World, Tiagunenko remarked that

> in the liberated countries, where the
> religious factor is an important aspect of the real existing situation,
> it would be adventurism to ignore it.
> Opposing the practice of religious
> rites in these conditions means insulting the religious feelings of believers, completely isolating oneself
> from the masses, and discrediting the
> idea of social liberation.[59]

Tiagunenko later expanded this thesis in a book on
Problems of the Contemporary National-Liberation
Revolution, warning somewhat frankly that in view
of the above considerations, "it is not accidental
that the leaders of almost all the young states give
religion a place of honor in one way or another."[60]

The Soviet Communists remain convinced that
scientific atheism will eventually triumph over religion in Africa. They caution, however, that any
direct governmental action to expedite this process
might well be counterproductive; the only approach
open to African regimes is the indirect one of relying on the spread of education and the material development of society to undo what decades--and cen-
turies--of religious socialization have accomplished.[61] These strictures against overt action
are especially applicable in the case of Islam,
for, ironically enough, the Soviet authorities seem
to have adopted the views of M. Sultan-Galiev, a
Muslim Communist who was criticized by Moscow in
the 1920's for his allegedly Pan-Islamic tendencies.
He advocated a program of "anti-religious propaganda,
and not of anti-religious struggle," whereby party
representatives of Muslim origin would carry on discussions of religious topics among the Muslim workers in towns and factories, giving them new information which would be gradually passed on to the villages. Above all, he reminded his superiors that

> when we conduct anti-religious propa-
> ganda among the Muslims, we must not
> forget for a moment that their cul-
> tural backwardness and their position
> as a politically and morally down-
> trodden people are their main evil.
> . . . As long as we do not break
> these chains [of political backward-
> ness], as long as we do not make
> these peoples truly free and equal
> citizens of the Soviet republic, no
> anti-religious propaganda can be suc-
> cessful. The improvement in the edu-
> cation of the Muslim peoples; the

> extensive drawing of these peoples
> into economic and administrative,
> and also political, organs of the
> government, whenever that is pos-
> sible; the widening of party work
> among them--these are the tasks of
> the day.[62]

Such a program would, of course, require decades before any concrete successes were achieved; the Soviet authorities were not willing to wait that long
at home, but, in Africa, they have little choice.

Soviet analysts have adapted very well to the
dim prospects of short-range religious reform: They
have turned their attentions to an analysis of the
contributions that religion might render to the anti-
imperialist struggle.   Historically, they have recognized that religious leaders have been in the fore-
front of the independence struggle, especially in
predominantly Muslim countries such as Guinea and
Mali.   They see this Muslim radicalism as a progressive factor today in pro-Western states such as
Senegal, where "the vast majority of the Muslim
clergy, who have always adhered to positions of
militant nationalism," have risked the hatred of
the ruling clique to take an independent stand
against foreign domination.[63]   Such analyses, of
course, neglect to mention that the Muslims may
have domestic political reasons for opposing Senghor
and that perhaps they are not motivated primarily by
foreign policy considerations.   However, to the Soviet authorities, any activity that might spur
Senghor to adopt a less conservative position is
welcome.   (Perhaps they feel that the Senegalese
Communists could exploit Muslim radicalism as a
lever to power in the way the Bolsheviks used the
Muslim nationalists, the Jadids, in Tashkent in
1918.)

A second positive aspect of religion is that
it sometimes provides a familiar, and therefore,
less suspect, vehicle for the transmission of radical political ideas to the masses.   It may be

possible either to use traditional religious leaders to lend legitimacy to a national regime or to
divert long-standing religious hostilities (for example, Muslim-Christian) into channels of political
action against the colonial powers. Soviet theorists often resort "ritualistically" to Lenin's dictum that "political protests in a religious cloak
are common to all peoples at a certain stage of
their development," striving, in Tillett's words,
to "dismiss the obvious contradiction of a progressive movement with a reactionary cause."[64] Of
course, whether this device is ideologically consis-
tent or not, it has been applied successfully by
the CPSU at home and, in view of political realities,
cannot be discarded in the African context. For,
although the retention of religion as an integral
element in the nationalist ideology can be bent to
the purposes of the reactionaries, it nevertheless
represents one main hope of the progressives:

> First, in the conditions of the gen-
> eral cultural backwardness of coun-
> tries long ruled by the colonialists
> and feudalists, religion remains the
> most popular and generally understood
> form of world view; secondly, con-
> sciousness of belonging to one reli-
> gious community here is often identi-
> fied with consciousness of national
> community, in the sense that religion
> can be used as an ideological weapon
> in the struggle against heterodox
> oppressors.[65]

Thus, the progressives must learn to work within
the constraints imposed by African realities if they
are to communicate their ideas to the masses. Furthermore, they must learn to collaborate with "lib-
erally inclined" religious leaders, for, in many
African countries, the clergy provides the only communications link between large segments of the
masses and the outside world. Collaboration is the
only realizable way to strengthen the national democratic front and to isolate the "reactionary feudal-
theocratic forces."[66]

A final reason for a positive Soviet assessment of religion--in this case, Islam--is that it thwarted the impact of the West upon African culture and society. It is apparent that Soviet Africanists borrowed this approach from the British analyst, J. S. Trimingham, for they have reviewed his works in Soviet Ethnography and have applied his criteria to their own studies of traditional African religions. Thus, E. Ia. Batalov has described how Christianity was able to oust local African religions, thereby subjecting the people to the full brunt of Western ideas,[67] whereas, according to L. Kubbel', Muslim law, the Arabic language, and the concept of community insulated the Muslims of West Africa against any such Western inroads.[68] This imperviousness, of course, is applauded by the Soviet authorities, as it means that, in dealing with the Muslims, the African "progressives" will not have to strip away a long-established system of Western political ideas. This optimism is, however, unwarranted, for the network of beliefs that protected the Muslims against the West might also render the Soviet ideology impenetrable.

Nevertheless, Soviet authorities must continue to direct their thoughts toward the possible positive ramifications of religion in Africa, for, in effect, they have no other choice: Their own analysts have described its continued strength, while the staunchest supporters they have had in Africa, such as Gamel Abdul Nasser and Sekou Toure, have made religion an integral part of their modernizing ideologies. It can be hoped that religion will help instill in the masses a sense of national community, thereby strengthening the few remaining pro-Soviet regimes until such a time when the believers can "decide for themselves whether socialist construction is compatible with religious prejudice."[69] Meanwhile, to alter Academician Zhukov's pronouncement only slightly,

> The logic of resisting imperialism's
> constant provocations and the need to
> repulse its encroachments on the sov-
> ereign rights and vital interests of

new states force them [and the Soviet
Union] to seek mutual support and encourage them to take coordinated actions, regardless of their fundamental differences.[70]

CULTURE

The term "fundamental differences" as it applies to the social sphere subsumes not only the
category of approaches to the religious question
but also the issues of the use of culture as an integrative factor, and the attempts of African leaders to develop this culture through idealization of
the African traditional heritage. In 1917, the Soviets themselves abandoned their ideological hostility to allowing national cultures to flourish,
but this was only a temporary aberration--a tacti-
cal measure designed to win over the various non-
Russian minorities to the Bolshevik cause. Their
true strategy remained the one advanced by Lenin in
his "Theses on the Problem of Nationality" (1913):

> From the point of view of national
> democracy, it is inadmissable to put
> forward the slogan of national cul-
> ture either directly or indirectly.
> The slogan is wrong, since the whole
> economic, political, and spiritual
> life of mankind has become more and
> more internationalized under capi-
> talism. Socialism will interna-
> tionalize it completely.[71]

According to Marxist-Leninist thought, it would
have been a reactionary and counterrevolutionary
move to rely on the national cultural heritages to
integrate the nation. Such activity would have
legitimized nationalism, thereby creating a further
obstacle to the eventual establishment of the international culture of the world proletariat. The
only correct solution was to stress the economic
development of the various regions, thereby uniting

the country through economic ties and through the
progressive culture of materialism. The only group
qualified to "manage" this process was the party,
for it alone could be trusted "to avoid any spontaneity and any kind of laissez-faire attitude and to
direct this process along a channel useful to the
people." In other words, the party was the one organization with sufficient cadres (that is, Russians)
and discipline (that is, democratic centralism) to
guide the country's cultural development in a "clearly expressed ideological direction."[72]

The Soviet Union is aware that African states
share neither its organizational assets nor its
level of economic development--elements that operate as important functional impetuses to national-
cultural integration. In fact, B. S. Erasov, apparently the resident Soviet expert on the role of culture in the African integrative process, has conceded in several articles that the peculiarities of
the problem have "called forth new conceptions of
culture affirming the priority of cultural values,
beliefs, ethical norms, historical traditions, and
institutions as the basis for social cohesion."[73]
Efforts to develop and promulgate the idea of a common cultural heritage are useful in the African context in view of the fact that the extensive political, ethnic, and religious heterogeneity often nul-
lify attempts to present any other idea as a unifying agent. Furthermore, symbols and traditions can
aid the regime in transmitting important political
and social information in an acceptable and compre-
hensible form.

Of course, in adopting this approach, African
leaders must be careful "to avoid the Scylla of extreme traditionalism and the Charybdis of 'cultural
revolution' in the Maoist sense."[74] It is undoubtedly difficult on the abstract level for Soviet
authorities to decide which of these prospects is
the most distasteful; however, since African socialism is stronger than Maoism in black Africa at the
present time, its tenets on culture are the ones
that have been singled out for attack. This

criticism has been highly selective, however, depending on the relation of the Soviet government
with the African socialist leaders during a particular period.[75]

Nevertheless, this selectivity cannot be interpreted as a renunciation or abandonment of ideological concerns: If it is at all possible to steer
the African governments onto a path closer to the
Soviet position, then this will certainly be attempted. On the issue of African culture, Soviet
authorities have directed all their analytical and
persuasive talents toward swaying the Africans from
the "Scylla of extreme traditionalism." They applaud the concept that certain traditional African
values must be emphasized in order to develop the
dignity of the African, for, in so doing, they can
criticize the Western imperialists for having destroyed this dignity. However, Soviet authorities
do not approve of the implication of this emphasis,
the implication that there is a uniquely black African culture. This they claim is racism, and they
deem it dangerous for several reasons. First, it
opposes black people to white, thereby replacing the
Soviet promoted dichotomy of socialist-imperialist
with a racial one from which the USSR cannot profit
at all. Second, a uniquely black culture is a concept that is exploitable by the Communist Chinese,
for they can claim that all "colored" peoples should
unite against the white oppressors. (Soviet fears
on this score have not proved unjustified, for the
Chinese have derived a great deal of political mile-
age from the color issue. They have had significant
success in promoting the idea of an Afro-Asian Solidarity Movement in which they would be represented
while the [white] Russians would be excluded.)
Third, the stress on black culture in Africa could
provide fertile ground for the efforts of certain
American blacks to divert the attention of the Africans from the national liberation movement at home
to the more general cause of ending black oppression
everywhere. Finally, the cultural emphasis could
function as yet another deterrent to the development
of class consciousness.

Such calculations have prompted Soviet authorities to strive to persuade the African socialists to modify their cultural programs. Their argument is that, while the traditional culture could function as a very effective medium for the transmission of new political and social values--that is, as a politicization tool--its incorporation into the value system would actually retard the politicization process. The masses would view this incorporation as legitimization of what Erasov terms their "myths and totems," thereby giving them no impetus whatsoever to modernize. The only solution to the problem of utilizing these traditions without perpetuating them is to abandon the view that they represent "an unchangeable 'heritage' which exists only to crown the governmental apparatus with new sanctions." Rather they should be seen as an instrument of mass mobilization. For, as Erasov urges,

> the existing culture is an important means of transmitting socially significant information, it acts as a mediator in social relations, its forms should be used to make events understandable to the people.[76]

If the traditional culture is viewed in this way, it could indeed provide African radicals with a very important weapon to induce the masses to join organizations aimed at the political modernization of society, and at the integration of all the various ethnic groups into the national community. Tribal members could identify with the national ethic, if it contained elements that were familiar to them, and, conversely, only the creation of an acceptable national ethic could wean people away from their disparate and localized traditions. In sum, the national government can succeed in its cultural integration drive only to the extent that it is able to persuade the masses that it respects their traditional heritage, that it incorporates only the more progressive, democratic elements in this heritage, and that it promotes interaction between the various local cultures. Here, of course,

the cultural interaction program of the USSR is
viewed as instructive, for Soviet officials have
consistently stressed the publication of works of
national literature in all the local languages, the
celebration of festivals of the culture of a certain republic in other republics, interrepublic meetings of authors and artists, and the exchange of
cadres in all the cultural spheres.[77]

Soviet Africanists point out, however, that the
use of culture as an integrator is a very complicated procedure and one that is subject to several
pitfalls: It might be exploited by separatist elements; it might lead to the exclusion of valuable
elements from other cultures; or the program might
not be keyed to the needs of future development.
These dangers must be faced by all African governments, but it is interesting to note the Soviet
statement that "progressive" regimes have a greater
chance of coping with them successfully. For, according to Erasov, the success ratio is a function
of the social orientation of the ideology (that is,
conservative or radical), the presence or absence
of a "higher culture," the character of existing
ties with the culture of other countries, and, finally, the "degree of democracy (or hierarchical
isolation) of the system of cultural values, which
directly depends on the democratic nature of the
social structure."[78]

However, Soviet authorities concede that an African regime, regardless of its political coloring,
might encounter difficulties in preventing separatist elements from capitalizing on its cultural program. These reactionary elements might be ethnic
groups or they might be the feudal and bourgeois
classes, as any of these has a vested interest in
preventing national consolidation. Thus ethnic
leaders could appeal to the traditions embodied in
the national cultural ethic to ensure that the basis
of legitimacy for their power would not be under-
mined: They could manipulate the old beliefs, myths,
and religious norms to glorify the local culture,
thus ensuring that their fellow tribesmen would not

transfer their allegiance to the national leadership.   In fact, some Soviet analysts believe they are aided in this reactionary effort by certain ethnographers, "especially those of the so-called functional school," who idealize the sacralization of chiefs and kings in Africa.

> They affirm that this is an autoch-
> thonous tradition which is vitally
> linked to the existence of the peo-
> ples who elaborated it.   It is use-
> less to contest the autochthonous
> character of this tradition.   However
> that is not to say that every tradi-
> tion is good and should be maintained
> only because of its local origin.
> . . .   The sacralization of the power
> of chiefs and kings is not only a
> theme of historical or ethnographic
> research; it is an actual political-
> social problem whose solution will
> require a great deal of effort and
> political wisdom.[79]

Both researchers and politicians should realize that, although sacralization is doomed to disappear as African society develops, traditions and myths can be sustained for a long time through the conscious or inadvertent efforts of members of both these groups.   It is admirable that they should attempt to satisfy the interest of the African in his past--an interest that has become particularly strong "with the rise of the struggle for liberation."   However, it is both wrong and harmful for authorities to declare that

> the tribes, the tribal chiefs, and
> tribal relations in general are an
> integral part of this "African way
> of life."   This conclusion is due
> to a lack of insight into the laws
> of social development.[80]

For, as Iordanskii notes, in a prime example of the functional approach criticized above by Charevskaia,

only if the tribal structure is allowed to die out
will the masses be susceptible to any national integration program. In other words, there is a direct "relationship between the degree of disintegration of the internal tribal structure of an ethnic
group and its readiness to enter into contacts with
other ethnic groups."[81]

Soviet analysts will concede that the African
nationalist leaders do have more than a passing interest in promoting national integration. However,
they claim that this interest is sometimes sacrificed to the preservation of the alliance with the
feudal-bourgeois elite. In most African countries,
this alliance is crucial to the functioning of the
one-party system, for, in order to obtain the support of the tribalized masses, the party has coopted ethnic leaders into the leadership network.
This maneuver is often crucial to the operation of
any national integration program, but it also has
serious disintegrative consequences. For, in effect, it means that the political structure and
ideology characteristic of the tribal or semifeudal
social system has been transferred onto a wider,
all-national formation.[82] Furthermore, it often
means that the leaders of both the traditional and
modernized sectors are the only ones involved in
formulating the national programs. As a result,
these programs are elitist, providing only a formal
basis for communication between the "upper crust"
of a society and the masses.

To Soviet Africanists, Negritude provides a
good example of elitism; in fact, Erasov has described Senghor's ideology as "the 'anti-European'
elitist variant of the interpretation of culture."[83]
Its stress on the dignity of the African at any
level of society lends cultural support to the efforts of the bourgeoisie to retain its position
without attempting any further efforts to promote
the economic and political development of society--
in other words, it makes the position of the elite
dependent upon cultural values, rather than upon its
fulfillment of modernization programs or attention

to the political demands of the masses.   Furthermore, _Negritude_ ensures that the masses will not
make too many demands, since it represents a glori-
fication of things as they always have been, rather
than a proclamation of what might be achieved in
the future.   In this way, the continued dominance
of the present elite is assured.

Also, although the conceptions of a uniform
black culture and of black dignity have had positive ramifications for the integration of black African countries, they, too, have been shared only
by the elite.

> The error of Leopold Senghor's posi-
> tion lies in the fact that he supposes
> that one can regard spiritual culture
> as an autonomous entity which can move
> at will . . . from one society to an-
> other. Leopold Senghor's critics
> rightly point out the concealed elit-
> ism of such a point of view, since a
> synthesis of this kind can only fall
> to the portion of the educated circles
> revolving in the sphere of European
> culture.[84]

This same criticism, of course, could also be applied to Sekou Toure's or Nkrumah's theories.   However, the fact that Erasov has praised their understanding of culture and placed it in the same class
with the works of Frantz Fanon indicates that his
criticism of Senghor's "elitism" is really a denunciation of his basic pro-Westernism.   For, if
Senghor's ideology were to be so influential as to
catapult him to prominence (or dominance) in any
French West African organization, this would be
very deleterious to the prospects for Soviet influence.   Soviet awareness of this danger is reflected
in the statement that political integration should
serve "as a means for subsequent cultural integration"; Toure might have some chance for dominance
in this process, whereas the opposite approach
might ensure Senghor's hegemony.[85]

This Soviet concern about the strengthening of
certain African culture movements is also demonstrated by warnings against the danger of a glori-
fication of African culture to the exclusion of valuable elements from the cultures of other peoples.
Soviet analysts, however, display the same ambiva-
lence toward African culture as they do toward African religion: On the one hand, a preoccupation
with things African might inure the Africans against
incursions by the West; on the other hand, though,
it might also render them impervious to the Soviet
development model and to Soviet ideology. It is apparent that Soviet scholars have deemed the dangers
of African culturism to be greater than any possible
benefits, for their writings on the optimal cultural
program for Africa have repeatedly inveighed against
it. It seems that they are aware that the dichotomy
that the African culturists have set up between African and Western may well be a long-lasting one
and, furthermore, that it summarily lumps the Soviet
Union with the other Western countries. In view of
this dichotomy, Soviet authorities consider it necessary to convince the Africans that certain Western
values are positive ones--at the risk of facilitating the expansion of "capitalist" Western culture.
Thus, Erasov urges that, for the "radicals" (that
is, progressives),

> there could be no contradiction be-
> tween "West" and "Africa," and instead
> of counting on the revival of ancient
> traditions, they unfailingly endorsed
> the necessity of using the experience
> of other countries and peoples which
> was applicable to African conditions.[86]

Once this conflict between Westernizers and African-
izers is resolved, as was its "counterpart"--the
Slavophile-Westernizers struggle in nineteenth-
century Russia--then the moderate, less ethnocentric faction can begin to select the best features
of Western culture. This process will lead them to
involvement with the Soviet model, for, if they are
truly working in the best interest of their country,

then the choice is obvious "between the aristocratic
or democratic elements of Western culture, between
the 'consumer' and scientific-technical, between
bourgeois European culture and that of the socialist countries."[87]

Thus, Soviet analysts view the evolution of
African culturism as a two-step process: from eth-
nocentrism to some form of Westernism, and then
from Westernism to the socialist subtype. However,
there is a much more noticeable note of confidence
in Soviet statements regarding the _type_ of Western
model that will be chosen than in their analyses of
whether the Western model will be chosen at all.
In fact, in order to convince the Africans to moderate their stress on African culture and the African
personality, Soviet writers have tried every con-
ceivable approach: from the reasoned arguments of
Erasov to the attacks of E. A. Veselkin, who accused the African leaders of being afraid to face
the future.

> Intensive ideological exchange is an
> objective process today. A wish to
> shut oneself off spiritually is noth-
> ing but fear of the difficulties of
> growth, a desire to avoid the need of
> solving the complicated tasks of the
> times. . . . The past should be an
> aid in the struggle and not a fetter
> in action.[88]

Since neither of these approaches to persuading the
Africans of the benefits of the Western model has
been very successful, Soviet analysts instead have
begun to emphasize the drawbacks of the African approach. Their chief criticism, and obviously an
all-inclusive one, is that the African culture program is not keyed to the needs of future development.

They are careful to explain that, in the early
days of independence, a strong emphasis on culture,
heritage, and traditions was a necessity, and

perhaps the only way to promote a sense of national
solidarity among the masses: Economic ties had not
been established and the modern state, with the new
identity it assumed on independence day, had a very
weak symbolic capability. Therefore, in this sense,
they concur in Ursula Hicks's observation that any
effective integration in the early years was largely a result of "the growth of a national 'myth'
which [looked] forward to the emergence of a nation . . . based on the traditions (real or largely
imaginary) of a great nation of the past."[89] Furthermore, they concede that the African regimes
have often demonstrated great wisdom in trying to
make use of communal traditions--for instance, village or nomad councils--in their modernization programs, for this has been "a very effective way of
awakening the political consciousness of the peasantry."[90] Finally, they acknowledge that, since
traditions are so deeply engrained in the masses,
great caution should be used in attempting to eliminate them. Since they form one of the pivotal
points of identification between the masses and the
regime, to try to extirpate them in less than a century would mean the overthrow of most African governments. If the regime did manage to survive the
initial rebellion, it would be overburdened by demands previously handled by the traditional native
institutions.

However, in spite of these realities, Soviet
analysts still assert that the Africans must "selectively" discard many of their traditions if they
are to succeed in their development programs. Thus,
although there has been considerable debate among
Soviet Africanists regarding the retention of the
commune,[91] the consensus seems to be that it should
be discarded. The underlying values of cooperation
and the lack of a concept of private property should
be retained, but, since the institution emphasizes
cooperation in consumption but not in production,
it would not be a viable basis for the collectivi-
zation--and hence, modernization--of society. Similarly, on a broader scale, while the concept of mutual obligation is admirable--and often useful,

since it shifts to the kinship group demands that otherwise might be made on the government--the fact that it often results in the dependence of several persons on the wages of one individual means that little is generated for the country's gross national product. A final example from the political realm is that, while Soviet authorities would like to see traditional institutions retained in form, they feel that both membership and outlook must be changed if these institutions are to contribute to the politicization effort. Thus, they applaud the fact that, in the case of the administrative councils of Mali's cooperatives, the traditional membership of tribal chiefs and patriarchs has been all but by-passed in an effort to involve agricultural and financial experts.[92]

Soviet writers point to the events of 1966 in Ghana as an example of the dire consequences of ignoring this selectivity principle. According to E. Zhukov, Nkrumah's overthrow

> showed that one must approach the slogan of reviving the democratic tradition of the commune with extreme caution. . . .   [An] overreliance on the slogan of communal traditionalism led to an outright underestimation of the real external and internal enemy of the workers--the bourgeoisie. . . . Appeals to collectivism of the old type did not correspond to the changing social conditions sufficiently to serve as a stimulus to the expanding struggle.[93]

Implicit in this analysis is the suggestion that Nkrumah erred in thinking that traditions could be relied on to direct mass allegiance to his regime; also implicit is irritation that Soviet recommendations regarding the transformation of the Convention People's Party (CPP) into a vanguard party were so blatantly ignored.

In addition to claiming that traditionalism may not further the political development of the regime (that is, in the direction of a socialist-type elitist party), Soviet writers also charge that it may hamper national integration.

> The consciousness of national com-
> munity--which could not serve as a
> basis for nationalism--is not born
> in village communes. This kind of
> conviction is usually born in the
> minds of people with a broader so-
> cial outlook who therefore under-
> stand the inevitability and useful-
> ness of consolidating on a country-
> wide scale.[94]

It is essential in the early days of independence for the regime to rely on traditions to legitimize its ruling position among the masses. However, continued reliance on mass appeal is dangerous, as it will take decades and, perhaps, centuries to overcome particularistic loyalties and make of these people genuine national citizens. Meanwhile, the intelligentsia, the petty proprietors, and the traders--men who were so important to the nation-building effort in the West--will have become almost irrevocably alienated from the regime. Their noninvolvement and nonconsideration in the formulation of the country's development programs not only will deny the regime their nation-building talents but also perhaps their political support as well. Thus, although traditionalism may have an initial integrative effect, its focus on culture rather than economics may be ultimately disintegrative or, at the very least, stultifying.

Economic activity and the involvement of the various socioethnic sectors in production is the only ultimate solution to national conflicts.[95] Admittedly, it is a long process and not always completely successful (witness the continued problems of the U.S. and USSR), but it provides the best opportunity for promoting national integration

while at the same time moving the country along the
path of economic growth.   Soviet authorities do not
recommend either the "nihilistic negation of national culture" or the elevation of culture into a
form of "ideological mystification and hypnosis."
Rather, they remind the Africans that "traditions
only serve the development of a nation when they
are not made into ends in themselves and an object
of simple admiration, but are augmented by the new
achievements of the people."[96]

NOTES

1.   V. Kudriavtsev, "Fighting Africa's Daily
Round," International Affairs, 10 (October, 1962),
54.

2.   N. I. Gavrilov, ed., Nezavisimiye strany
Afriki (The Independent Countries of Africa) (Moscow:
Nauka, 1965), pp. 237-38.

3.   V. I. Peredentsev, "The Influence of Ethnic Factors on the Territorial Redistribution of
Population," Izvestia Akademii Nauk SSSR, seriia
geograficheskaia, 4, 1965; trans., Central Asian
Review, XIV, 1 (1966), 54.

4.   N. S. Babintseva, "O sootnoshenii tempov
kapitalovlozhenii i podgotovki kadrov v osvobodivshikhsia stranakh" ("On the Correlation Between the
Rates of Capital Allocation and the Preparation of
Cadres in the Liberated Countries"), in S. I.
Tiul'panov, ed., Itogi i perspektivi sotsial'no-
ekonomicheskogo razvitiia molodikh suverennikh
gosudarstv (Conclusions and Perspectives on the
Socioeconomic Development of Young Sovereign States)
(Leningrad: Izd'vo Leningradskogo Universiteta,
1965), p. 5.

5.   Xenia Eudin and Robert Slusser, Soviet Foreign Policy, 1928-1934 (University Park: Pennsylvania State University Press, 1966), I, p. 145.

6.   V. Iordanskii, "Sotsial'nye sdvigi v gorodakh Tropicheskoi Afriki" ("Social Shifts in the Towns of Tropical Africa"), Mirovaia ekonomika i mezhdunarodnye otnosheniia, 10 (October, 1967), 83.

7.   V. Kudriavtsev, "Real and Fictitious Diffi-culties," Izvestia, November 2, 1968, p. 4; trans., CDSP, XX, 44 (November 20, 1968), 23; see also R. A. Ul'ianovskii, "Aktual'nye problemy natsional'no-osvoboditel'nogo dvizheniia (po itogovomu dokumentu mezhdunarodnogo soveshchania kommunisticheskikh i robochikh partii, 1969)" ("Actual Problems of the National-Liberation Movement [According to the Final Document of the International Conference of Commu-nist and Workers' Parties, 1969]"), Narody Azii i Afriki, 4 (1969), 10.

8.   L. Iablochkov, "Socio-Demographic Dispro-portions of Africa in the Modern World," in V. G. Solodovnikov, ed., Africa in Soviet Studies, 1968 (Moscow: Nauka, 1969), p. 187.

9.   Gavrilov, op. cit., p. 238. See also Cuba: A Giant School, a pamphlet released by the Information Department of Cuba's Ministry of For-eign Affairs in 1969.

10.   B. G. Gafurov, and G. F. Kim, et al., Natsional'no-osboboditel'noe dvizhenie v Azii i Afrike, Vol. III (Na Novom Puti) (The National-Liberation Movement in Asia and Africa [On a New Path]), Moscow: Nauka, 1968, p. 307.

11.   F. Konopikhin, "Guinea Looks Ahead," New Times, 40 (October, 1968), 10.

12.   See, for example, S. A. Demianchuk, "Voca-tional Guidance for Students in Rural Schools," Shkola i proizvodstvo, 1, 1969; trans., Soviet Edu-cation, XII, 1 (November, 1969), 31-42.

13.   Richard Pipes, "The Forces of Nationalism," Problems of Communism, XIII, 1 (January-February, 1964), 3.

14.   Geoffrey Wheeler, "National and Religious Consciousness in Soviet Islam," Survey, 66 (January, 1968), p. 69.

15.   J. Ornstein, "Soviet Language Policy: Continuity and Change," in Erich Goldhagen, ed., Ethnic Minorities in the Soviet Union (New York: Praeger, 1968), p. 140.

16.   L. M. Zak and M. I. Isaev, "Problemy pis'mennosti narodov SSSR v kul'turnoi revoliutsii" ("Problems of the Written Languages of the Peoples of the USSR in the Cultural Revolution"), Voprosy istorii, 2 (February, 1966), 6-8.

17.   M. S. Dzhunusov, "Soviet Autonomy and the Vestiges of Nationalism," Istoria SSR, 1, 1963; trans., Soviet Sociology, II, 1 (Summer, 1963), 22; cf. Carl Freidrich, "Federalism and Nationalism," Orbis, X, 4 (Winter, 1967), 1012.

18.   Alec Nove and J. A. Newth, The Soviet Middle East (New York: Praeger, 1967), p. 127.

19.   For a Soviet explanation of this, see B. G. Gafurov, "Reshenie natsional'nogo voprosa v SSSR" ("The Solution of the National Question in the USSR"), Azia i Afrika Segodnia, 1 (January, 1962), 7.

20.   I. I. Potekhin, "Some Aspects of the National Question in Africa," World Marxist Review, IV, 11 (November, 1961), 41.

21.   Gavrilov, op. cit., p. 232.

22.   Interview with the author, November, 1969.

23.   G. B. Starushenko, Natsiia i gosudarstvo v osvobodaiushchikhsia stranakh (Nation and State in the Liberated Countries) (Moscow: Mezhdunarodnye Otnosheniia, 1967), p. 257; A. Nikanovov, "Kamerun: u vulkana preobrazovanii" ("Cameroon: On the Volcano of Change"), Azia i Afrika Segodnia, 8 (August, 1968), 7.

24. I. I. Potekhin, Gana Segodnia (Ghana Today) (Moscow: Izd'vo geograficheskoi literatury, 1959), pp. 73-77, 146-58.

25. S. Bruk and N. Cheboksarov, "Sovremennyi etap natsional'nogo razvitiia narodov Azii i Afriki" ("The Current Stage of National Development of the Peoples of Asia and Africa"), Sovetskaia etnografiia, 4 (July-August, 1961), 98.

26. Potekhin, "Some Aspects of the National Question in Africa," p. 43.

27. I. I. Potekhin, Africa's Future: The Soviet View, an abridgement of Afrika smotrit v budushschee (Moscow: Izd'zo Zostochnoi literatury, 1960), printed as a supplement to Mizan, III, 4 (April, 1961), 12.

28. A. B. Letnev, "Novoe v Maliiskoi derevne" ("New Developments in the Malian Village"), Sovetskaia etnografiia, 1 (January-February, 1964), 87-88.

29. I. I. Potekhin, Stanovlenie novoi Gany (The Establishment of New Ghana) (Moscow: Nauka, 1965), p. 318.

30. Ibid., p. 323. (Italics mine.)

31. J. Clyde Mitchell, "Tribalism and the Plural Society," in John Middleton, ed., Black Africa: Its Peoples and Their Cultures Today (New York: Macmillan, 1970), p. 264.

32. Starushenko, op. cit., p. 239. (Italics mine.)

33. M. O. Mnatsakanian, "Natsiia i natsional' naia gosudarstvennost" ("The Nation and National Statehood"), Voprosy istorii, 9 (September, 1966), 29.

34. V. I. Kozlov, "O razrabotke teoreticheskikh osnov natsional'nogo voprosa" ("Elaboration of the Theoretical Foundations of the National Question"), Narody Azii i Afriki, 4 (1967), 84.

35. Albert Zanzolo, "The National Question and Nigeria," The African Communist, 36 (First Quarter, 1969), 20.

36. Starushenko, op. cit., p. 257.

37. V. Iordanskii, "Tropicheskaia Afrika: o prirode mezhetnicheskikh konfliktov" ("Tropical Africa: On the Nature of Interethnic Conflicts") Mirovaia ekonomika i mezhdunarodnye otnosheniia, 1 (January, 1967), 42.

38. V. I. Lenin, Selected Works, XI, p. 679; quoted in Stefan Possony, ed., Lenin Reader (Chicago: Regnery, 1966), p. 91. (Italics in the original.)

39. See A. Bennigsen and C. Lemercier-Quelquejay, Islam in the Soviet Union (New York: Praeger, 1967), p. 139.

40. Walter Kolarz, Religion in the Soviet Union (New York: St. Martin's Press, 1961), p. 412.

41. V. I. Lenin, O natsional'nom i natsional'no-kolonial'nom voprise (On the National and National-Colonial Question) (Moscow: 1965), pp. 478-79; quoted in Kolarz, op. cit., p. 407.

42. "The Soviet Approach to Islam," Mizan, II, 8 (September, 1960), 2; also Richard Pipes, The Formation of the Soviet Union (Cambridge, Mass.: Harvard University Press, 1964), p. 192.

43. Quoted in Jane Degras, ed., The Communist International, 1919-1943 (3 vols.; London: Oxford University Press, 1956-65), I, p. 143.

44. S. M. Gadzhiev, "Popytki modernizatsii islama v sovremennikh usloviakh" ("Attempts to Modernize Islam in Contemporary Conditions"), Voprosy filosofii, 12 (1961), 119.

45. A. Akhmedzianov and V. Li, "Dve tendentsii 'musul'manskogo natsionalizma'" ("Two Tendencies of 'Muslim Nationalism'"), Azia i Afrika Segodnia, 1 (January, 1964), 58.

46. I. I. Potekhin, "Etnograficheskie nabliudeniia v Gane" ("Ethnographic Observations in Ghana"), Sovetskaia etnografiia, 3 (May-June, 1958), 125.

47. R. A. Ul'ianovskii, "Agrarnye reformy v stranakh blizhnego i srednego Vostoka, Indii, i ivgo-vostochnoi Azii" ("Agrarian Reforms in the Countries of the Near and Middle East, India, and Southeast Asia"), Narody Azii i Afriki, 2 (1961), 17.

48. V. G. Solodovnikov, Antiimperialistiches-kaia revoliutsiia v Afrike (The Anti-Imperialist Revolution in Africa) (Moscow: Nauka, 1967), pp. 289-90.

49. See B. I. Sharevskaia, Starye i novye religii tropicheskoi i iuzhnoi Afriki (Old and New Religions of Tropical and Southern Africa) (Moscow: Nauka, 1964); also M. T. Stepaniants, "Islamskaia etika' i ee sotsial'naia smysl'" ("The 'Islamic Ethic' and Its Social Purport"), Voprosy filosofii, 2 (February, 1966); trans., Central Asian Review, XIV, 4 (1966), 294-305.

50. This absence is notable in view of the Western analyses of the effect of religion on Pan-Africanism. See, for example, Dennis Austin, "Pan-Africanism 1957-1963," in Dennis Austin and Hans Weiler, eds., Inter-State Relations in Africa (Frieburg im Bresgau, 1965), pp. 1-29. The only significant Soviet reference to this is found in E. Zhukov, "Natsional'no-osvoboditel'noe dvizhenie narodov Azii i Afriki" ("The National-Liberation Movement of the Peoples of Asia and Africa"), Kommunist, 4 (March, 1969), 41.

51.   I. I. Potekhin, "O nekotorikh zadachakh afrikanisitiki v sviazi c konferentsiei narodov Afriki" ("On Certain Tasks of African Studies in Connection with the Conference of the Peoples of Africa"), Sovetskaia etnografiia, 2 (March-April, 1959), 15-16.

52.   V. Kudriavtsev, "Africa's Hopes and Anxieties," International Affairs, 11 (November, 1963), 42; on religious separatism in the Cameroon, see V. G. Grafskii and B. A. Strashun, Federalism v razvivaivshchikhsia stranakh (Federalism in Developing Countries) (Moscow: Mezhdunarodnye Otnosheniia, 1968), p. 210.

53.   Arthur Klinghoffer, Soviet Perspectives on African Socialism (Rutherford, N.J.:   Fairleigh Dickinson University Press, 1969), p. 75.   The author cites Kudriavtsev's article, "Fighting Africa's Daily Round" (International Affairs, 10 [October, 1962], 51-57), as the earliest example of this realistic approach.

54.   V. D. Zotov, "Sotsialisticheskie preobrazovaniia v Srednei Azii i religioznyi vopros" ("Socialist Transformations in Central Asia and the Religious Question"), Voprosy filosofii, 11 (1967), 61.

55.   R. A. Ul'ianovskii, "Nekotorye voprosy nekapitalisticheskogo razvitiia" ("Certain Questions Regarding Noncapitalist Development"), Kommunist, 1 (June, 1966), 117.

56.   L. Polonskaia and A. Litman, "Vlianie religii na obshchestvennuiu mysl' narodov Vostoka" ("The Influence of Religion on the Social Thought of the Peoples of the East"), Narody Azii i Afriki, 4 (1966), 10.

57.   Wheeler, op. cit., p. 75.

58.   Zotov, op. cit., pp. 61, 67.

59. V. Tiagunenko, "Sotsialisticheskie dok-
triny obshchestvennogo razvitiia osvobodivshchikhsia
stran" ("The Socialist Doctrines of Social Development of the Liberated Countries"), Mirovaia ekonomika
i mezhdunarodnye otnosheniia, 8 (August, 1965), 83-84.

60. V. Tiagunenko, Problemy sovremennikh
natsional'no-osvonoditel'nikh revoliutsii (Problems
of the Contemporary National-Liberation Revolution)
(Moscow: Nauka, 1966), p. 213.

61. Interview with A. B. Letnev, Historian,
Africa Institute, Moscow, Fall, 1969. See also Iu.
Bochkarev, "Kommunisty--samye stoikie bortsi za
natsional'nuyu nezavisimost'" ("Communists--The
Staunchest Fighters for National Independence"),
Kommunist, 5 (March, 1963), 105-13.

62. M. Sultan-Galiev, Metody anti-religioznoi
propagandy sredi musulman (Methods of Anti-Religious
Propaganda Among the Muslims) (Moscow: 1922); ex-
cerpted in Xenia Eudin and Robert North, Soviet
Russia and the East, 1920-1927 (Stanford, Calif.:
Stanford University Press, 1957), pp. 47-48.

63. C. Amidou and M. Dienne, "Senegal Marches
Forward," World Marxist Review, VIII, 6 (June,
1965), 55.

64. Lowell Tillett, The Great Friendship:
Soviet Historians on the Non-Russian Nationalities.
(Chapel Hill: University of North Carolina Press,
1969), p. 133.

65. S. N. Grigorian, ed., Ideologiia sovre-
mennogo natsional'no-osvoboditel'nogo dvizheniia
(The Ideology of the Contemporary National-
Liberation Movement) (Moscow: Nauka, 1966), p. 97.

66. Tiagunenko, Problemy . . ., p. 214.

67. E. Ia. Batalov, "Osnovnye napravleniia
razvitiia filosofskoi mysli v stranakh Azii i Afriki" ("Basic Trends in the Development of Philo-
sophical Thought in the Countries of Asia and
Africa"), Voprosy filosofii, 12 (1964), 17.

68.   L. Kubbel', "J. S. Trimingham, Islam in West Africa, (Oxford: Clarendon, 1959)," Sovetskaia Etnografiia, 6 (November-December, 1960), 165.

69.   Kudriavtsev, "Fighting Africa's Daily Round," p. 54.

70.   E. Zhukov, op. cit., p. 41.

71.   V. I. Lenin, "Theses on the Problem of Nationality," Works, 2d ed., Vol. 16, p. 512; quoted in Solomon Schwarz, "The Soviet Concept and Conquest of National Cultures," Problems of Communism, II, 6 (1953), 41.

72.   A. Arnoldov, "Sotsializm i kul'turnyi progress" ("Socialism and Cultural Progress"), Izvestia, October 3, 1968, p. 4.

73.   B. S. Erasov, "Kontseptsii kul'tury v ideologii natsionalizma razvivaiushchikhsia stran" ("Concepts of Culture in the Ideology of Nationalism of Developing Countries"), Narody Azii i Afriki, 2 (1969), 118.

74.   Ibid., p. 116.

75.   For example, in the early 1960's, criticism was leveled at Senghor's theory of Negritude, while Nkrumah's concept of the African personality escaped similar denunciation.   Later, in 1966, when Soviet-Senegalese relations underwent a noticeable improvement, Soviet artists participated in Senegal's World Festival of Negro Arts.   Klinghoffer, op. cit., p. 75; Robert Legvold, "The Soviet Union and Senegal," Mizan, VIII, 4 (July-August, 1966), 166-67.

76.   B. S. Erasov, "'Mify i totemy'ili real'noe edinstvo" ("'Myths and Totems' or Real Unity"), Voprosy filosofii, 3 (1969), 84.

77.   N. I. Matiushkin, "Razreshenie natsional'nogo voprosa v SSSR" ("The Resolution of the National Question in the USSR"), Voprosy istorii, 12 (December, 1967), 17.

78. B. S. Erasov, "Kontseptsii kul'tury . . .," pp. 122-23.

79. B. Charevskaia, "Sacralisation du pouvoir des rois et des chefs dans l'Afrique au sud du Sahara," in M. A. Korostovtsev, ed., Essays on African Culture (Moscow: Nauka, 1966), p. 182.

80. Radio Moscow broadcast, July 2, 1960; quoted in Fritz Schatten, Communism in Africa (London: George Allen and Unwin, 1966), p. 111.

81. Iordanskii, "Tropicheskaia Afrika . . .," p. 50.

82. B. S. Erasov, "Tropicheskaia Afrika: dva podkhoda k kul'ture" ("Tropical Africa: Two Approaches to Culture"), Azia i Afrika Segodnia, 6 (1969), 6.

83. Erasov, "Mify i totemy . . .," p. 87.

84. B. S. Erasov, "Leopol'd Sengor i ego kontseptsiia kul'tury" ("Leopold Senghor and His Conception of Culture"), Narody Azii i Afriki, 2 (1967), 96.

85. See Erasov, "Kontseptsii kul'tury . . .," p. 122.

86. Erasov, "Mify i totemy . . .," p. 91.

87. Erasov, "Kontseptsii kul'tury . . .," p. 123. For a comparison of the Slavophile-Westernizer controversy in Russia and the modern African cultural debate, see I. I. Potekhin, Africa's Future: The Soviet View, an abridgement of Africa smotrit v budushchee (Moscow: Izd'vo Zostochnoi literatury, 1960), printed as a supplement to Mizan, III, 4 (April, 1961), p. 17.

88. E. A. Veselkin, "The African Personality," in Korostovtsev, ed., op. cit., pp. 86-87.

89.   Ursula Hicks, ed., <u>Federalism and Economic Growth in Underdeveloped Countries</u> (London: George Allen and Unwin, 1961), p. 14.

90.   I. Andreev, "Novoe v obshchine Mali" ("The New in the Mali Commune"), <u>Azia i Afrika Segodnia</u>, 11 (November, 1965), 19.

91.   This is explored in Chapter 6.

92.   Andreev, <u>loc. cit.</u>

93.   E. Zhukov, <u>op. cit.</u>, p. 198.

94.   L. D. Iablochkov, "Evolution of African Nationalism as a Political Ideology," Papers Presented by the USSR delegation to the Second International Conference of Africanists, Dakar, 1967, p. 9.

95.   See B. S. Erasov, "The Ideological Challenge in Tropical Africa and Cultural Traditions," Papers Presented by the USSR Delegation to the Second International Congress of Africanists, Dakar, 1967, p. 14.

96.   P. M. Rogachev and M. A. Sverdlin, "On the Concept 'Nation'," <u>Voprosy istorii</u>, 1 (January, 1966), 44; trans., <u>CDSP</u>, XVIII, 21 (June 15, 1966); also E. Parnov, "Traditsii i sovremennost" ("Traditions and Modernity"), <u>Azia i Afrika Segodnia</u>, 4 (April, 1967), 6-9.

5

THE QUESTION OF NATIONAL BOUNDARIES

The solution that was first proposed by Moscow to the problem of ethnic heterogeneity in black Africa was the revision of national boundaries. In the first years of the African nationalist movement, this proposal seemed both appropriate and realistic: It would bring greater correspondence between the ethnic and political boundaries of the African states and it could be worked out by political leaders who shared the common bond of having served under the British or French colonial system. Furthermore, the proposal seemed perfect for Soviet propaganda purposes: By continually discussing the arbitrariness of African state boundaries, Soviet writers could illuminate yet another negative consequence of imperialist rule.

However, African political realities soon forced an abandonment, or at least a postponement, of Soviet projections regarding the redrawing of African state frontiers. First of all, it was apparent that discussions of the incompatibility between ethnic and national boundaries were only providing grist for the imperialist propaganda mill.

Potekhin was aware of this danger as early as 1957:

> The most curious element in this im-
> perialist propaganda is that the im-
> perialists represent the artificiali-
> ty of colonial boundaries as an ob-
> stacle to independence but at the same
> time do not want to correct these
> boundaries. . . . A vicious circle
> obtains. It is impossible to free
> the colonies because their borders
> are artificial, but rectifying the
> borders is impossible without the
> liquidation of the colonial regime.
> . . . National demarcation is inev-
> itable, but this is [now] a matter
> for the future. . . . Life will show
> how this is to be done.[1]

In view of the fact that the Soviet leaders deemed
African independence to be in their best interests
(it would at least provide them with some chance
for influence) and that African nationalist leaders
considered it so important, the tenor of Soviet
writings was adapted to the parameters established
by the West. In other words, because the West continued to list ethnic heterogeneity as a reason for
denying the African independence, Soviet theorists
were forced to claim that the existing state units
could, in fact, form viable nations.[2]

A second factor that necessitated a revision
in Soviet attitudes regarding African boundaries
was the realization that the existing territorial
units had already become a strong focus of national
pride and chauvinism. The rapid demise of the 1959
Union of Independent African States (composed of
Ghana, Guinea, and later, Mali) indicated the
strength of these territorial nationalisms, for, if
they were so intense after only a year or two of
independence, it was probable that time and the
trappings of international prestige would consolidate them permanently. The establishment of the
Organization of African Unity in 1963 caused a

brief flurry of optimism in certain African and Soviet circles, evoking visions of African states
joining to form larger and more rational units.
However, the final draft of the OAU charter soon
dispelled such illusions. Its codification of respect for the sovereignty and territorial integrity
of all states according to the boundaries inherited
from the colonialists indicated that the byword of
the OAU was cooperation, not amalgamation. This
meant, according to Potekhin, that "there is only
one, rather long, but reliable method of solving
this complex problem [of boundaries]: an all-out
effort to bring the peoples within the confines of
one state together."[3]

This was deemed the sole available solution in
view of a third African reality--that any attempted
frontier revision would probably result in inter-
state or civil war. In the words of Julius Nyerere,
"our boundaries are so absurd that they must be regarded as sacrosanct."[4] It is unlikely that any
two contiguous states could agree on border changes,
while an attempted unilateral move by one state
would evoke a hostile reaction from the other. Soviet authorities would like to think that "progressive" regimes would be willing to compromise, while
one could hardly expect "conservative, bourgeois
elements" to rise above national egoism and the
drive for power. In reality, however, they admit
that there are very few "progressive" African regimes in the Soviet sense of the term, and even
they have not been converted to the spirit of proletarian internationalism. Since imperialist circles could exploit the outbreak of territorial conflicts, "one must recognize the correctness of the
decision of many African states to preserve the
territorial status quo."[5]

Furthermore, any attempt at boundary revision
could result in civil war. In spite of the urgent
problems of national centrifugalism confronting
many black African states, there are several forces
and factors that would render any demarcation along
ethnic-historical lines even more dangerous: There

is a sizeable national bourgeoisie in each existing
unit, which profits by its continued existence;
there are ethnic groups that would resist the reim-
position of precolonial domination by other groups
(for example, the Fanti, who were subjected to re-
peated subjugation attempts by the Ashanti in the
early nineteenth century), and, finally, precolonial units were extremely fluid. As Khrushchev
noted in his proposal to conclude a treaty renounc-
ing the use of force in resolving territorial conflicts, "If we were to take as a basis for solution
of a boundary problem the history of several thou-
sand years, then evidently, everyone will agree
that in many cases we would come to no solution at
all."[6]

A fourth reality of African politics is that
boundary conflicts have been relatively rare in the
postindependence era.[7] It is true that the 1960's
witnessed disputes between Ghana and Togo, Morocco
and Algeria, Somalia and Kenya, and Somalia and
Ethiopia. However, this last conflict is the only
one that has proved insurmountable. Most other
states have found their internal political problems
too pressing to allow for the diversion of energies
and resources into interstate conflicts. Schatten
claimed in his Communism in Africa that these internal problems would induce the African governments to stir up frontier conflicts in order to
distract their populations;[8] however, because these
internal problems are largely attributable to tribalism and because frontier disputes would only call
national loyalties further into question, most African regimes have wisely resisted this temptation.
They have chosen to concentrate on the attenuation
of tribal conflicts, reserving the question of
boundary revision for a time when the existence of
a United Africa might make the whole issue irrelevant. Soviet authorities, ever eager to coordinate
their political emphases with the issues preoccupy-
ing the African nationalists, have also turned
their attentions to the problem of tribalism and
national centrifugalism.

Initially, Moscow was hampered in its analysis
of tribalism by its insistence that the extent of
the problem had been exaggerated by the imperialists in order to forestall the granting of independence and, furthermore, that, if it were not for
imperialist machinations, the problem would not
exist at all. However, by 1962 (the year of the
switch from optimism to realism in Soviet views of
Africa), this emphasis on the role of imperialism
in _creating_ the problem had been replaced by a
stress on the possibility of their exploiting the
problem if it were not eliminated as soon as possible. Thus, Kudriavtsev blamed the colonialists
for fanning tribal strife in the Sudan and Nigeria,
for example, all the while admitting that the

> existence of tribes, and the strife
> which is present between them (which
> expresses itself in the most diverse
> forms, even to the tribal principle
> in forming governments in modern
> states which regard themselves as
> democratic and even as being based
> on the principles of "African so-
> cialism") is an objective factor
> which cannot be left out of account
> and cannot be disregarded.[9]

The fact that, at the 1969 International Communist
Conference, Brezhnev alluded to the way "nationalism and separatism" could be exploited by the imperialists to make the "contacts" of Third World
nations with the socialist world more difficult indicates that this continues to be a prime area of
Soviet concern.[10]

But the problem of devising effective political measures to eliminate tribalism also continues
to be a vexing one. The Soviets still cling to the
hope that the adoption of the progressive ideology
of socialism will result in basic improvements in
the African sociopolitical structure. However,
this is a matter for the future--a future that will

be even further delayed if the reactionary tendencies bred by tribalism are not removed.

> The Communist movement in the East
> is faced with many difficulties of a
> subjective and objective character.
> Scientific socialism, the goals which
> it has, correspond to the interests
> of the working masses of the liber-
> ated peoples. But in conditions of
> the wide dissemination and, at times,
> predominance of bourgeois-nationalistic,
> religious, and other traditional forms
> of ideology, of the great influence of
> tribal, patriarchal-feudal, and caste
> survivals, in conditions where the
> basic tasks of the national-liberation
> revolution are unsolved, scientific
> socialism in its entirety cannot be
> adopted in such a short time by the
> subjugated and exploited masses.[11]

Since the adoption of socialism as a long-term solution to the oppression of the masses has been
forestalled by the ramifications of this oppression,
it is essential that more rapid political answers
be devised.

REGULATION OF THE TRIBAL CHIEFS

A short-term solution that immediately suggested itself to Soviet authorities was the regulation of the tribal chiefs--the prime carriers of
"patriarchal-feudal survivals." In the early years
of their contact with Africa, they defined regulation as elimination. Thus, in the meetings of the
United Nations Trusteeship Council that convened in
1948, the Soviet representative invariably intro-
duced recommendations calling for the replacement
of the tribal system with a democratic government.[12]
The premises underlying this proposal were three-
fold: (1) that chieftaincy owed its survival only
to the "artificial" support of the colonialists;

(2) that the masses were ready and willing to have
a system of participatory government; and (3) that
the nationalist regimes had sufficient power and
organization to by-pass the chiefs in their bid for
mass allegiance.

Closer examination, however, revealed these
assumptions to be fallacious. Thus, whereas, in
1959, Potekhin was still echoing the view that the
tribal form of organization would disintegrate as
soon as the imperialists were ousted, after only a
few years of direct contact with Africa, Soviet
analysts realized that their hopes did not corre-
spond to reality. They observed that, while a
country like Mali may not have had any strong traditional chiefs--either because the sociopolitical
structure precluded their emergence (for example,
among the Dogono and Bozo) or they had "perished in
the struggle with invaders" (for example, among the
Bambara and Songhai)--this was clearly an exception.[13] In most African states south of the Sahara,
prefeudal tribal relations predominated.[14] These
tribal organizations--and the chiefs' role within
them--were preserved by the rights of the chiefs
over the community's land and funds, the traditional respect for chiefs as ancient kinsmen, and the
movement of the chiefs into such "modern" areas as
trading and other forms of commercial activity. As
M. Frenkel' lamented in 1968,

> it would seem that since the chiefs
> play a negative role and since they
> symbolize all that is conservative
> and old in African society, they
> should be stripped of all power as
> soon as possible. However, things
> are not that simple. The chief is
> also a symbol of group society, a
> symbol of national influence. Be-
> sides, the chief also wields great
> influence.[15]

In other words, the predominance of the chief in the
village areas is assured not only by his skillful

manipulation of both old and new instruments of power, but also by the continued socialization of the African into the traditional structure.

Thus, although Soviet analysts would prefer to believe that the masses are ready to oust the chiefs in favor of a system of participatory government, they now acknowledge in textbooks written for their own students that the survival of such institutions as age groups, maternal succession, ancestor worship, and kinship mutual aid implies that the majority is content to live within the existing sociopolitical framework.[16] Certain villagers chafe under this system, to be sure, but they are relatively few in number and resolve the conflict by migrating to urban areas. This means that the traditional system continues relatively unchallenged, for the departure of the dissidents has deprived the system of a major internal force for change. External forces such as agrarian reform and over-all economic development, might be expected to effect some attenuation of the chiefs' power. However, in most African states economic development programs are so slow and produce such dislocations that the reliance of the people on the traditional support systems is actually intensified.[17] In other words, although a traditional outlook hinders economic progress, the halting and often ill-conceived governmental projects often persuade the villager that only from the old system can he expect sustenance and a modicum of economic security.

In view of the continued dependence of the African villager on the traditional system, it is difficult to conceive how the national government could enlist his support without working through the chiefs. However, the majority of Soviet Africanists continue to urge that the new regimes bypass the chiefs, even though scholars such as Frenkel' remind them that

> tens and hundreds of thousands of
> party members . . . join the party
> because their chief ordered them to

> do so . . . and they vote for whom
> they are told. In a word, the chief
> in these countries is a leading type
> of "party worker" and the political
> activism of the majority of members
> is practically nil.[18]

Many Soviet scholars find this argument unconvinc-
ing, especially since they have long been urging
the abolition of the mass party in favor of a vanguard party structure. In fact, they use Frenkel''s
data to support their own case, claiming that a political party that contains so many tradition-bound
members could not possibly serve the cause of progress. They then proceed to discuss Nkrumah's
overthrow, claiming that if he had emulated Mali
and Guinea in ousting the chiefs at the outset, the
opposition could not have used them as a power base
for their coup.[19]

However, such arguments beg the question in
several ways. First of all, they neglect to mention that the position of traditional rulers in
Mali was never very strong, and that Toure could
probably never have ousted them in Guinea if he had
not been helped by the French colonial administration. Secondly, they overlook the fact that Nkrumah relied relatively little on the traditional
chiefs. He replaced scores with men whom he deemed
more "progressive" and tried to use mass rallies,
propaganda, and so on to appeal to key sectors of
society over the heads of their traditional rulers.
In spite of these measures, the traditional chiefs
still retained enough power to serve as a buttress
for the National Liberation Council--an indication
that mass loyalties were still largely oriented toward the traditional sector. Finally, such arguments are evasive because they fail to distinguish
between the need for the regime to rely on the traditional sectors for over-all support and the tendency to recruit party members from this stratum.
Even if the government were to restrict party membership to an elite, it would still have to enlist
mass support somehow, lest the opposition appeal to

these segments in its bid for power. For, as
Solodovnikov noted in 1967,

> if the socioeconomic and political
> role of feudal elements is relatively
> small in the former French colonies
> south of the Sahara, then in North
> Africa, and also Central Ghana,
> Northern and Western Nigeria, Uganda,
> Zambia, Ruanda, Burundi, and Ethio-
> pia, the feudals represented and
> represent a serious economic and po-
> litical force.[20]

If they are this strong in so many African countries and if the various regimes do not have the
power simply to declare the institution of chieftaincy dissolved, then methods must be devised
whereby the support of the chiefs can be enlisted,
while efforts to neutralize their influence are
simultaneously underway.

COOPTATION OF ETHNIC LEADERS

One such method would be to coopt the ethnic
leaders into the political system. The 1921 Soviet
policy of Korenizatsiia or "indigenization" may be
cited as a variant of this, as may the establishment of the People's Commissariat of Nationalities
(Narkomnats) in 1918. Under this latter policy,
each nationality was assigned a corresponding commissariat. The national commissariats and sections,
in turn, acted on instructions from their respec-
tive local Communist Parties, each of which was af-
filiated with and subordinated to the All-Russian
Communist Party.[21] Thus, the primary reason that
the Bolshevik government conceded some administrative autonomy to the nationalities was because the
party existed as a cohesive and dominant unit.
Organizational federalism was never a characteristic of the CPSU; instead it was consistently maintained as a highly centralized (and Russian) institution.

The Bolsheviks were able to maintain this party centralism in the face of minority pressures because (1) the Russians comprised the majority of both the population and party members; (2) Lenin and Stalin had sufficient charisma and/or coercion to counteract any centrifugal tendencies in the party; (3) the Bolsheviks had destroyed the power of the traditional ruling elements through land expropriation, exile, or murder;[22] and (4) the economic program was sufficiently successful to deflect mass loyalties from the traditionally dominant forces to the party regime. As a result of these factors, the Bolsheviks could coopt ethnic leaders into the party without the fear that it would disintegrate into a mere reflection of the societal fragmentation on a higher scale.

However, these factors are not operative in black African politics. As a result, "it is not a rare occurrence when the supporters of this or that party are joined in ethnic associations, such that the internal structure of the party resembles a conglomerate of different ethnopolitical blocks."[23] The inability of the government to effect any far-reaching political or economic inroads on the traditional structure has meant that tribalism continues to be the basic mass loyalty; this foundation, in turn, is mirrored at all levels of the administrative and party apparatus.

Furthermore, one might wonder if things could be otherwise. Economic development is usually cited by Western and Soviet analysts alike as the final solution to the problem of ethnicity in Africa. However, when an examination of the African urban area is undertaken--and this is where economic progress is most apparent--the question arises whether financial growth will contribute to detribalization at any time in the foreseeable future. For economic development has been substantial enough to lure certain villagers to the towns, but not sufficient, in most cases, to provide for them once they arrive. In other words, the government has sufficient resources to construct a few firms

and industrial plants and to fund a limited number
of social services; however, its resources are
hardly adequate to provide jobs for all the migrants or to help alleviate the dislocations resulting from urban unemployment. As a result, the
person who rebels against the village tribal structure by emigrating is actually "supertribalized" in
the urban environment: He must appeal to tribal
associations and mutual help organizations if he is
to survive at all.[24] His only alternative is to
return to the village, where, of course, he will
again be involved in the tribal system. Either
way, the government's inability to help him will
alienate him from the existing regime; his anger
and disillusionment will be fertile ground for any
traditional opposition forces.

Because the dissatisfaction index in most African countries is so high, it would be extremely
dangerous for a regime to ignore or exclude potential opposition groups in forming its governing
system. Most groups, therefore, are brought into
the system through the cooptation of their leaders
--a process that is especially carefully applied
to tribal and ethnic rulers. This has the advantage for the regime of assuring that potential op-
ponents--and, indirectly, their followers--will be
kept under official aegis and public exposure.
Furthermore, it might be expected to have the additional advantage of actually integrating both
leaders and supporters into the national system if
it were not for the absence of one crucial element:
sufficient economic and power resources. For the
most serious strains on political integration are
imposed

> not only by the static strength of
> ethnic or national loyalties but by
> the competitiveness that arises among
> ethnic groups as they modernize and
> struggle to divide the meagre re-
> sources of new countries. . . . An
> individual elector has tended to vote
> for that party which he thinks will

> best represent his community in the
> sense of securing for it what ameni-
> ties are available from the government
> and protecting it against the domina-
> tion of strangers.[25]

If the elector has this attitude, then so does his
representative; for not only will he reflect the
outlook of his constituents, but it is also likely
that he will be faced with the same scramble for
government amenities, albeit on a more official
level. Both state and party bureaucracies have
expanded enormously in the postindependence era,
making government the biggest business and largest
employer in most African states; however, no state
apparatus has been able to keep pace with the demand. This has resulted in great competition for
jobs among individuals and ethnic groups--not only
to secure an income for themselves, but also to
support the nepotism that is endemic to most developing countries. The result of this competition--
and the mutual suspicion it breeds--has been that
governmental systems have become mirrors, rather
than eliminators, of the ethnic centrifugalism that
plagues their societies.

POLITICAL PARTIES: MASS PARTIES
VERSUS VANGUARD ORGANIZATIONS

In their early writings on African political
parties, the Soviets hoped that the mass party
could compensate for the deficiencies of the administration. These parties were touted as the only
effective means of harnessing the universal drive
for liberation and as the answer to imperialist efforts to split the movement by foisting the multiparty system upon the former colonies. This attitude, in fact, was formalized by the Declaration of
the 1960 Moscow Conference of Representatives of
Communist and Workers' Parties:

> the urgent tasks of national rebirth
> in the countries that have cast off

the colonial yoke can be successfully
accomplished only given a resolute
struggle against imperialism and the
vestiges of feudalism through the
unification of all patriotic forces
of the nation in a single national
democratic front.[26]

Thus, the single-party system was deemed the most
effective way to ensure the political integration
of the entire population. Nor did Moscow worry at
this time that the bourgeois-reactionary elements
would predominate in this organization; the convic-
tion remained strong that the African nationalists
would adopt a progressive and anti-Western posture.

In other words, whereas the existence of a
multiparty system might intensify the influence of
the pro-Western and procapitalist strata (because
the parties would be weaker and therefore more susceptible to Western manipulation), the single-party
system would have a strong proletarian bias as a
result of its mass membership. This would facilitate the development of communism in Africa, for,

as long as it is possible for the
working class to play an effective
part in the mass national party, to
defend its class interests, to put
forward its own ideas concerning all
aspects of national development, to
study, discuss and propagate Marxist
concepts, then the maintenance of the
single mass party and its progressive
development into a party based on
scientific socialism will be possible.[27]

The role of the working class was viewed as the key
element in this entire process, for, by the mid-
1960's, the Communists still had not discarded
their opinion of the African proletariat as an extremely class-conscious, progressive, and rapidly-
growing segment of the population. Most African

regimes interested in receiving Soviet aid took
full advantage of this ideological partiality by
claiming to operate in the best interests of the
proletariat and to do everything possible to ensure
its rapid expansion; the Parti Democratique de
Guinee (PDG) was one of the most skillful practi-
tioners of this campaign, developing it with great
success for several years.[28]

The Soviets also lauded the role that the
single-party system could play in effecting national integration. In contrast to the multiparty system, which would encourage each ethnic group to
sponsor its own political instrument, it was felt
that the single mass party could "rise above tribal
limitations" and unite all the people in the struggle against colonialism.[29] Through the vehicle of
a charismatic leader, mass rallies, and the creation of national symbols, it was hoped that the
single party could hold the country together in the
face of already alarming centrifugal tendencies.
It is interesting to note that this view was shared
by many African leaders and also by certain Western
analysts.[30] They considered the multiparty system
to be a dangerous luxury that would fail to take
advantage of the unity forged during the nationalist revolution. Instead, it would result in an extremely fragmented political arena and a needless
waste of monetary and human resources. Furthermore
--and most importantly--it would create an incred-
ible strain on the still fragile network of
governmental-legal institutions. In fact, it was
precisely because the apparatus and power of the
new states were so underdeveloped that Soviet Africanists urged that an increasing amount of nation-
building responsibility devolve on the mass political party.[31]

They still recommend this procedure as an initial step for countries like Cameroon, which have
made little or no progress on the path to national
integration or political development;[32] however,
such recommendations are a rarity in present-day
Soviet analyses of Africa. For the most part, they

display an increasing dissatisfaction with the mass
single-party systems and a growing awareness of
their shortcomings--such as the way they can be
manipulated for reactionary purposes by pro-Western
regimes, their lack of contact with the masses,
their inability to prevent military coups, and, finally, their tendency to mask or thwart the development of classes. Admittedly, one can find a few
examples of such criticism in Soviet writings of
the early 1960's; however, they were usually confined to pro-Western regimes. Thus, in March, 1961,
shortly after the Tananarive Conference on the Belgian Congo, K. Ivanov complained that, in the Congolese nationalist movement,

> as often happens in a mass movement,
> shortcomings were revealed--primi-
> tiveness, localism, poor organiza-
> tion, and the habit of individual
> patriotically-minded intellectuals to
> act on the principle that everyone
> can be a smart fellow in his own
> way.[33]

It can be inferred from the selected targets of
such criticism that Soviet ideologues were relatively confident that a mass party in a pro-Soviet
or even socialist-type regime would have the "political wisdom" to avoid such damaging mistakes.
In fact, the validity of this inference is borne
out by the description of mass parties in states on
the noncapitalist path penned by Kremnyov in 1963.
Thus, in contrast to the poorly regarded Congolese
party, the mass parties in Guinea, Mali, and Ghana
were extolled for

> uniting various sections of the popu-
> lation and unquestionably expressing
> the interests of the broad masses.
> Their programs reflect the desire of
> the overwhelming majority of the pop-
> ulation for a higher standard of liv-
> ing, social justice and collective
> forms of economic endeavor. These
> programs, of course, do not rest on a

> Marxist foundation. But one can en-
> visage the possibility of the influ-
> ence of the growing working class in-
> creasing in these parties and turning
> them into mass parties of the Marxist-
> Leninist type.[34]

It was hoped that the leaders of these parties would
recognize the need for a more compact, elitist
structure, and would more or less automatically move
their organizations in this direction. The success
of these socialist-type parties in meeting their
countries' needs would, in turn, inspire the
capitalist-oriented regimes to be more tolerant of
Communists and communism.

These Soviet expectations regarding African
mass parties were not fulfilled: The parties were
exploited for reactionary ends in several countries,
while, in the states of national democracy, the
leaders who relied on them were hardly successful
in promoting either economic or political development. Thus, in pro-Western countries such as Senegal, Niger, and Upper Volta, mass single-party systems were used as the nucleus for what Soviet writers term "presidential republics." It is interesting that the only major work that appraised the
presidential parties favorably was written in 1963
--the year when Soviet optimism regarding all of
Africa was rising once more. Thus, V. P. Verin's
Presidentskie Respubliki v Afrike (Presidential Republics in Africa) describes even the creation of
these highly authoritarian, nonproletarian parties
as "understandable" in view of the "mass illiteracy
and ignorance of the population," its separatist
tendencies, and the need to resist the concerted
economic and political pressure of France. He considers these regimes to have great "progressive"
potential:

> In the struggle for national democracy,
> a broad front of national forces is
> formed, and representatives of the
> nation's progressive forces come to
> power. In these conditions, the

> presidential form of government may
> receive democratic content and become
> a transitional form on the road to a
> state of national democracy. The
> state of national democracy, in its
> turn, opens the prospect of transi-
> tion to the road of socialist develop-
> ment--the road that sooner or later
> all the young states of Africa will
> take.[35]

Verin concludes, of course, that the Francophone
states could be moving faster along the noncapitalist path, and that certain of them, such as Congo-
Brazzaville, had made no progress at all. However,
he remarks that states such as Niger and Upper Volta had made great strides in strengthening their
ties with the workers and with the world socialist
system.

Such hopeful views were soon relegated to the
dustbin of history. Kudriavtsev launched a new type
of analysis in November, 1963, when he reported that,
although a one-party system can be progressive in
countries on the noncapitalist path, these merits
should not be ascribed "schematically" to all mass
parties. He points out that, with the exception of
Algeria, the ruling class in all the former French
colonies is not working for a true anti-imperialist
revolution and the liberation of the masses from all
forms of economic and political oppression. Instead, this elite "regards the acquisition of state
independence as the culminating point of the
national-liberation movement."[36] Independence provides these leaders and their French masters with
the simplest way of quieting the masses, while at
the same time freeing them to continue their exploitative policies.

MASS PARTIES AND MILITARY COUPS:
GHANA, A CASE STUDY

This negative look at presidential mass parties was inspired by the wave of military coups

that was beginning at this time.   The early coups
seemed to be directed only at countries that were
pro-Western, capitalist, and long-established presidential republics--Dahomey, the Central African
Republic, Congo-Brazzaville, Niger, Upper Volta, and
so on.   The pattern was so clear that for a while
it deluded Soviet analysts into thinking that the
coups must be a result of weaknesses peculiar to
these pro-Western regimes.   Prominent Africanists
such as G. B. Starushenko began to attribute a
"positive significance" to these coups, looking to
the military to grant the power and privileges to
the working masses that had long been denied them
by the authoritative rulers.[37]   Kudriavtsev joined
in this denunciation of the deposed regimes (and,
indirectly, of V. P. Verin's favorable treatment of
them) by claiming that these governments had long
denied the people any outlet for political expression; in fact, "prior to the coups, one could speak
about democracy in these countries only by much
stretching of the point."   He concluded rather
smugly that

> current events in a number of African
> countries exactly reflect the dis-
> crepancy between the capitalist path
> of development with all its inherent
> political attributes and those common
> national interests whose satisfaction
> is inconceivable without the decisive
> overcoming of the entire legacy of
> colonialism.[38]

The implication of Kudriavtsev's analysis was
that despotic rule, the stifling of democracy and
opposition, and presidential dictatorships were
characteristics restricted to capitalist mass party
systems and that, in view of these shortcomings,
one could hardly expect any but the progressive
governments to escape military overthrow.   However,
less than six weeks after the publication of his
remarks, Kwame Nkrumah was deposed.   This event was
shattering to Soviet propagandists, for no sooner
had they learned to explain the rash of military
coups as part of a big "swing to the left" in

Africa[39] than one of the most touted leftist regimes itself was overturned. Furthermore, Ghana
was not only a state that was deemed leftist in its
foreign policy, but it had also been named a state
of national democracy--an accolade accorded only to
those governments with the strongest noncapitalist
orientation. Soviet authorities could not simply
acknowledge that all their hopes for such states
had been ill-founded, but neither could they avoid
the reality that Nkrumah had been replaced by a
military junta. Their solution to this dilemma was
three-staged: For the first ten days they attributed the coup to a CIA plot;[40] next, they admitted
that Nkrumah had made mistakes in his governing of
the country; and, third, they declared that perhaps
the instrument of a mass party was not at all the
most suitable for progressive-type regimes.

Thus, shortly after the coup, a whole spate of
articles began to appear chronicling the deficiencies in Nkrumah's administration. It must be admitted that Soviet analysts had made some criticisms of his regime before the coup of February 22;
however they were usually incidental to the entire
analysis and were not of a systemic nature. For
example, Potekhin had carefully remarked that
"Ghana, like all the young African states, also
suffers from 'nepotism,' connected with the out-
dated concepts of family and kinship," while a 1965
book on Ghana took note of the economic dislocations produced in the course of the development
program.[41] There is evidence that the Soviets had
more than a passing concern for the increasing
bureaucratization of the party, but they seem to
have been mainly worried that this would have an
effect on economic growth;[42] they appeared confident that Nkrumah's regime could escape the political catastrophe visited on so many procapitalist
regimes.

After the February events, Soviet Africanists
began to analyze the shortcomings of Nkrumah's regime as a political system; in fact, they were so
thorough that, by the time all the articles were

in, Nkrumah had been accused of mishandling every
sector of the population: (1) By taking only half-
way measures against the tribal chiefs, he had left
them ample room for their reactionary activities;
(2) by attempting to attract the peasant masses
through traditional symbols and ideologies, he had
intensified their links with the survivals of the
past and made them only "passive observers" of the
country's modernization; (3) by tolerating bribery
and corruption in the state administration, he had
exacerbated the workers' dissatisfaction with their
own economic plight; (4) by attempting to take over
the management of small businesses, without the
necessary staff and planning resources, he had
alienated the all-important middle class; and (5),
by failing to undertake the necessary political
work among the army and internal security forces,
he had left this group free to exploit existing
popular dissatisfaction for extralegal purposes.
In sum, as Mirskii declared, the coup was effected
because Ghana lacked a leader "who stood at the
height of popularity and enjoyed the complete support of the dominant sectors of the population."[43]

Once Soviet analysts had concluded that Nkrumah had lost contact with the masses, an examination of the primary means he used to try to redress
this--the mass party--was unavoidable. It is true
that prior to Nkrumah's overthrow Communist analysts had urged that the mass party not be accepted
as the best instrument for building socialism; however, even though they advocated "the further evolution of the one-party system in the direction of
the leading role of the working class," they still
praised mass parties such as Nkrumah's for their
"revolutionary-democratic character."[44] However,
after the 1966 coup, even this somewhat general accolade fell away in the face of the realization
that the mass party was a perfect cover-up for any
leader bent on neglecting the interests of the
burgeoning proletariat.

Soviet Africanists began to realize that Nkrumah's overthrow would never have been greeted by

such remarkable passivity on the part of the masses
and, indeed, collusion by certain sectors of society, if his party had been an effective and democratic one. Instead, the Convention People's Party
(CPP) was ineffective by virtue of its size, lack
of ideology, and reliance on charismatic leadership
to hold it together, and undemocratic by virtue of
its attempts to maintain the illusion of class solidarity while masking the dominance of the bureaucratic bourgeoisie. By relying on a party type
more suited to the early days of the independence
revolution, when all classes are united in the
struggle against the colonial oppressors, than to
the present, when nascent class divisions are exacerbated, Nkrumah had made a fatal mistake. For

> coincidence of interests of various
> layers of the populace, however pro-
> longed, does not prove the homogeneity
> of African society. The right to
> make decisions on matters of state is
> usually assumed by a party or an or-
> ganization which represents the in-
> terests of the dominating social
> group, whether it forms the majority
> of the population or not.[45]

The dominating social group in most African countries is the bureaucratic bourgeoisie. Nkrumah
could have neutralized its reactionary tendencies
if he had made the workers the central element of
his political apparatus and program; by clinging to
the mass party, however, the potential influence of
the workers was undercut. Furthermore, as a result
of the ineffectiveness of the CPP, Nkrumah had to
rely increasingly on the governmental network--a
reliance that only intensified the power of the
bureaucratic stratum to the detriment of the interests of other classes.[46]

Soviet authorities concluded from this analysis
of the party-class relationship in Ghana that the
African progressives had erred in predicating their
retention of a mass party on the assumption that

there were no classes in their societies. The assumption may have been warranted in the early days
of the nationalist struggle;[47] however, this union
of all grups in search of a common goal had been
only a temporary one. A noticeable process of
class formation was proceeding in African society,
and one ignored this in establishing a political
party only at the risk of transferring society's
contradictions to the internal organizational
structure. This had seriously weakened the CPP.
Nkrumah's insistence on including everyone--even
fourteen-year-olds--in the party seriously strained
the already tenuous lines of political control;
more and more bureaucratic echelons were added to
redress this, with the result that the more activ-
ist bourgeoisie completely swamped the working
masses.

> This hindered the democratic election
> of the leadership even at the party's
> grass roots. Party secretaries were
> frequently appointed from the top. . . .
> As a result, the citizen was deprived
> of any possibility of free expres-
> sion. . ."[48]

This proved dangerous for the CPP, not because the
masses rebelled in order to regain their political
rights (they were not politically aware enough for
this), but because they retreated into the political apathy from which the mass party was supposed
to rouse them. Nkrumah himself was thus responsible for cutting off a potential source of political
support in the battle with the bourgeois reactionaries.[49]

Thus, organizationally, the mass party structure had failed Nkrumah (and Keita of Mali) because
it supported their illusions regarding the unity of
society and the politicization of the people.
Ideologically, it had not served to advance the
cause of socialism, because the need to appeal to
so many thousands of people had necessitated the
sacrifice of new political ideas to the more

familiar themes of traditional life. In other
words, a "lowest-common-denominator" process had
set in:

> The attempt to make the ideas of so-
> cialism understandable to the masses,
> the majority of whom were neither
> literate nor acquainted with the po-
> litical struggle in the class sense
> of the word, led to a certain over-
> simplification of the real social
> meanings, and even to their dis-
> tortion.[50]

Soviet authorities admit that it is essential that
a leader explain his political philosophy to the
general citizenry; however, they assert that this
should be accomplished through the work of front
organizations. The party, meanwhile, would be composed only of workers with the highest level of political consciousness, for only this group is capable of absorbing the essentials of Marxism-Leninism
and utilizing them to restructure society.

The mass party structure led certain leaders
to overlook the role of the workers and to exaggerate their own importance. Soviet analysts acknowledge that, in the early days of the independence
struggle, the party head had an important role to
play as a symbol of the party's unity and perma-
nence. However, the threat always existed that
collective leadership would be sacrificed to a
"dangerous identification of state and party with
the personality of the national leader."[51] This is,
in effect, what occurred in Ghana, to the extent
that Nkrumah, rather than the ideology of socialism,
became the unifying factor in the CPP. This "cult
of personality"[52] was deleterious to the socialist
cause in that it worked to increase the masses' devotion to Nkrumah, rather than their level of political consciousness; it finally proved to be disastrous because, once Nkrumah was overthrown, his
allegedly "mass" political structure simply disin-
tegrated. The Soviet rulers were not only deprived

of a sympathetic political leader, but their "state
of national democracy" was shown to be little but a
figment of their own (and Nkrumah's) active political imagination.

Ideally, according to Soviet analysts, the
only solution to this situation is to create an entirely different type of political party, to abandon the mass party in favor of an elite or vanguard
organization. This structure could absorb the ethnic and local leaders--a measure that should be
adopted in order to defuse any potential opposition,[53] but it could unite these leaders on an entirely new basis. The cementing element would be a
progressive ideology, rather than traditional symbols, and the party would be able to utilize existing loyalties, while simultaneously neutralizing
them, as its proletarian orientation would enable
it to enact the reforms necessary to eliminate
tribalism--and tribal chiefs--from the African social structure.

This new vanguard party is viewed as the only
appropriate structure for the second stage of the
anti-imperialist revolution--the stage where the
masses have moved beyond the battle for formal autonomy to the struggle for a socialist regime that
alone can guarantee their true political and economic independence. Soviet analysts would like to
see the Africans follow the model of the CPSU--a
cohesive organization with a maximum of ideological
purity, which at the same time functions as the
main integrator of society. Here, the vanguard
concept is realized in two ways: First, CPSU membership is granted to only 12 million people, or
5 percent of the total population; secondly, even
with this select group, yet a further distinction
is made between members and elite. The elite is
the party's principal means of serving as an integrator of the entire political network and acquir-
ing the information necessary "to govern the principal decision-making processes of the system."
Therefore, the people in this group are either supervisory party members who have been extremely

"skillful" in the practice of politics or leaders
coopted from an important functional group, such as
the military, industry, or the scientific establishment.[54] Control over this elite--and over the
entire population--"is largely accomplished through
supervisory and administrative agencies but is sup-
plemented by the extensive political education program."[55] However, the danger remains that, in the
long run, the effect of the attitudes of the functional elite on the character of the party will be
greater than its ideology is able to combat.

        This analysis of the CPSU is extremely germane
to any discussion of the possibility of constructing a vanguard party in Africa, for, if the danger
exists, according to Gehlen, that the coopted elite
might affect the ideological level of the CPSU,
then how much greater would the danger be for the
less stabilized and firmly rooted parties of Africa.
Furthermore, if the CPSU, with its large number of
well-organized cadres, is able to reach only 25 to
30 percent of the urban population through its direct political education program--and less than
half that percentage in the country as a whole[56]--
the question arises whether an African vanguard
party could ever maintain contact with the masses,
especially in view of the fact that it lacks the
communications media that the Soviet Union uses to
buttress its insufficient agitprop mechanism. The
efforts of mass parties such as the CPP to reach
the people through mass rallies, parades, and so
on, were designed to redress this lack, but popular
support still could not be enlisted and maintained;
how then will a much smaller vanguard party be able
to overcome this obstacle? For, as I. Diarra, Political Secretary of Mali's Sudanese Union, declared,

            In addition to the purely practical
            problems that the development would
            engender, it would result in sub-
            jective contradictions arising from
            the expelling of large numbers of
            members being added to the objective

> contradictions and conflicting inter-
> ests. Ex-party members may well be
> expected to retain some influence and
> to reinforce the core of the opposi-
> tion. At best they could be a vacil-
> lating group likely to ally itself
> with the opposition at any time. This
> aggravation of the political contra-
> dictions could affect the armed forces
> and impel them to embark on hazardous
> adventures.[57]

Thus, vanguard parties could result in an aggravation of the very conditions that Soviet analysts
expect them to resolve, eventually leading to military coups in the few countries fortunate enough to
have escaped them.

The validity of Diarra's opinion is, of course,
open to question--especially since his superior,
Modibo Keita, was also overthrown in November, 1968.
Nevertheless, it is interesting that, although Soviet authorities allowed his views to be aired in
the World Marxist Review, they still found it necessary to misquote him completely in later books.
Thus, whereas Diarra asserted that a mass party
could "carry the socialist revolution through to
the end," Solodovnikov quoted him as saying that,
although a mass party could begin the construction
of socialism, only a vanguard party could complete
it.[58] The only explanation for what must be construed as a deliberate misrepresentation of Diarra's
views is that the overthrow of Nkrumah turned Soviet analysts against the mass party structure so
completely that they felt they needed all available
support for their total advocacy of the vanguard
concept. This explanation is substantiated, in
fact, by articles that began to appear in the Soviet Union after Nkrumah's downfall referring to the
"vanguardization" of the Union Soudanaise[59]--a process that was hardly noticeable at all, as a Soviet
writer later ruefully acknowledged.[60] However,
during the 1966-68 period, Moscow was still hopeful
that the passivity of the Ghanaian masses in the

face of the overthrow of their national-democratic
regime could be interpreted more as a result of deficiencies in the mass-party structure than as evidence of lack of preparedness for the noncapitalist
path.

Keita's overthrow, however, necessitated a
further Soviet confrontation with the realities of
African politics. As M. Frenkel' commented,

> Today one can say that the all-
> national parties have outlived their
> usefulness. Class parties will in-
> evitably replace them. But this will
> not happen soon as the process of
> class formation is slow. In the mean-
> time, the all-national party will
> serve as a cover for the new elite,
> which is following its narrow group
> interests.[61]

It was now deemed senseless to try to undermine the
influence of this reactionary elite by creating a
vanguard party, because neither the political capabilities of the party nor the level of political
consciousness of the masses were high enough to
tolerate such a strain. The best way to cope with
this reactionary challenge was to concentrate on
building a mass base of power and on meeting the
basic economic needs of the population; not until
these prerequisites were met could the African regimes hope to emulate the CPSU in its function as
not only the vanguard, but the integrator, of society.[62] Africa was not ready for anything but a
"firm union" of all anti-imperialist forces. As
Ul'ianovskii warned, "attempts at monopolistic control of state power, at ignoring other anti-
imperialist, progressive forces often leads to a
disruption of political stability and even to a
loss of power."[63]

Thus, in their ten years of active political
involvement in black Africa, the Soviets had come
full circle: They began by praising the mass party

as the best way to capitalize on the unity generated by the independence struggle, then urged the
progression to a vanguard party in order to overcome the lags in Africa's political development,
and, finally, returned to the position that, in
view of these lags, the mass party was the only
workable organizational structure. The possibility
remained that the mass party could eventually
evolve into a higher form, but, under the present
conditions, it was necessary to bring all the
forces of the unitary state structure to bear on
the solution of Africa's material problems.

The party could accomplish a great deal in
this regard, since, although Soviet authorities did
not consider that it should assume administrative
power itself, they did feel that only the party
could guarantee the state's effective functioning.

> The role of the political party is
> especially significant where the pro-
> cess of establishing the national
> state has not been completed, when
> the governmental-legal institutions
> still are not definitely formed, when
> the state apparatus is not always
> sufficiently effective.[64]

By uniting all of the population strata into one
institution, while at the same time concentrating
on diffusing the progressive forces (that is, the
workers, the peasants, and the "working intelligentsia"), the party could give invaluable support to
the state's efforts to establish a unitary, and not
a federal, administration. For, according to Soviet Africanists, choosing the correct governmental
form is one of the most important factors in promoting political integration.

FEDERALISM OR A UNITARY STATE?

Marxism-Leninism has traditionally been opposed to the federal principle as a basis for state

organization. It is true that Lenin agreed in 1917
to the adoption of a federal constitution for the
USSR, but his insistence that the party remain centralized, plus the dominance of the Russian Republic in national politics, worked to ensure that the
Soviet Union was, in fact, a unitary state. This
accorded completely with Lenin's views on the best
way to advance the socialist revolution and unite
the people in the spirit of proletarian internationalism, for a federal system would work to advance the self-determination of peoples rather than
the self-determination of the working class within
each nationality.[65] A unitary system, on the other
hand, would focus people's attentions and loyalties
on a level above their own nationality, thereby facilitating the transition to socialism.

Soviet leaders, of course, have had difficulties even with the facade of federalism that they
have set up: Various nationality groups have developed strong attachments to administrative units
that were meant to be completely artificial. These
realities have perhaps intensified their ideological aversion to federalism, for, if strictly formal
autonomy could arouse such loyalties, it is con-
ceivable that a true federal system could create
regional loyalties that would be impossible to
overcome. Furthermore, if the CPSU has problems
responding to this challenge, the much less centralized African parties would have extreme difficulties even coping with separatist tendencies--to
say nothing of moving the masses in the direction
of proletarian internationalism.

Soviet Africanists see the fact that three of
the four existing African federations (Uganda,
Cameroon, and Nigeria) were set up by the colonialists as evidence that the departing rulers wanted to
"paralyze the work of the whole machinery of government" in order that they might return and exploit the ensuing crisis.[66] Their plan was relatively easy to carry out, for three reasons: First,
they could present it to the Africans--and to the
world--as an effort to ensure that the rights of
all key nationality groups would be respected;

secondly, they could depend on the support of feudal elements, such as the Ashanti chiefs or Hausa
emirs, who feared that their power would be diminished in any unitary system; and third, these countries had not had anti-imperialist revolutions,
which might have aroused the political consciousness of the masses. The colonialists, therefore,
were free to impose their bourgeois federations--
federations that Starushenko charges, "did not even
set up for themselves the task of helping to solve
the national problem." If they had, he continues,
they would have contained more than two or three
units, granted the "right of free exit" to these
units, and ensured equal representation for all.[67]

Starushenko's advocacy of the "right of free
exit" must be considered in light of the theme of
all Soviet works on African federalism: that the
important thing is not "the form of the state, but
its class essence."[68] If a federation, such as
Tanzania or Nigeria in the late 1960's, serves the
interests of the proletariat (or the Soviet Union),
then the demand for "free exit" would be deemed secession, and would be unalterably opposed by all
progressive forces. If, on the other hand, the
federation is designed only to serve the interests
of colonialism, that is, to impede the country's
industrialization, to preserve feudal power, and to
intensify localism, then Moscow will derive great
propaganda value from the fact that "free exit" is
not allowed. For the class essence of such a federation is bourgeois; it allows the neocolonialists
so much freedom of maneuver that the workers are
impeded in their drive to join the world proletarian movement. Why else would no federal states
have been included in the ranks of "states of national democracy," or even had strong systems of
one-party rule? According to Grafskii and Strashun,
the connection between the form of state structure
and the nature of the political movement is too
strong to be denied.[69]

The assertion of such a connection allows
Soviet authorities to link their concern for
nation-building in Africa with their concern for

development along the noncapitalist path: They can
point out not only that African federal states are
usually reactionary states, but also that the federal states are the ones that have been involved in
the most drastic civil conflicts in modern Africa.
This is not because the Africans do not possess the
necessary political acumen to operate a federal
system ("as Western analysts such as Carl Friedrich
have alleged:), but rather because the division of
powers implicit in this system provides too many
openings for imperialist maneuvering. The fact
that federalism can work to alleviate national contradictions in Switzerland and the Soviet Union,
but not in Canada, shows that the essential element
is not economic or political development, but rather the ability to prevent the adoption of "a chauvinistic course by a ruling national group."[70] The
African states, beset by internal and external reactionaries, do not have this ability.

However, a unitary state might provide the instrument by which this inability could be eliminated. Soviet Africanists acknowledge that this
form of government can also aggravate separatist
tendencies and fall prey to the forces of reaction,
as in the Ivory Coast,[71] but, if it is directed by
a "progressive" regime, it can advance the consolidation of a strong nation-state. For the wide constitutional powers of the government can be used to
ensure that (1) popular loyalties are directed toward the national system, rather than toward any
regional subunit; (2) local and traditional rulers
are directly subordinate to the central authority;
(3) no powerful and difficult-to-control federal
governments will be accessible to neo-imperialist
machinations; (4) the existing particularistic loyalties will not be legitimized by being enshrined
in a federal constitution; and (5) the national
planning that is essential to the development of
the noncapitalist path can proceed. In view of
these factors, and in spite of the potential dangers, the unitary state is the form that Moscow
recommends: "The future belongs to those political
forms which aid the movement of peoples along the
path of socialist progress."[72]

THE EVOLUTION OF SOVIET VIEWS
ON NIGERIAN FEDERALISM

However, an analysis of the evolution of Soviet views on the Nigerian state structure indicates that, for Moscow, the issue of political form is often completely dwarfed by considerations of advancing "socialist progress" and, furthermore, that the progress of the Soviet state is more important than that of any African people. Thus, whereas federalism was heartily denounced when it was set up by the departing British colonialists and retained by the pro-Western Nigerian capitalist bourgeoisie, it was appraised positively by 1967 when it represented the administrative choice of this same bourgeoisie now deemed Moscow's friend. Admittedly, there had been several changes in the leadership of Nigeria--from Balewa to General Ironsi to General Gowon, but Gowon represented essentially the same interests from the Northern and Western regions that Moscow had decried as "feudalists" and "comprador bourgeoisie" in an earlier period.[73] What had changed was that, whereas prior to late 1966, the policies of this North-West axis had provided Moscow with little opportunity for influence, the need for outside support occasioned by its battle against the Eastern rebels meant that the possibilities for Russian influence over Africa's richest state had vastly increased.

Soviet Africanists had been wont to describe these same Eastern forces, represented by the NCNC (National Congress of Nigeria and Cameroon) as "progressive," interested in a unitary state "which would be based on genuine consideration of the interests of the national minorities."[74] The East's move against the North-West reactionaries in the military coup of January, 1966, to effect these unitary proposals was praised strongly by the Kremlin:

> Although these measures do not
> change the social structure of the
> country or affect very seriously
> the economic domination of foreign

> companies, they can undoubtedly im-
> prove the situation and lay a founda-
> tion for further ways of creating and
> strengthening an independent Nigeria.
> The military have been welcomed every-
> where.[75]

Moscow obviously hoped that, in spite of the dangers and difficulties involved in imposing a unitary structure on peoples long used to federal expression, Ironsi's government could use this mechanism eventually to diminish the power of the reactionary elements, thereby breaking up the alliance
of these groups with Western forces. Thus, his
regime--although a military one--might be expected
to inaugurate a so-called "swing to the left" at
least in the class character of the Nigerian government, if not also in its foreign policy orientation.

Within a few months, however, it was obvious
to Moscow that the progressiveness of General
Ironsi's ideas on the state structure was more than
counterbalanced by the reactionary nature of official policy. By May, Moscow radio was lamenting
that, contrary to all expectations,

> very little has changed in the country
> in recent months. The state machinery,
> though slightly reduced, is still in
> the hands of those who served the old
> regime and the foreign monopolies.
> What is more, the government has made
> it clear that it will encourage for-
> eign capital in Nigeria. This point
> of the government's program has
> caused approval in the West.[76]

Any regime that continued in close association with
the capitalist states and whose policies, moreover,
allowed no room for the expansion of Russian trade
and/or influence was to be decried. Ironsi's overthrow, therefore, was greeted by Moscow with remarkable equanimity. The possibility existed that

his successor, General Gowon, might pursue policies
more favorable to the Soviet Union; as a result,
the typical Soviet cycle of a terse report on the
coup, followed by a denunciation of the deposed regime, favorable commentary on the new government,
and magnification of all signs of potential progressiveness, began anew.

Thus, whereas earlier Soviet commentary had
spoken of "the feudalists and comprador bourgeoisie
of the Northern and Western regions" resisting the
"progressive" policies of the Eastern leaders and
their party, the NCNC, Soviet analysis eventually
underwent a complete volte-face. It was now this
same NCNC that was said to embody the comprador
element.[77] Gowon, of course, represented the
North-West alliance, and, if he were to be courted
by Moscow, previous criticism would have to be completely redirected.

This redirection applied not only to personal-
ities, but also to policies. Gowon wanted to return
to the federal structure of government, and, as a
result, Moscow altered its previous denunciation of
this system. Ironsi was now charged with having
been insensitive to Nigerian realities in imposing
a unitary structure,[78] for, although it was a com-
mendable idea in principle, it failed to take into
account the problems of tribalism and feudal domi-
nance--problems that could only be eliminated by
socioeconomic change.[79] The best way to effect
this change was not to indulge in the adventurist
action of eliminating the long-familiar, if ill-
functioning, system but rather to modify it. For,

> the strong dissatisfaction in the
> country with the federal system, the
> action of the army against it in
> 1966, the ensuing civil conflicts
> between different national groups,
> were not the results of the organiza-
> tion of the state on a federal basis,
> as certain Western jurists and sociol-
> ogists claim, but the consequence of

>the inconsistent and sometimes per-
verted execution of the principle of
federalism, and the ignoring of local conditions.[80]

Thus, by 1967, Soviet analysts had chosen to ignore
completely their earlier indictments of the suit-
ability of the federal system for Nigeria,[81] to attribute such negativism to the West (which had been
criticized earlier for sponsoring federalism), and
to proceed to applaud Gowon's attempts to increase
the number of units from three to twelve.

Admittedly, this expansion would redress the
previous identification of political parties with
regional sentiments--an identification that Soviet
authorities had long denounced as a barrier to national development. However, it is extremely noteworthy that they hardly mentioned the existence of
political parties, much less their nature, in their
haste to praise Gowon and his policies.[82] They
were willing to accept his view that the military
government reduced the importance of such institutions, for their concern with developing good relations with the Nigerian government overshadowed
their concern for the nature of its internal political development.

While the civil war continued, Soviet tolerance of the military regime, the reinstatement of
federalism, and Gowon's view that "Nigerian development could be attained only by remaining in the
system of world capitalism"[83] could be attributed
to respect for the exigencies of war (a war so bit-
ter that little time was left for ideological rumi-
nations or systemic change) and to Moscow's hesitancy to bring up politics until its position as
Nigeria's ally had been solidified. However, the
war is now over, but still Moscow's tolerance continues. This provides yet another example of
Brezhnev and Kosygin's willingness to subordinate
the interests of communism to those of the Soviet
state. Considerations of Nigeria's wealth (total
revenues will reach $1 billion by 1975), and the

Soviet Union's need for markets for its manufactured goods have been given priority--a priority
vindicated, perhaps, by the recent launching of a
Soviet-Nigerian Trade Organization to sell Soviet
trucks and automobiles and the formulation of plans
for a large steel plant to be constructed by the
Russians.[84] Moscow justifies such trade on the
grounds that it will "consolidate Nigeria's economic independence"[85]--a prelude, of course, to eventual political liberation. However, it appears
that the USSR considers its own economic development to be of far greater importance.

NOTES

1. I. I. Potekhin, "Zadachi izucheniia
etnicheskogo sostava Afriki v sviazi s raspadom
kolonial'noi sistemy" ("Tasks of Studying the Ethnic Makeup of Africa in Connection with the Fall of
the Colonial System"), Sovetskaia etnografiia, 4
(July-August, 1957), 104.

2. See Russia Looks at Africa (London: Central Asian Research Centre, 1960), p. 21.

3. I. I. Potekhin, Stanovlenie novoi Gany
(The Establishment of the New Ghana) (Moscow:
Nauka, 1965), p. 316; also his "Legacy of Colonialism in Africa," International Affairs, 3 (March,
1964), 20. Note the change from his 1960 statement
in Africa's Future: The Soviet View, an abridgement of Afrika smotrit v budushchee (Moscow: Izd'zo
zostochnoi literatury, 1960), printed as a supplement of Mizan, III, 4 (April, 1961) that the creation of regional federations was the only realistic
solution to the boundary problem. This change is
noted in "Potekhin on African Frontiers," Mizan, VI,
4 (April, 1964), 11.

4. Quoted by Rupert Emerson, "African States
and the Burdens They Bear," African Studies Bulletin, X, 1 (April, 1967), 2; see also Ia. Ia. Etinger,

Politicheskie problemy Afrikanskogo edinstva (Political Problems of African Unity) (Moscow: Nauka, 1967), p. 80.

5.   R. A. Tuzmukhamedov, ed., Organizatsiia Afrikanskogo edinstva (The Organization of African Unity) (Moscow: Mezhdunarodnye Otnosheniia, 1965), p. 56.

6.   Quoted in Potekhin, "Legacy of Colonialism in Africa," p. 18.

7.   See Ravi Kapil, "On the Conflict Potential of Inherited Boundaries in Africa," World Politics, XVIII, 4 (July, 1966), 656-73.

8.   Fritz Schatten, Communism in Africa (London: George Allen and Unwin, 1966), p. 51.

9.   V. Kudriavtsev, "Afrika kak ona est'" ("Africa As It Is"), Izvestia, August 30, 1966, p. 2.

10.   Speech by L. I. Brezhnev at the International Conference of Communist and Workers' Parties in Moscow, Pravda and Izvestia, June 8, 1969; trans., CDSP, XXI, 23 (July 2, 1969), 9.

11.   R. A. Ul'ianovskii, "Aktual'nye problemy natsional'no-osvoboditel'nogo dvizheniia (po itogovomu dokumentu mezhdunarodnogo soveshchania kommunisticheskikh i rabochikh partii, 1969)" ("Actual Problems of the National-Liberation Movement [According to the Final Document of the International Conference of Communist and Workers' Parties, 1969]"), Narody Azii i Afriki, 4 (1969), 9-10.

12.   Vernon McKay, Africa in World Politics (New York: Harper and Row, 1963), p. 233.

13.   Compare I. I. Potekhin, "O nekotorikh zadachakh afrikanisitiki v sviazi c konferentsiei narodov Afriki" ("On Certain Tasks of African Studies in Connection with the Conference of the Peoples of Africa"), Sovetskaia etnografiia, 2

(March-April, 1959), 14-15; and I. L. Andreev, "Obshchina i sotsial'nye protsessy v osvobodaiu-shcheisia Afrike," ("The Commune and Social Processes in Liberated Africa"), Voprosy filosofii, 8 (1965), 56-67.

14. K. Ivanov, "The National-Liberation Movement and the Non-Capitalist Path of Development," International Affairs, 12 (December, 1964), 12.

15. M. Frenkel', "Rol' vozhdei v Sierra-Leone" ("The Role of the Chiefs in Sierra Leone"), Azia i Afrika Segodnia, 7 (July, 1968), 21.

16. N. N. Liubimov, ed., Afrika v mirovoi ekonomike i politike (Africa in World Economics and Politics) (Moscow: Mezhdunarodnye Otnosheniia, 1965), pp. 57-58.

17. V. Kudriavtsev, "Afrika: Novoe rozhdaetsia v mukakh" ("Africa: The New Is Born in Pain"), Azia i Afrika Segodnia, 11 (November, 1966), 28-29.

18. M. Frenkel', "Plemena--partii--biuro-kratiia" ("Tribes--Parties--Bureaucracies"), Mirovaia ekonomika i mezhdunarodnye otnosheniia, 11 (November, 1968), 113.

19. See V. Iordanskii, "Ghana: Power Crisis," New Times, 25 (June 21, 1967), 12-14; also V. Kudriavtsev, "Afrika kak ona est" ("Africa As It Is"), Izvestia, August 30, 1966, p. 25.

20. V. Solodovnikov, ed., Antiimperialisti-cheskaia revoliutsiia v Afrike (The Anti-Imperialist Revolution in Africa (Moscow: Nauka, 1967), p. 289.

21. Xenia Eudin and Robert North, eds., Soviet Russia and the East, 1920-1927 (Stanford, Calif.: Stanford University Press, 1957), pp. 22-23.

22. See Charles Wilber, The Soviet Model and Underdeveloped Countries (Chapel Hill: The University of North Carolina Press, 1969), pp. 23-24.

23. V. Iordanskii, "Tropicheskaia Afrika: cherty novogo goroda," ("Tropical Africa: Characteristics of the New Town"), Narody Azii i Afriki, 1 (1969), 23.

24. V. Iordanskii, "Tropicheskaia Afrika: o prirode mezhetnicheskikh konfliktov" ("Tropical Africa: On the Nature of Interethnic Conflicts"), Mirovaia ekonomika i mezhdunarodnye otnosheniia, 1 (January, 1967), 52.

25. James O'Connell, "Political Integration: The Nigerian Case," in Arthur Hazelwood, ed., African Integration and Disintegration (New York: Oxford University Press, 1967), pp. 131, 149. This view is shared by V. Korovikov, "Nigeriiskii Krizis" ("Nigerian Crisis"), Pravda, June 16, 1967, p. 5.

26. Pravda, December 6, 1960, pp. 1-4; trans., CDSP, XII, 49 (January 4, 1961), 2; see also G. Starushenko, "Cherez obshchedemokraticheskie preobrazovaniia k sotsialisticheskim," ("Through All-Democratic Transformations to the Socialist"), Kommunist, 13 (September, 1962), 104-9.

27. Jack Woddis, The Way Ahead (New York: International Publishers, 1963), p. 105.

28. See M. A. Krutogolov et al, Stanovlenie natsional'noi gosudarstyennosti v nezavisimikh stranakh Afriki (The Establishment of National Statehood in the Independent Countries of Africa) (Moscow: Mezhdunarodnye Otnosheniia, 1963), p. 76.

29. V. Iordanskii, "Reading Africa's Contemporary History," International Affairs, 11 (November, 1965), 97; also Potekhin, Stanovlenie novoi Gany, p. 255.

30. See R. C. Pratt, "The Future of Federalism in British Africa," Queen's Quarterly, LXVII (1960), 200; quoted in R. L. Watts, New Federations: Experiments in the Commonwealth (Oxford: The Clarendon Press, 1966), p. 344.

31. Iu. Iudin, "Politicheskie partii i odno-partiinie sistemy v nezavisimikh stranakh Tropi-cheskoi Afriki" ("Political Parties and One-Party Systems in the Independent Countries of Tropical Africa"), Sovetskoe gosudarstvo i pravo, 12 (December, 1966), 49.

32. A. Nikanovov, "Kamerun: u vulkana preobrazovanii" ("Cameroon: On the Volcano of Change"), Azia i Afrika Segodnia, 8 (August, 1968), 7.

33. K. Ivanov, "Kongo i Afrika" ("The Congo and Africa"), Pravda, March 30, 1961, p. 3.

34. M. Kremnyov, "Africa in Search of New Paths," World Marxist Review, VI, 8 (August, 1963), 75-76. (Italics in the original.)

35. V. P. Verin, Prezidentskie respubliki v Afrike (Presidential Republics in Africa) (Moscow: Mezhdunarodnye Otnosheniia, 1963), quoted in "Re-gimes of French-Speaking African Countries," Mizan, VI, 7 (July-August, 1964), 1-10.

36. V Kudriavtsev, "Africa's Hopes and Anx-ieties," International Affairs, 11 (November, 1963), 40.

37. G. B. Starushenko, Natsiia i gosudarstvo v osvobodaiushchikhsia stranakh (Nation and State in the Liberated Countries)(Moscow: Mezhdunarodnye Otnosheniia, 1967), p. 223.

38. V. Kudriavtsev, "African Tremors," Iz-vestia, January 15, 1966; trans., CDSP, XVIII, 2 (February 2, 1966), 31. (Italics mine.)

39. See Lev Stepanov, "Third World in Three Dimensions," New Times, 2 (January 10, 1966), 3-5; cited in "The Soviet Dilemma," Mizan, VIII, 2 (March-April, 1966), 49.

40. This allegation has since been scaled
down to a claim that the CIA "participated in the
preparations for the coup in Ghana." See V. G.
Solodovnikov, "Zadachi sovetskoi afrikanistiki"
("The Tasks of Soviet African Studies"), Narody
Azii i Afriki, 3 (1968), 6.

41. I. I. Potekhin, "Problemy bor"by c perezhitkami proshlogo na Afrikanskom kontinente" (Problems
of Struggling Against the Survivals of the Past on
the African Continent"), Sovetskaia etnografiia, 4
(July-August, 1964), p. 192 (italics mine); also L.
Alexandrovskaia, Gana (Moscow: 1965), pp. 119-20;
cited in "The Soviet Dilemma," p. 50.

42. See A. Ramzi and A. Levkovsky, "The Petty-
Bourgeois Masses in the Revolutionary Movements of
the Third World," World Marxist Review, IX, 1 (January, 1966), 63; cited in "The Soviet Dilemma,"
p. 50.

43. G. Mirskii, "Politicheskaia rol' armii v
stranakh Azii i Afriki" ("The Political Role of the
Army in the Countries of Asia and Africa"), Narody
Azii i Afriki, 6 (1968), 7; see also B. G. Gafurov,
G. F. Kim, et al., Natsional'no-osboboditel'noe
dvizhenie v Azii i Afrike, Vol. III (Na Novom Puti)
(The National-Liberation Movement in Asia and Africa,
Vol. III [On a New Path]) (Moscow: Nauka, 1968),
p. 205; E. M. Zhukov, Sovremennye teorii sotsializma
"natsional'nogo tipa" (Modern Theories of Socialism
of the "National Type") (Moscow: Mysl, 1967), p.
198; V. Shelepin, "Africa: Why the Instability?"
New Times, 52 (December 30, 1968), 24; Kudriavtsev,
"Afrika kak ona est," p. 25; "Ghana's New Government Faces Economic Chaos," Moscow Radio in Hausa
to Africa, 1830 GMT, October 7, 1969.

44. Liubimov, op. cit., p. 125; also V.
Midtsev, "Gvineaia na novom puti" ("Guinea on a New
Path"), Kommunist, 12 (August, 1965), 85-93; Woddis,
op. cit., pp. 101-5.

45. L. D. Iablochkov, "Evolution of African Nationalism as a Political Ideology," Papers Presented by the USSR Delegation to the Second International Congress of Africanists, Dakar, 1967, p. 11.

46. Frenkel',"Plemena . . .," p. 114.

47. Iu. Bochkarev, "The Guinea Experiment," New Times, June, 1960, p. 26; quoted in Arthur Klinghoffer, Soviet Perspectives on African Socialism (Rutherford, N.J.: Fairleigh Dickinson University Press, 1969), p. 115.

48. N. Gavrilov, "Africa: Classes, Parties and Politics," International Affairs, 7 (July, 1966), 42-43.

49. R. A. Ul'ianovskii, ed., Nekapitalisticheskii put' razvitiia stran Afriki (The Non-Capitalist Path of Development of the Countries of Africa) (Moscow: Nauka, 1967), pp. 369-70; see also G. Kim and A. Kaufman, "Non-Capitalist Development: Achievements and Difficulties," International Affairs, 12 (December, 1967), 74.

50. E. M. Zhukov, op. cit., p. 198.

51. Ul'ianovskii, ed., op. cit., p. 165.

52. On the cult of personality in Africa, see R. Andreasian, "Revoliutsionnye demokraty Azii i Afriki" ("The Revolutionary Democrats of Asia and Africa"), Azia i Afrika Segodnia, 10 (October, 1966), 4; J. Bellamy, "Testing Time For Ghana," The African Communist, 27 (Fourth Quarter, 1966), 26; Ul'ianovskii, ed., op. cit., p. 369; A. Zanzolo, "Crisis in Africa," The African Communist, 26 (Third Quarter, 1966), 27.

53. Interview with V. G. Grafskii and B. A. Strashun, Institute of State and Law, Moscow, September, 1969. See also N. Mitrofanov, "Edinstvo v

mnogoobrazii" ("Unity in Versatility"), Azia i
Afrika Segodnia, 6 (June, 1963), 14.

54. Michael Gehlen, The Communist Party of
the Soviet Union (Bloomington: Indiana University
Press, 1969), pp. 27, 67.

55. Ibid., p. 140.

56. Ibid., pp. 84-85.

57. I. Diarra, "The Mass Party and Socialist
Construction," World Marxist Review, X, 1 (January,
1967), 33.

58. Cf. ibid., p. 31; and Solodovnikov, Antiimperialisticheskaia revoliutsiia v Afrike, p. 302n.

59. For example, see F. Tarasov, "Otkuda
iskhodit'opasnost'" ("Whence the Danger?"), Pravda,
December 18, 1967, p. 5; also Gavrilov, "Africa:
Classes, Parties and Politics," p. 42.

60. V. Shelepin, "Africa: Why the Instability?" New Times, 52 (December 30, 1968), p. 24.

61. Frenkel', loc. cit.   (Italics mine.)

62. V. Kudriavtsev, "Afrikanskie isbergi"
("African Icebergs"), Azia i Afrika Segodnia, 5
(May, 1969), 10; also Interview with M. Bourdakin,
Soviet Embassy, Accra, Ghana.

63. Ul'ianovskii, "Aktual'nie problemy
. . . ," p. 10.

64. Iudin, "Politicheskie partii," p. 49;
also Starushenko, op. cit., p. 228.

65. V. I. Lenin, "The National Question in
Our Program," Selected Works, II, p. 322; quoted in
Stefan Possony, Lenin Reader (Chicago: Regnery,
1966), p. 229.

66. V. G. Grafskii, "Federalizm v Tropicheskoi Afrike" ("Federalism in Tropical Africa"), <u>Sovetskoe gosudarstvo i pravo</u>, 9 (September, 1967), 116; Starushenko, <u>op. cit</u>., p. 267; I. Potekhin, "Novoe Afrikanskoe gosudarstvo--Gana" ("A New African State--Ghana"), <u>Sovetskaia etnografiia</u>, 2 (March-April, 1957), 113-14.

67. Starushenko, <u>Natsiia . . .</u>, p. 267.

68. <u>Ibid</u>., p. 275; V. G. Grafskii and B. A. Strashun, <u>Federalizm v razvivaiushchikhsia stranakh</u> (<u>Federalism in Developing Countries</u>) (Moscow: Mezhdunarodnye Otnosheniia, 1968), pp. 6-7.

69. Grafskii and Strashun, <u>op. cit</u>., p. 25.

70. Starushenko, <u>Natsiia . . .</u>, pp. 266-67.

71. <u>Ibid</u>., p. 275; also <u>New York Times</u>, February 24, 1970, p. 22.

72. Grafskii and Strashun, <u>op. cit</u>., p. 223.

73. Krutogolov <u>et al</u>., <u>op. cit</u>., p. 146.

74. <u>Ibid</u>.

75. Moscow Radio, February 11, 1966; quoted in "Nigeria," <u>Mizan</u>, VIII, 3 (May-June, 1966), 130. See also L. Fedorov, "Nigeriia do perevorota i posle" ("Nigeria Before the Coup and After"), <u>Azia i Afrika Segodnia</u>, 6 (June, 1966), 49.

76. Moscow Radio, May 13, 1966; quoted in "Nigeria," p. 130.

77. Cf. Krutogolov <u>et al</u>., <u>op. cit</u>., p. 146; and Grafskii and Strashun, <u>op. cit</u>., p. 25.

78. Kudriavtsev, "Afrika kak ona est'," p. 2.

79. See V. Kudriavtsev, "Nigerian Tragedy,"

Izvestia, March 21, 1967; quoted in "Soviet Views on Nigeria," Mizan, IX, 2 (March-April, 1967), 72; see also Korovikov, op. cit., p. 5.

80.   Starushenko, Natsiia . . ., p. 273.

81.   Admittedly, Potekhin had declared in 1964 that a unitary state might not be suitable for Nigeria, but this was exceptional and did not become a theme of pre-1967 Soviet analyses. (See his "Legacy of Colonialism in Africa," p. 20.)

82.   Moscow Radio in Hausa to Africa, 1830 GMT, December 30, 1969.

83.   V. G. Solodovnikov, ed., Afrika segodnia (Africa Today) (Moscow: Znanye, 1969), p. 34.

84.   Moscow Radio in Hausa to Africa, 1730 GMT, December 29, 1969.

85.   Moscow TASS International Service in English, 1457 GMT, May 3, 1970.

6

Soviet Africanists deem economic development
the ultimate long-range solution to African nation-
building problems, for only if the total resources
of the state are increased can steps be taken to
eliminate the inequality between regions and the
scramble for employment that so intensify ethnic
rivalries--rivalries that perpetuate the power of
reactionary traditional and neo-imperialist forces.
However, they caution that the issue is not simply
one of accumulating capital and marketing the growing industrial output, for, on the surface, capitalism provides results that are as good (or better)
than those that socialism can produce for the underdeveloped world. Only if an examination is made of
the groups that benefit from this economic growth,
and of the durability and reality of the higher
growth indexes, can the qualitative differences between the two systems be discerned. If the African
states want true economic independence, freedom
from domination by foreign capital, and a real improvement in the quality of life for their citizenry, then a political decision must be made: The
noncapitalist path must be chosen.

In this sense, then, the Soviet Marxists as-
cribe to the theory of the primacy of politics, to

the view that "the supposedly spontaneous operation
of economic 'rules' could be altered by deliberate
political action."[1] They apply this theory not
only to the problem of economic growth, but also to
the entire realm of national development:

> An absolute requirement for the trans-
> formation of a people into a developed
> nation is the establishment of indus-
> trial centers and, based on them, cul-
> tural centers, and, what is most im-
> portant, the formation of national
> detachments of the working class and
> the intelligentsia as the basic
> forces for the consolidation of the
> nation and the development of a na-
> tional culture.[2]

In other words, a political commitment to the tenets
of socialism is the sole way to ensure the best economic policy for the country and the assignment of a
leading role to the progressive forces. Once this
commitment is made, of course, then noncapitalist
economics will in themselves become a driving force
in societal transformation; production relations
will affect not only the generation of ideas, but
also the actual distribution of power. Thus, the
Marxists bring their followers full circle, from an
injunction to begin with the correct political ideology to a reminder that, in the final analysis, the
basis of any struggle is economic.[3] In any event,
Third World leaders are assured that only a denial
of capitalism as both a political and economic system will ensure a permanent solution to their development problems.

These problems, of course, are numerous; however, discussion here will of necessity be limited
to the prospects that socialism holds for the elimination of national centrifugalism. Soviet authors
have written volumes on the success of the socialist
path in creating a strong multinational state in the
USSR and would like to believe that the same success
could rather automatically be achieved in the African

countries. In the early 1960's, before socialist
methods were actually applied by certain African
leaders, Soviet Africanists could avoid any discussion of specifics by simply stating that capitalism
was responsible for the "oppression and exploitation of small peoples by large"--a situation that
socialism, by its very nature, would preclude.[4]
Socialist-type regimes would smash the forces of
feudalism and reaction, adopt the principle of national equality, abjure the use of force and favor-
itism, and achieve such economic development that
class formation would proceed apace and the progressive classes would be ushered into power. In sum,
the correct national policy would be adopted at the
correct time.[5]

Needless to say, the proper policies were not
developed so easily. Moscow watched in dismay as
the ethnic conflicts continued, the socialist-type
regimes floundered, and elements of the Soviet
model, such as the single-party system, proved
rather unsatisfactory. Ethnic particularism was a
causal factor in the downfall of such pro-Soviet
leaders as Nkrumah, while new adherents to socialism such as the People's Republic of the Congo
(Brazzaville)--so named in January, 1970--have had
such problems with tribalism that it is questionable how long the regime, much less the People's
Republic, will last. Even a cursory survey of the
African scene was sufficient to elucidate the groud-
lessness of Moscow's earlier optimism regarding the
ability of socialist regimes to cope with African
centrifugalism. As Leonid Brezhnev remarked in 1967:

> History shows that the elimination of
> backwardness and the advance to social-
> ism, bypassing capitalism, presuppose
> the solution of many complicated so-
> cial problems and require the creation
> of modern productive forces. The peo-
> ples of the countries which have
> chosen a socialist orientation still
> have to solve these problems.[6]

This pessimism about the ability of socialism to provide direct political answers to African nation-building problems has become a keynote of Soviet commentary under the Brezhnev-Kosygin regime, culminating in the recent statement by K. Brutents in _Pravda_ that "the social forces of the developing countries are encountering tasks <u>that considerably outstrip, sometimes by many decades</u>, the degree of formation of the socioeconomic prerequisites adequate for these tasks."[7] Perhaps the single most effective way to strengthen these progressive states and establish the necessary base for their performance is to concentrate on socialism as an economic system.

THE RELEVANCE OF ECONOMIC ASPECTS OF
THE SOVIET NATION-BUILDING MODEL
TO BLACK AFRICA

However, the question immediately arises whether the economic aspects of the Soviet nation-building model are applicable to black Africa. The Bolsheviks could make extensive economic aid to poorer regions of the USSR one of the key elements of their integration program, while such an option is not available to an African government. Soviet authorities acknowledge that, "in order to liquidate the inequalities between regions, capital allocation in the economy of the national republics exceeded that of the Soviet Union as a whole."[8] Only a country that by 1914 had received a substantial amount of foreign capital and ranked as Europe's largest oil-producer, third in machine construction, the fourth largest producer of steel, and, in sum, was the fifth most powerful industrial nation in the world[9] could afford such a diversion. As Kurt Muller has indicated, Lenin as early as 1899 acknowledged that the Industrial Revolution, still hardly noticeable in the Third World today, was a reality in Russia even at that time.[10]

Soviet analysts have admitted that the economic aspect of the Soviet nation-building model might not

be entirely applicable to the African setting.   K.
Ivanov inaugurated this trend in 1964 by remarking
that, even in the Soviet Union, the national question could not be resolved "by a mechanical transfer of organization and methods from the advanced
Soviet republics to the backward ones."   It was
necessary to adapt the model to new conditions and
to depend on "the fraternal unity of nations and
the help of the working class"--that is, economic
aid[11]--to effect any real change; theories were
simply not enough.

In 1968, Gafurov and Kim stated openly that
the situation of the Soviet Union in the early years
and that of today's underdeveloped nations are strikingly dissimilar. First of all they pointed out
that the magnitude and duration of the wars of national liberation nullified any efforts to create a
modern military-industrial base comparable to that
of the Soviet Union. Secondly, the USSR was economically more advanced:

> In the mid-1930's, the Soviet Union
> already had the necessary objective
> conditions for creating a more or
> less self-sufficient economy. . . .
> None of the young Asian or African
> states can now or in the near future
> reach such a high level of technical
> competence. The Soviet government,
> using a rather small, but well-
> prepared technical intelligentsia
> remaining from prerevolutionary Rus-
> sia, could in a short time establish
> a whole army of engineers and tech-
> nicians. . . . [Finally,] the Soviet
> Union, occupying a huge territory,
> had almost all the most important
> types of mineral and agricultural raw
> materials. . . . Enterprises optimal
> in size could be created [while]
> Asian and African states can only do
> this in certain districts.[12]

In other words, the Soviet Union had sufficient economic resources to withstand the expenditures and
dislocations that a program of integrating backward
nationality groups entailed. The African states do
not; therefore, it is clear that "the lessons of
Soviet experience should not be automatically applied."[13]

INDUSTRIALIZATION AND URBANIZATION

However, this realization developed very slowly. Thus, in the early 1960's, industrialization
was deemed the ultimate solution to African centrifugalism. As a result of Moscow's optimism regarding
the industrial potential of African countries, the
rapidity with which the resulting benefits would be
extended to the countryside, and the rate of detribalization of the ever growing corps of industrial
workers, neither sociopolitical factors nor the
problem of the isolation of the peasant masses was
accorded much attention. Ethnographers and political economists alike based their work on the premise
that industrial development was liquidating the age-
old tribal conflicts: Thus, while Gavrilov strove
to show how this process facilitated "the strengthening of unity on the basis of a recognition by the
people of a community of state and class interests,"[14]
ethnographers such as Ismagilova and Braginskii were
compiling supportive data. Braginskii drew on a 1956
UNESCO report to prove that "the disintegration of
tribal relations was proceeding apace":

> In the African sector of the town of
> Elizabethville (Congo) [now Lubum-
> bashi], 40 percent of the population
> had not returned to their tribes over
> the course of 10-20 years, and 20
> percent of the adult population left
> [pokinulo] their tribes more than
> twenty years ago.[15]

Braginskii cited these figures to substantiate his
thesis regarding the correlation between industrialization and urbanization, on the one hand, and

detribalization, on the other. He did not mention
that the time span involved in this process might
be dangerously long or that the rate of population
growth in the urban areas might outstrip the rate
of industrial construction. Furthermore, he ignored
the fact that urban settlement patterns in Elizabeth-
ville (as in other African cities) were based on
tribal affiliation, making it completely unnecessary
to return to the village to maintain one's ethnic
loyalties.

Western specialists on African urbanology were
analyzing these aspects in detail by 1960,[16] but Soviet preconceptions regarding industrialization combined with the relative newness of African Studies
as an area of specialization to ensure that their
negative conclusions would be overlooked. Thus,
L. D. Iablochkov criticized Max Gluckman's conclusions regarding the persistence of tribalism in African towns (although, interestingly enough, the
editors of <u>Sovetskaia etnografiia</u> did publish a
complete translation of his article):

> In a number of places, perhaps inad-
> vertently, he gives the false impres-
> sion of a stable balance of popula-
> tion interchange between the town and
> the village; the villager going to
> the town is detribalized, the worker
> returning to the village is de-
> urbanized. Even to a person only
> slightly acquainted with dialectics,
> it should be obvious that the pro-
> cess of the dying out of the old
> tribal structure is irreversible and
> the growth of the towns inevitable.
> His odd statement regarding the ex-
> istence of tribalism in the town is
> also doubtful. One can hardly call
> a new phenomenon, not tied to the
> tribal structure in the village local-
> ity, tribalism. . . . The town out-
> strips the village in social progress
> and actively influences its develop-
> ment.[17]

Ismagilova continued this positive treatment of the
effects of urbanization on detribalization in her
classic work on The Peoples of Nigeria, published
in 1963.[18] However, an article written by Potekhin
in 1964 signaled the beginning of a new approach to
the study of urban ethnicity. He still was not prepared to acknowledge that urbanization might work
to intensify tribalism in African conditions, but
he did admit that its effects had not been so thorough as to eliminate all the "negative survivals of
the past"[19]--survivals such as the extended family,
men's unions, town societies, and age classes. They
not only inhibited the development of national consciousness but also represented a definite brake on
economic growth.

K. Ivanov, a frequent contributor to International Affairs, amplified Potekhin's concern by sug-
gesting that the limelight be shifted away from "the
urban struggle" to a study of village life. He
noted that "no clear answers" had been given to the
question of how the village was to be induced to
take the new path--a neglect that might eventually
give rise to severe difficulties for progressive
regimes. In his words, "to focus attention on the
town is much easier but entirely insufficient today
and may lead to vulgar simplification and error."[20]
The warning was clear, and both author and journal
were authoritative; unfortunately, however, the
Kremlin was still committed to the industrialization-
urbanization policy. Therefore, the rapid shift in
research priorities that he advocated went unrealized.

THE DEVELOPMENT OF AGRICULTURE AND THE
RURAL AREAS: A NEW EMPHASIS

The inauguration of the Brezhnev-Kosygin regime
brought about a new preoccupation with the state of
the Soviet economy.[21] The consequences for Soviet
analysis of the Third World were far-reaching. If
domestic growth was the foremost internationalist
duty of the USSR, then the Kremlin's reluctance to
increase foreign aid necessitated achieving the maximum possible effectiveness from current programs.

This, however, was not occurring. By following a
path of rapid industrialization to the neglect of
agriculture, the underdeveloped areas had suffered
setbacks in both areas. On the one hand, the sup-
ply of capital, tax revenues, and the proper raw
materials essential to industrialization had fallen,
while food shortages, poverty, and subsistence farming were still endemic to the rural areas. It was
clear that agricultural development had to be given
priority if over-all economic growth was ever to be
achieved.

Interestingly enough, this new official stress
on agriculture and the problems of the rural areas
brought about a surge of articles on the realities
of African urban life. Perhaps the fact that industrialization had been de-emphasized meant that
the previous pressure to elucidate its positive aspects no longer existed; alternatively, it is possible that the overthrow of Nkrumah, combined with
Brezhnev's emphasis on economic rationality, evoked
an investigation of the deficiencies of existing African development programs. At any rate, it is
noteworthy that two weeks after Brezhnev's speech
and the Ghana coup, <u>Pravda</u> published a somber article by Ul'ianovskii warning that the ongoing economic programs were ill-conceived and did not take
into account the "unpreparedness of the popular
masses to support the reforms." Continued efforts
to proceed on the noncapitalist path when the necessary economic base and mental attitudes were lacking
could only "lead to the growth of conflicts, and to
the disturbance of the economic relations between
town and country, and between industry and agriculture."[22]

Ul'ianovskii's allusions to the role that the
disaffection of the urban worker could play in fo-
menting political instability were amplified by
Vladimir Iordanskii in a series of scholarly articles on ethnicity and the urban poor. His principal observations were three: (1) that the rate of
migration of villagers into the towns far outstripped
the rate of increase in job opportunities; (2) that
unemployment caused a reliance on ethnic associations

for survival; and (3) that this renewed ethnicity
hampered national integration, impeded the growth
of class consciousness, and rendered the city-
dwellers susceptible to the reactionary machinations of tribal opponents to the regime. He concluded that African leaders must recognize "the
limited 'absorption' capability of contemporary urban society, [and] its weakness as an assimilator."[23]
To fail to acknowledge these realities was to court
political upheaval and tribal conflicts--disasters
that could be averted only by stemming the rate of
rural emigration through a concentrated program of
agricultural development.[24]

Agricultural development, it was hoped, would
lead to a modernization of village society and hence
to the liberation of the peasant masses from tribal
politics and ethnic consciousness. For, according
to Marxist analysis of the transformation of ethnic
units, the most significant precipitating factor is

> the change in the structure of the pri-
> mary formations: the development of
> productive forces and the social dif-
> ferentiation among tribes and between
> tribes which it entails, the rise of
> the institution of labor leading to
> the decomposition of the tribal struc-
> ture and the disappearance of one of
> the most important prerequisites of
> its existence--territorial integrity
> of the tribe.[25]

If tribalism could be eliminated among the peasantry, the political and economic advantages would be
numerous. Economically, the size of the internal
market would increase markedly: (1) The chiefs
would no longer receive such a large percentage of
the output as tribute; (2) the mutual aid concept
would be attenuated, impelling the individual to be
more productive, as he could no longer rely on the
kinship structure for support. Politically, the
index of peasant participation in political unrest
would be substantially decreased: (1) Reactionary

chiefs and ethnic leaders could no longer win adherents to antigovernment manifestations by appealing
to ethnic particularisms; (2) the peasantry could
be socialized into the national political community
and, hopefully, into the ethos of the ruling regime.

THE ROLE OF THE VILLAGE COMMUNE

It was clear that the optimum method of village transformation would be one effecting agricultural development and also the detribalization (or
increase in class consciousness) of the peasantry.
It was also clear that the existing socioproductive
structure of the rural areas would have to be considered in the formulation of new programs, for the
work of Soviet researchers had convinced them that
the ties of the peasants to the primitive-communal
structure were still strong.[26] However, several approaches to the existing structure were available:
(1) rapid elimination; (2) retention of the structure as the basis for the transition to higher
forms of productive relations (i.e., socialism); or
(3) rejection of the structure, while retaining the
underlying values. Soviet analysts have successive-
ly considered the merits of each approach, finally
settling on the last one as the optimum.

The first suggestion, that the entire precapitalist formation of African agriculture should be
rooted out as rapidly as possible, was not given
serious consideration by Soviet Africanists. There
seem to have been several reasons for this reti-
cence. First, it was felt that the African regimes
lacked the necessary cadres, legitimacy, and re-
sourcefulness to effect a rapid substitution of a
new outlook for the old without risking widespread
peasant unrest. Secondly, it was feared that the
premature dissolution of the peasant community
(obshchina) might result in the conversion of the
peasants to private farming--a conversion that
could be exploited by the imperialists to foist the
capitalist system of development on sub-Saharan Africa.[27] Thirdly, Moscow was aware that one of the

key tenets common to the many variants of African
socialism was the belief that the communal attitudes
and patterns of traditional society could be the
foundation for the construction of a new order.
Therefore, to urge the extirpation of the traditional system would incur the wrath--and perhaps,
alienation--of certain of the continent's most
prominent leaders.

These calculations prompted Africanists such
as Potekhin to disregard Lenin's oft-quoted injunc-
tions against any populist idealization of peasant
society and to declare instead that, "in the view
of the founders of Marxism," the village commune
can, under certain conditions, become a starting
point for the noncapitalist development of a country and for the building of socialism.[28] The early
1960's witnessed the publication of a spate of similarly optimistic articles in Soviet publications.
Certain drawbacks of the communal system were men-
tioned--for instance, the support it lent to the
preservation of the power of the chiefs--but such
negative aspects were discussed only in passing.
The major emphasis of this period was a positive
one, culminating in the fulsome praise heaped on
the commune in an article in Voprosy istorii in
1965. Here, Andreev remarked that the commune
could provide the same benefits for the underdeveloped countries that it provided for the backward
areas of the USSR. Although it was responsible for
a somewhat slower tempo of socialist construction,

> the existence of these communes pro-
> vided the especially backward peoples
> definite sociopsychological advan-
> tages of development. This factor
> should not be underrated . . . as
> socialism assumes not only the crea-
> tion of developed industry, but also
> the inculcation of a consciousness
> of responsibility among people, de-
> sire for labor, [and] a friendly,
> brotherly relationship of one person
> to another.[29]

The implication of Andreev's statement was that the communal structure--both in the Soviet Union and in Africa--could help to develop the New Socialist Man. It could school the peasant in patriotism and the more practical fields such as food production, and finally, through its political manifestations (for example, the village and communal councils), it could integrate the individual into the national political life.

Andreev's article marked the end of the writings recommending that the communal structure could be retained as the basis for the transition to socialism. Counterarguments had been advanced in the pages of Soviet journals for some time, but, spurred by the emphasis on realism and rationality so evident in Brezhnev's speeches to the 23d CPSU Congress, these arguments become dominant. Soviet political commentators now urged that the structure be bypassed in an effort to construct new forms of agricultural cooperation on the basis of the old communal values. The period of overt sympathy with the views of the African socialists now seemed over, swamped by the Kremlin's desire to see African agriculture develop at a rate and manner that would be most advantageous to its own economic needs. These needs include both large amounts of raw materials for the expansion of Soviet industry and the conclusion of trade, rather than aid, agreements. The satisfaction of both these requirements depends on the expanded output of African agriculture--a goal toward which the activities of all Soviet Africanists are now directed.

V. G. Solodovnikov, in his capacity as the Director of the Africa Institute and one of the Soviet Union's most prominent political economists, seems to have been selected as the natural articulator of these new concerns. Conversations with his research staff, perusal of his speeches, and analysis of his more academic writings all reveal the same general theme: "The African community has outlived itself and is no longer in keeping with the modern level of social organization of production."[30]

He rejects the view that the traditional structure
provides a good schooling for socialism for the individual or that it might function as a foundation
for the building of a socialist society. He re-
turns, instead, to the theories of traditional
Marxism-Leninism--that is, that socialism does not
imply a "modernization" of the old, but rather "a
genuine revolution in the development of productive
forces, a radical transformation of relations of
production as well as efficient economic activity."[31]
This transformation will be neither automatic nor
painless, as many African socialists believe; instead, it will require a concerted attack against
the outmoded social and political survivals that
the commune sustains.

These survivals are numerous: (1) the communal
structure in general, which isolates the peasants
from each other (thereby inhibiting the growth of
class consciousness) and from their leaders (thereby providing them free rein to enact their reactionary ideas); (2) the chauvinistic view that, by relying on the commune, Africa can avoid the general patterns and laws of socialist development; (3) tribal
organization; (4) the institution of tribal chiefs
and clan elders--men who function as exploiting landlords under the guise of traditionalism; (5) the tendency of the peasantry to cooperate in consumption,
but not in production, thereby hindering the growth
of the internal market and evoking a concept of private property; (6) the reluctance to adopt new production methods because the old ones are hallowed
by tradition; (7) the persistent poverty that this
breeds--a poverty that drives large numbers to the
towns, where they become not only a financial drain
on the regime, but also a prime source of political
instability; and (8) the intensification of ethnic
centrifugalism, for "closed village communes scattered in savannahs [can only] increase the inherent
suspicion towards the neighboring alien population."[32]

In view of all these negative manifestations of
communalism, the question arises whether there are
any positive values that can serve as the basis of

the new agricultural organizations that Moscow is
recommending. Admittedly, the positive aspects are
few, but Soviet authorities deem them significant
nevertheless. They include the traditions of collective labor and democratic decision-making and
the fact that the widespread practice of communal
landholding would free the African regimes from
undertaking any forced redistribution of land in
order to collectivize agriculture. These factors
represent a tremendous positive force--provided
that they are acted upon by progressive social
forces:

> Dualism is the law of the self-
> movement (and self-destruction) of
> the commune--the unity and struggle
> of two contradictory sources: the
> collective and the individual, the
> social and the private. . . . In
> view of its dual nature, the commune
> can be (and historically is) a tran-
> sitional form either to private
> property (in different forms) or to
> the social (socialist) form of prop-
> erty. . . .
>   However, the commune of itself
> can give birth only to those social
> forms based on some type of private
> property. It absolutely cannot give
> rise of itself (spontaneously) to the
> highest social (socialist) form of
> production and property (although the
> Russian Populists in the past and
> certain ideologues of "African so-
> cialism" cannot understand this).
> Which path it takes depends on the
> level of development of the socio-
> economic and historical sphere in
> which the commune exists and devel-
> ops.[33]

Zak's analysis of the dualism inherent in the commune is essentially a mirror of the ideas of Western specialists--specialists who have long cautioned

that the African peasant will retain his belief in the value of cooperative patterns only as long as they have demonstrable benefits for him and are upheld by a system of sanctions.[34] In other words, if modernizing African leaders wish to destroy the old communal structure while retaining certain traditional values, they will have to develop new monetary and ideological forms of persuasion to replace those inherent in the old system of tribal loyalties and mutual aid.

The proposed monetary incentives are of two types: indirect and direct. The indirect incentives include signs that the government is as committed as the peasantry to bettering agricultural conditions and the nation's economic situation. Thus, the regime is expected to liquidate usury, decrease unproductive and ostentatious spending, and institute a system of progressive taxation that will weigh heavily on the wealthy landowners and feudal chiefs. According to V. L. Tiagunenko's somewhat optimistic assessment, the institution of these reforms would make it possible "to double the investment in agriculture."[35] This increase would, in turn, facilitate the granting of direct economic inducements to the peasants to bring them into the cooperatives--inducements such as the provision of seed, tools, and fertilizer, the advice of agrotechnical specialists, and higher prices for products than those obtainable on the open market.[36]

This stress on prices, profits, and material inducements is extremely revealing of the economic and political rationality that characterizes current Soviet analyses of the African peasantry and African agriculture. Soviet writers are not advocating the collectivization path adopted by Stalin, nor even the establishment of sovkhozy or state farms in which each peasant would be an employee of the state, for, in the absence of the requisite power and cadre resources, either method would result in widespread political instability and a sharp decrease in agricultural output--factors that would be disastrous for the African regimes and,

coincidentally, for the economic development plans
of the USSR. Therefore, the Russians content themselves with proposing the establishment of collec-
tives--a rather vague African variant of the kolkhoz,
or collective farm, which will be set up in two
stages. First, marketing cooperatives will be
formed, and later, producers' cooperatives in which
there will be "authentic socialist ownership of
land and equipment."[37] The transition will be extremely gradual, as African revolutionary regimes
do not have the talent, tools, or the strong party
necessary for any rapid progression. To paraphrase
the words of one Soviet Africanist, if Tanzania is
having difficulties in spite of the moderation of
Nyerere's program, the diffusion of party cadres
throughout the country, and the relative absence of
ethnic conflicts, it is questionable whether the
other black African states can achieve any appreciable collectivization in the foreseeable future.[38]

Thus, pragmatism has replaced ideological considerations as the keynote of Soviet writings on
African agricultural development: The emphasis has
shifted from collectives to cooperatives, and then
from producers' cooperatives to marketing coopera-
tives--to even the most minimal system if it would
only work to increase output and productivity. However, the Soviet economists now complain that the
Africans lack sufficient finances to provide tools
and staff for even this basic system. Thus, an
analysis of Soviet writings on agricultural development envelops the reader in a vicious circle:
The lack of agricultural development retards economic growth, but the low level of economic growth
hinders agricultural development. Soviet analysts
have attempted to break out of this circular argument by claiming that, instead of an expensive
process of agricultural mechanization, improved
hoes and kerosene lamps could initially work won-
ders in many parts of Africa.[39] However, even
these primitive implements are costly--especially
in the quantities necessary for any significant
agricultural growth--and are often beyond the means
of many African countries. Therefore, Soviet

economists have concluded that "the experience of
the last ten to fifteen years suggests that essential changes in the African economic structure are
rather improbable in the forthcoming decade as
well."[40]

In view of the basic Marxist premise regarding
the inverse relation between economic development
and tribalism, it is apparent that a vicious circle
obtains here as well: Tribalism slows down economic
growth, but the slow rate of economic growth hampers
the elimination of tribalism. Extraeconomic methods,
such as coercion or ideological work by the party,
have been suggested in the past to replace the in-
centive to joining the national production community
that economics might have provided. However, all of
the scholars and diplomats that I interviewed warn
that the use of force must be eschewed, lest peasant
unrest similar to that evoked by collectivization in
the Kekedou-Kissidou area of Guinea in 1960 erupt
throughout sub-Saharan Africa.[41] Furthermore, they
do not expect party work to prove very effective,
since that, too, requires funds. Since these funds
are not being generated by the African economies,
nor are they forthcoming from the developed countries, it is apparent that the African peasant will
continue to live in a political-economic framework
similar to that which has endured for centuries.

The consequences of this situation are significant both for the African regimes and for the Soviet
Union. First, since "consciousness of national identity cannot originate within the commune,"[42] the African peasantry will retain its particularistic loyalties to tribe and clan, frustrating the regimes'
efforts to integrate it into the national community.
Therefore, the instability potential of the peasantry will remain high. Soviet analysts have long
recognized this fact and have actually termed the
village "to all appearances sleepy and conservative," "the cradle of revolt."[43] They fear for the
stability of current African leaderships and also
for the effect that any overthrow might have on
their own fortunes in Africa. However, they have

apparently decided that the risk pales in significance when compared to the magnitude of the resources needed for Soviet domestic development.
The requirements of the domestic economy are so
great that financial aid to modernize Africa's villages cannot be justified.

Secondly, since the Gross National Products of
the states on the capitalist path are generally
higher than those of the states traditionally associated with Moscow, it is likely that the former
would have more money to invest in establishing
agricultural cooperatives. This would raise their
agricultural output vis-à-vis the noncapitalist
countries, thereby hindering Moscow's efforts to
present the adoption of the capitalist path and
association with the capitalist countries as counterproductive. In fact, the pro-Western African
states, such as Uganda, Senegal, and the Ivory
Coast, have made "substantial progress" in the cooperative movement, as Moscow has publicly--and
ruefully--acknowledged.[44] However, here again the
propaganda value that might be gained from sponsoring the successful cooperativization of Guinean agriculture, for example, is far outweighed by considerations of the financial drain that this would
impose on the USSR.

Finally, if the resources that the African
states can devote to agricultural modernization are
limited, then this money will have to be used selec-
tively--that is, to bring at least minimal improvements to all village areas or to concentrate almost
exclusively on the development of one region.
Since the economic rationality of the former approach is questionable and since most African
states are victims of some type of regional polarity, it is probable that the latter course will be
adopted. This has occurred in such countries as
Cameroon, where cooperativization programs have
been concentrated on the South.[45] This serves to
intensify an existing ethnoreligious bifurcation
by increasing the economic disparity between North
and South, with the result that economic development

hardly fulfills the Soviet prediction of furthering
national integration.

Most Soviet Africanists, of course, continue
to insist that economic growth is the ultimate answer to African centrifugalism, for this tenet is
indeed basic to Marxism. However, the past few
years have witnessed a significant decrease in Soviet optimism on the rapidity of this process in
African conditions--a decrease that has not only
affected the analyses of prominent political commentators but has also spawned outright negativism
on the part of certain lesser known nationalities
specialists.

Thus, among the prominent writers who now display an increasing reluctance to make any sanguine
predictions about the nature of economic processes
in Africa, we can list V. Kudriavtsev, E. Zhukov,
and B. G. Gafurov. These men concur in the judgment that economic development will eventually lead
to the establishment of a stable national community
in the countries of Africa. However, they decline
to claim that this process will be finalized in the
near future or that the difficulties involved can
be eliminated by the choice of the noncapitalist
path. In fact, Gafurov and Kim offer this assessment of Africa's prospects:

> The countries in Tropical Africa can
> either take the capitalist path,
> . . . which leads to long decades of
> suffering by the people, foreign ex-
> ploitation and the formation of a
> national bourgeoisie--that exploit-
> ing class currently not found in many
> African countries. Or they can take
> the noncapitalist path . . . which
> will not bring a rapid easing and im-
> provement in the life of the masses,
> and will demand of them great effort,
> but which will be based on the fra-
> ternal international assistance of
> the socialist countries and will ex-
> clude the formation of a national
> bourgeoisie.[46]

If Gafurov and Kim held out no hope for a rapid improvement in the life of the masses even with the
help of the Soviet bloc, it is obvious that this
process will be even further delayed by the downgrading of aid to Africa on the scale of Soviet
priorities. Furthermore, Kudriavtsev will not even
grant African states the possibility of by-passing
the problems of class contradictions and degenera-
tion of economic life--consolations that at least
had punctuated Gafurov and Kim's rather grim analysis. Instead, he sees a persistence of tribalism
and feudal relations and a period of worsening economic conditions--factors that leave the masses in
a situation that "differs little from that of the
preindependence era."[47] If more than ten years of
independence have accomplished little in the area
of economic growth or national integration, it is
likely that this situation will persist into the
twenty-first century.

THE CORRELATION BETWEEN NATIONALISM
AND ECONOMIC GROWTH

Recently, a second group of lesser-known scholars has begun to advance the view that perhaps even
a successful economic development program will not
effect the disappearance of nationalism and ethnic
particularism. Admittedly, these men are not Africanists, but it is likely that their sociological
studies of prejudice and ethnicity will eventually
influence Soviet writings on Africa. A. G. Agaev
seems to have inaugurated this new critical trend
by pointing out the dogmatic nature of the entire
Marxist theory of nation-building.

> It is well-known that in historical
> materialism there is a thesis regard-
> ing the connection of the tribal
> form of community with primitive
> structures and of the appearance of
> peoples and nationalities in the pro-
> cess of transition to slave-owning
> and feudalism, and nations--from
> feudalism to capitalism. However,
> from this undisputed theoretical

> statement have been drawn many mis-
> taken conclusions, and even the
> statement itself has been turned
> into a dogmatic scheme. This sche-
> matization . . . has led to ignoring
> the indisputable fact that, with the
> disappearance of feudalism, a na-
> tionality does not simultaneously
> and automatically disappear, and
> that neither under capitalism nor
> socialism does the socioeconomic
> development of nationalities lead
> unfailingly to the formation of
> self-sufficient nations.[48]

M. Dzhunusov proceeded to apply this view to the
national question in the Soviet Union, pointing out
that historical experience showed that "unfriendly
relations may arise between peoples even when there
are no longer any socioeconomic factors breeding
antagonisms between them." He concluded that "antipathies between nations that are rooted in history die hard."[49]

Although Soviet Africanists are certainly aware
that extraeconomic factors play an important role in
maintaining tribalism (witness their voluminous
writings on tradition, religion, language, and so
on), they are not prepared to admit that economics
will not ultimately render these factors irrelevant.
The Nigerian Civil War forced an acknowledgment that
an interesting parallel existed with the earlier
Congolese crisis, in that, in both cases, it was the
richest regions that attempted to secede;[50] however,
this similarity was attributed to the efforts of the
imperialists to dupe the inhabitants of Africa's
wealthiest mineral areas. In other words, Soviet
analysts did not, and perhaps could not, deduce that
there might be a positive correlation between nationalism and economic growth, rather than the negative one predicted by Marxist analysis.

Such a deduction would not only have extensive
theoretical ramifications, but it would also affect

the domestic and foreign relations of the Moscow
regime. For, if the premise that nationalism is a
function of poverty proved to be questionable, it
would frustrate the efforts of the Russians to claim
a purely fraternal interest in the development of
the backward Soviet peoples. Similarly, it would
hamper the attempts of the Soviet government to contrast its friendly concern for Africa with the chauvinistic designs of the bourgeois-nationalist powers
of the West. The elucidation of this contrast has
been a basic--and valuable--weapon in the Soviet
propaganda arsenal for years, one that the government would loathe to see tarnished by the findings
of a few academics. Therefore, in the interests of
doctrinal purity, preserving the myth of domestic
national relations, and not disturbing the tenor of
Soviet propaganda abroad, it is probable that Soviet
Africanists will continue to present economic growth
as the ultimate, if painfully slow, impetus to African national integration.

NOTES

1. Edouard Bustin, "The Quest for Political
Stability in the Congo: Soldiers, Bureaucrats and
Politicians," in Herbert Spiro, ed., Africa: The
Primacy of Politics (New York: Random House, 1966),
p. 16. See also, V. Kudriavtsev; "Real and Fictitious Difficulties," Izvestia, November 2, 1968, p.
4; trans., CDSP, XX, 41 (November 2, 1968), 23.

2. P. M. Rogachev and M. A. Sverdlin, "On the
Concept 'Nation,'" Voprosy istorii, 1 (January,
1966), 33-48; trans., CDSP, XVIII, 21 (June 15,
1966), 15.

3. Cf. K. Ivanov, "The National and Colonial
Question Today," International Affairs, 5 (May,
1963), 4; and L. V. Goncharov, ed., Stroitel'stvo
natsional'noi ekonomiki v stranakh Afriki (Building
a National Economy in the Countries of Africa)
(Moscow: Nauka, 1968), p. 3.

4. R. N. Ismagilova, in N. I. Gavrilov, ed., Nezavisimiye strany Afriki (The Independent Countries of Africa) (Moscow: Nauka, 1965), p. 268; quoted in "Soviet Thoughts on Nigeria's Crisis," Mizan, IX, 4 (July-August, 1967), 175-76.

5. V. Iordanskii, "Reading Africa's Contemporary History," International Affairs, 11 (November, 1965), 96-97; I. P. Tsamerian, "The International Significance of the Experience of the CPSU in Solving the National Question in the USSR," Voprosy istorii KPSS, 9 (September, 1968), 41-55, translated in Current Abstracts of the Soviet Press, I, 5 (October, 1968), 11; G. B. Starushenko, Natsiia i gosudarstvo v osvobodaiushchikhsia stranakh (Nation and State in the Liberated Countries) (Moscow: Mezhdunarodnye Otnosheniia, 1967), pp. 242-43.

6. I. Brezhnev, "Fifty Years of Great Victories of Socialism," Pravda and Izvestia, November 4, 1967, pp. 2-6; trans., CDSP, XIX, 44 (November 22, 1967), 13.

7. K. Brutents, "Rastushchaia revoliutsionnaia sila" ("A Growing Revolutionary Force"), Pravda, January 23, 1970, p. 4. (Italics mine.)

8. B. G. Gafurov, "Reshenie natsional'nogo voprosa v SSSR" ("The Solution of the National Question in the USSR"), Azia i Afrika Segodnia, 1 (January, 1962), 6.

9. R. Maxwell, Information USSR (London: Pergamon, 1962); quoted in R. Dowse, Modernization in Ghana and the USSR (London: Routledge and Kegan Paul, 1969), p. 3.

10. Kurt Muller, The Foreign Aid Programs of the Soviet Bloc and Communist China (New York: Walker, 1967), p. 194.

11. K. Ivanov, "The National-Liberation Movement and the Non-Capitalist Path of Development," International Affairs, 9 (September, 1964), 37.

12. B. G. Gafurov, G. F. Kim, et al., Natsional'
no-osboboditel'noe dvizhenie v Azii i Afrike, Vol.
III (Na Novom Puti) (The National-Liberation Movement
in Asia and Africa, Vol. III [On a New Path]) (Moscow:
Nauka, 1968), pp. 201-3.

13. Interview with V. I. Kaufman, Candidate of
Historical Sciences, Africa Institute, Moscow, Fall,
1969. This view was shared by certain Soviet diplomats, notably, by M. Bourdakin in Accra.

14. Gavrilov, ed., op. cit., p. 58.

15. "Aspects sociaux de l'industrialisation et
de l'urbanisation en Afrique au sud du Sahara,"
UNESCO, 1956, p. 239; quoted in M. I. Braginskii,
"Sotsial'nye sdvigi v Tropicheskoi Afrike posle
vtoroi mirovoi voiny" ("Social Trends in Tropical
Africa After the Second World War"), Sovetskaia
etnografiia, 6 (November-December, 1960), 37; see
also R. N. Ismagilova, "Etnicheskii sostav naseleniia Tanganiki" ("The Ethnic Makeup of the Population of Tanganyika"), Sovetskaia etnografiia, 3
(May-June, 1956), 102; S. Bruk and N. Cheboksarov,
"Sovremennyi etap natsional'nogo razvitiia narodov
Azii i Afriki" ("The Current Stage of National Development of the Peoples of Asia and Africa"),
Sovetskaia etnografiia, 4 (July-August, 1961), 77.

16. See, for example, Kenneth Little, The
Mende of Sierra Leone: A People in Transition
(London: Routledge and Kegan Paul, 1951); also
Michael Banton, West African City (London: Oxford
University Press, 1957).

17. L. D. Iablochkov, "Perevod i predpislovie
statiu Maks Glukman, 'Plemennoi uklad v sovremennoi
Tsentral'noi Afrike'" ("Translation and Introduction
to the Article by Max Gluckman, 'Tribal Structure in
Modern Central Africa'"), Sovetskaia etnografiia, 6
(November-December, 1960), 57.

18. R. N. Ismagilova, Narody Nigerii (The
Peoples of Nigeria) (Moscow: Izd'vo Vostochnoi
literatury, 1963), pp. 10-11.

19. I. I. Potekhin, "Problemy bor"by c perezhitkami proshlogo na Afrikanskom kontinente" ("Problems of Struggling Against the Survivals of the Past on the African Continent"), <u>Sovetskaia etnografiia</u>, 4 (July-August, 1964), 189-90.

20. Ivanov, "The National Liberation Movement and the Non-Capitalist Path of Development," pp. 40-41.

21. See especially the CPSU Central Committee Report delivered by L. I. Brezhnev to the 23d CPSU Congress, Moscow Radio, March 30, 1966; quoted in "Pointers from the 23rd CPSU Congress," <u>Mizan</u>, VIII, 3 (May-June, 1966), 95.

22. R. A. Ul'ianovskii, "Sotsializm i natsional'no-osvoboditel'-naia bor"ba" ("Socialism and the National-Liberation Struggle"), <u>Pravda</u>, April 15, 1966, p. 4; quoted in "Pointers from the 23rd CPSU Congress," p. 99.

23. V. Iordanskii, "Tropicheskaia Afrika: cherty novogo goroda" ("Tropical Africa: Characteristics of the New Town"), <u>Narody Azii i Afriki</u>, 1 (1969), 18; also "Tropicheskaia Afrika: o prirode mezhetnicheskikh konfliktov" ("Tropical Africa: On the Nature of Interethnic Conflicts"), <u>Mirovaia ekonomika i mezhdunarodnye otnosheniia</u>, 1 (January, 1967), 52; "Sotsial'nye sdvigi v gorodakh Tropicheskoi Afriki" ("Social Shifts in the Towns of Tropical Africa"), <u>Mirovaia ekonomika i mezhdunarodnye otnosheniia</u>, 10 (October, 1967), 81.

24. L. D. Iablochkov, "Socio-Demographic Disproportions of Africa in the Modern World," article in V. G. Solodovnikov, ed., <u>Africa in Soviet Studies, 1968</u> (Moscow: Nauka, 1969), p. 186; V. G. Grafskii, "Federalizm v Tropicheskoi Afrike" ("Federalism in Tropical Africa"), <u>Sovetskoe gosudarstvo i pravo</u>, 9 (September, 1967), 120.

25. V. I. Kozlov, "Tipy etnicheskikh protsessov i osobennosti ikh istoricheskogo razvitiia" ("Types

of Ethnic Processes and Peculiarities of Their Historical Development"), _Voprosy istorii_, 9 (September, 1968), 104.

26. For example, see I. I. Potekhin, "Pozemel'
nye otnosheniia v stranakh Afriki" ("Agrarian Relations in the Countries of Africa"), _Narody Azii i
Afriki_, 3 (1962), 16-31.

27. _Ibid_., pp. 30-31.

28. I. I. Potekhin, _Africa's Future: The
Soviet View_, an abridgement of _Afrika smotrit v
budushschee_ (Moscow: Izd'zo Zostochnoi literatury,
1960), printed as a supplement of _Mizan_, III, 4
(April, 1961), 5.

29. I. Andreev, "Obshchina i sotsial'nye
protsessy v osvobodaiushcheisia Afrika" ("The Commune and Social Processes in Liberated Africa"),
Voprosy filosofii, 8 (1965), 63 ff.

30. V. G. Solodovnikov, "Some Problems of
Economic and Social Development of Independent African Nations," Papers Presented by the USSR Delegation to the Second International Congress of Africanists, Dakar, 1967, p. 14.

31. A. B. Letnev, "The Neocolonialists as In-
terpreters of Socialism," in V. G. Solodovnikov,
ed., _Africa in Soviet Studies, 1968_ (Moscow: Nauka,
1969), p. 63.

32. L. D. Iablochkov, "Evolution of African
Nationalism as a Political Ideology," Papers Presented by the USSR Delegation to the Second International Congress of Africanists, Dakar, 1967, p.
9; see also A. B. Letnev, Estimation of Agricultural Produce Marketing Systems in Connection with
Agrarian Reforms (The Case of West Africa)," Papers
Presented . . . , pp. 9-10; Gavrilov, ed., _op. cit._,
pp. 108-21; N. N. Liubimov, ed., _Afrika v mirovoi
ekonomike i politike_ (_Africa in World Economics and
Politics_) (Moscow: Mezhdunarodnye Otnosheniia,
1965), pp. 57-58.

33. S. D. Zak, "Marksizm o prirode i sud'bakh obshchinoi sobstvennosti i razvivaiushchiesia strany" ("Marxism on the Nature of Communal Property and the Developing Countries"), in S. I. Tiul'nanov, ed., Itogi i perspektivi sotsial'no-ekonomicheskogo razvitiia molodikh suverennikh gosudarstv (Conclusions and Perspectives on the Socioeconomic Development of Young Sovereign States) (Leningrad: Izd'vo Leningradskogo universiteta, 1965), p. 37. (Italics in the original.)

34. Igor Kopytoff, "Socialism and Traditional African Studies," in William Friedland and Carl Rosberg, Jr., eds., African Socialism (Stanford, Calif.: Stanford University Press, 1964), p. 58.

35. V. L. Tiagunenko, Problemy sovremennikh natsional'no-osvonoditel'nikh revoliutsii (Problems of the Contemporary National-Liberation Revolution) (Moscow: Nauka, 1966), pp. 86-89.

36. V. Iordanskii, "Protivorechiia nekapitalisticheskogo razvitiia v Afrike" ("Contradictions of Non-Capitalist Development in Africa"), Narody Azii i Afriki, 3 (1968), 54.

37. A. Langa, "Socialism and Rural Revolution," The African Communist, 35 (Third Quarter, 1968), 73.

38. Gavrilov, ed., op. cit., p. 121; for a more recent discussion of Tanzania's problems, see the New York Times, December 14, 1969, I, p. 9.

39. Kudriavtsev, "Real and Fictitious Difficulties," pp. 22-23. See also L. Aleksandrovskaia, "Kooperativnoe dvizhenie v Afrike: problemy i perspektivi" ("The Cooperative Movement in Africa: Problems and Perspectives"), Mirovaia ekonomika i mezhdunarodnye otnosheniia, 3 (May, 1963), 39-51.

40. L. I. Alexandrovskaia and L. V. Goncharov, "Some Trends of Development of African Economics," in Solodovnikov, ed., Africa in Soviet Studies, 1968, p. 26.

41. Fritz Schatten, Communism in Africa
(London: George Allen and Unwin, 1966), p. 133.

42. Iablochkov, "Evolution of African Nationalism as a Political Ideology," p. 15.

43. V. Iordanskii, "Problems of Rural Africa,"
New Times, 28 (July 14, 1965), 18.

44. I. A. Svanidze, "Problems of Raising the
Productivity of Agriculture in Africa," Papers Presented by the USSR Delegation to the Second International Congress of Africanists, Dakar, 1967, p. 5.

45. V. Iordanskii, "Kamerun v chas vybora"
("Cameroon at the Hour of Decision"), Za rubezhom,
August 1-7, 1969, p. 18.

46. Gafurov, Kim, et al., op. cit., pp. 205-6.

47. V. Kudriavtsev, "Afrikanskie isbergi"
("African Icebergs"), Azia i Afrika Segodnia, 5
(May, 1969), 11; also his "Unity and Separatism,"
Izvestia, November 17, 1967, p. 12; trans., CDSP,
XIX, 46 (December 6, 1967), 17.

48. A. G. Agaev, "Narodnost' kak sotsial'naia
obshchnost" ("Nationality as a Social Community"),
Voprosy filosofii, 11 (1965), 26.

49. M. Dzhunusov, "The National Question:
Two Ideologies, Two Policies," International Affairs, 10 (October, 1966), 39. See also his article, "The Theory and Practice of the Development
of Socialist National Relations," Voprosy filosofii,
9, 1967; abstracted in CDSP, XIX, 46 (December 6,
1967), 31.

50. Iordanskii, "Tropicheskaia Afrika: o
prirode mezhetnicheskikh konfliktov," p. 47.

7

SOCIAL STRATA
AND
INTEGRATION

The past decade has witnessed an increasing
pragmatism on the part of Soviet analysts toward
the role of certain strata in the nation-building
process in black Africa. Thus, although Marxist
ideology may have predisposed the Soviet analysts
toward an emphasis on the African workers and peasantry, this predisposition was soon dwarfed by the
overwhelming evidence of reality. No amount of
statistical juggling or wishful thinking could possible elevate the masses into a vanguard position
in the construction of the nation just as--and be-
cause--they could not be assigned a leading role in
either economic or political development. As a result, Soviet commentators shifted their emphasis
toward the leadership groups, specifically, to the
African intelligentsia, the bureaucracy, and the
military.[1] It was concluded that these groups had
the dominant effect on integration policies, as
they form the nucleus of the power complex in most
African states.

THE AFRICAN PEASANTRY

Of course, Soviet writers have not abandoned
their concern with the African peasantry--and for

two reasons: First, the Chinese Communists have
made this group the focus of their revolutionary
program; second, this stratum forms the bulk of the
population of black African states and, by its
sheer size, merits close observation. In fact, it
might be said that the peasantry has received increasing attention in Soviet analysis of African
nation-building during the past decade, albeit primarily from a negative perspective. That is, as
Soviet analysts have become more aware of the persistence of ethnic particularisms among the peasant
population and of the continued isolation of this
group from the limited, but ongoing, national socialization process, they have become more conscious
of its centifugal potential. In other words, Soviet
commentary centers on the instability that the peasants might cause, rather than the integration that
they might help to promote.

In the early years of their contact with black
Africa, Soviet analysts were encouraged by the participation (or at least nonresistance) of the peasantry in the united anti-imperialist front. From
this supposed participation, two inferences were
drawn: first, that the African peasants were a
"progressive" social stratum and, second, that they
would be willing to abandon their traditional iso-
lationism and ethnic particularism to join in the
broader struggle for national development.[2] In
other words, these Soviet Africanists appeared willing to abandon the traditional Russian radical distrust of the peasantry in order to take full advantage of the peculiarities of the African revolutionary situation.

However, as the preceding chapters have shown,
closer examination and more detailed studies impelled the Africanists to tone down their sanguine
predictions. In fact, they came to identify the
African peasantry as the prime carrier of the most
primitive and patriarchal-feudal survivals in African society: for example, (1) the peasants adhere
to Syncretist or Muslim beliefs; (2) they cling to
their local dialects; and (3) they maintain a

belief in the legitimacy of the chieftaincy and the
entire kinship system. Although the collectivism
of the peasants may render them responsive to socialist teachings and progressive ideas, this potential must be activated by the proper leadership.
By themselves, the peasants will cling to the patterns of ethnicity and feudalism that have prevailed
throughout history.[3]

The activization role previously ascribed to
African leaders by Soviet scholars was a dual one:
On the one hand, these leaders would embark on a
program of economic development that would integrate the rural areas into the national production
community, while on the other hand, they would establish political parties that would involve the
peasants in the nation's political life. However,
political institutions have proved unequal to the
task. Regarding economic development, Soviet analysts now acknowledge that the original emphasis on
industrialization brought few tangible benefits to
the countryside, while the program of agricultural
development will not have appreciable immediate results. In the foreseeable future, African leaders
are advised that not even indirect economic methods
such as migrations will work to increase the interaction between city and village.

This negativism is interesting in view of the
integrative role formerly attributed to migrations
by Soviet scholars and can only be explained as an
offshoot of a re-evaluation of African realities.
Thus, in 1963, Ismagilova was extolling the positive impact of migrations on the African struggle
for national unity and the elimination of reactionary social tendencies, claiming that, when the migrants return to the village, they "carry with them
elements of a new social order, new norms of behavior, different outlooks on life, and a different
psychology, not connected with a sense of belonging
to a definite tribe."[4] She fully expected that
population mobility would achieve the same results
in sub-Saharan Africa that it had in the USSR,
where studies had indicated that the rate of

assimilation increased as the level of mobility increased.[5] However, further research in Africa was
to show that certain factors rendered this correlation inoperative.

The first factor, as we have seen, was the
tribal settlement pattern of African towns, which
absorbed the villager upon his arrival. The second
factor was the tendency of a large segment of the
migrants to return home as soon as they had accumu-
lated a certain amount of capital; their dedication
to this goal while they were in the cities worked
to immunize them to the new values of life around
them. On the other hand, those that did not return
to the villages actually contributed to the "slow
pace of social progress" there, as they were not
functioning as the carriers of new ideas. Thus,
the pattern of African migration was retrogressive
in all respects: The migrants who did return to
the countryside were so village-oriented that their
sojourn in the towns had not modified their attitudes at all, while those whose departure had been
motivated by antitribal feelings did not return for
precisely that reason. The result was that the rural way of life continued unchanged, unchallenged
by the viruses of nationalist and class consciousness, which were springing up in the cities.[6]

If direct and indirect economic methods were
deemed ineffective, the only way to reach the peasantry was through an alliance with the workers--an
alliance that would be embodied in a mass party.
This concept has been a constant thread in Soviet
commentary on independent Africa--one of the few
ideas to have been espoused by both Khrushchev and
the new Soviet leadership. As Brezhnev explained
at the 1969 International Conference of Communist
and Workers' Parties:

> The peasantry in that part of the
> world is a mighty revolutionary
> force, with all the fluctuations
> stemming therefrom and all the con-
> tradictions in ideology and policy.

> As a matter of fact, for the time be-
> ing it cannot be otherwise, inasmuch
> as the overwhelming majority still
> live in conditions of monstrous pov-
> erty, lack of rights, and feudal and
> sometimes even pre-feudal relations
> that have not yet been overcome.
> The experience of the revolu-
> tionary movement in various parts
> of the world has shown that the most
> reliable path for the effective in-
> volvement of the peasantry in the
> struggle against imperialism and for
> genuine social progress is the cre-
> ation of an alliance between it and
> the working class.[7]

As might be expected, Brezhnev is much less optimistic than earlier commentators about the speed
with which such an alliance might be forged, while
Solodovnikov, the Soviet Union's chief Africanist,
has admitted that the fact that "the interests of
the African workers and peasants do not fully co-
incide" might be listed as a specific impediment.[8]
However, in view of the oft-demonstrated passivity
of the peasant masses in the face of military coups
and the efforts of the Chinese Communists to convince the Africans of the "superrevolutionism" of
the peasantry,[9] thus touting their own brand of
communism, Soviet authorities insist that it is important to establish proletarian hegemony in the
national liberation movements as soon as possible.
This proletarian dominance would not only help to
ensure that the Soviet model of Communist development prevailed, but it would also catapult the more
progressive and national-minded African workers to
control of the anti-imperialist movement.

THE AFRICAN WORKERS

Communist nation-building theory assigns a
leading role to the working class--a class that,
along with the intelligentsia, is one of "the basic

forces of the unity of the nation and of the development of national culture."[10] The influence of
this theoretical bias upon Soviet Africanists has
been strong, especially since the workers are also
expected to play the dominant role in ushering in
the socialist revolution. However, analysis of the
evolution of Soviet writing on this topic reveals a
growing awareness of the incomplete detribalization
of the African worker, the numerical insignificance
of this stratum, the continuing state of only semi-
politicization, and the fact that other groups sur-
pass the workers in national consciousness and political acumen. Most Soviet theoretical analyses
continue to assign a leading role to the African
workers, but one suspects that this represents mere
ideological pandering, while the focus of Soviet
policy concentration shifts to other strata.

As support for their positive evaluation of
the African workers, however, Soviet commentators
can cite several points. The first is that any
basic statistical analysis will indicate that the
number of African workers has increased significantly since the end of World War II: Thus, whereas on
the eve of the war, there were approximately 4 million workers in sub-Saharan Africa, in 1961 there
were 11 million, and in 1966, 18-19 million.[11] In
other words, as Liubimov noted happily in 1965,
"the working class is forming faster than the national bourgeoisie"[12]--a fact that he interpreted
to mean that the working class would be able to outstrip the bourgeoisie in power as it had in numbers.

The second positive factor is the anti-
imperialism of the African workers. Having been
"cruelly exploited" by the colonialist monopolies,
they long ago developed a strong desire to rid
their country of this element. Furthermore, and
more importantly, they were willing to subscribe
to political means, such as strikes and party membership, in order to accomplish this goal. Their
anti-imperialism provided a convenient base for
forming an alliance with the peasantry--an alliance
that might otherwise not have been established in

view of the noncoincident interests and world outlook of these two strata. This ability to forge a
firm alliance will serve the workers well in their
mission of ushering their states along the path to
socialism and national unity:

> Success in the struggle in the field
> of ideology, especially against re-
> actionary forms of nationalism, de-
> pends to a large extent on the abil-
> ity to attract to one's side numerous
> and natural allies, both those who
> agree in general and those who agree
> on particular issues. . . . Without
> their support and sympathy, it is im-
> possible to win the fight.[13]

As long as the workers remain cohesive and firm in
their antichauvinist outlook--an outlook attributed
to the workers by the theories of Marxism-Leninism[14]--
they will contribute to the cause of ethnic harmony
and social progress.

African Trade Unions

A primary factor in the maintenance of this
cohesiveness is the African trade union movement.
Soviet commentators have been aware of the significance of this movement since the early days of their
contact with independent black Africa, writing as
early as 1960 that, "under certain conditions, the
labor unions, led by men trained in theory, may assume the role of leadership over the working class
and represent the latter in its relations with the
broad masses."[15] This faith in the progressivism
and abilities of trade union leaders is attributable to the general Soviet concern with the labor
movement--a concern formalized by the creation of
the communist-dominated World Federation of Trade
Unions after World War II. Efforts to extend the
influence of the WFTU brought the Russians into contact with the nascent labor organizations of colonial Africa--organizations that were surprisingly

strong, for, with the colonial prohibition of overt
political parties, many African radicals had turned
their attentions to the labor unions. Since these
unions often were not proscribed, they could serve
as both a front and focus for anticolonialist political activity. The unions thus became linked at
an early stage with extreme nationalism and anti-
imperialism.

Soviet observers were impressed with both the
organizational strength and ideological fervor of
the African trade unions. Their optimism led them
to exaggerate the ability of the unions to overcome
the ethnic orientation of the workers--an orientation that was a barrier to the development of class
consciousness. Soviet analysts predicted that the
unions could take hold even among the migrant workers and that they could turn the nonpolitical orientation of these and all workers to their advantage:

> In connection with the rapid growth
> in the ranks of the trade unions,
> not a few politically inexperienced
> workers have entered them who are
> not yet cast in the proletarian mold
> and who have not yet acquired mili-
> tant traditions, but who, to make up
> for this, are uncorrupted by reform-
> ist ideology. This to a certain ex-
> tent facilitates the dissemination
> of proletarian class ideology among
> the working masses.[16]

The Russians felt not only that the trade union membership could be imbued with the proper progressive
attitudes, but also that the union leaders would remain attached to these ideas, using their power to
keep their governments on the noncapitalist path.
They were encouraged by the "leading role" played
by the trade unions in overthrowing Fulbert Youlou
of the Congo (Brazzaville)[17] and by the support
that the Guinean unions had afforded to Sekou Toure.
Little mention was made of the fact that the labor
organizations might give rise not to true class
consciousness, but to the trade union consciousness

that Lenin had so often warned against--trade union
consciousness that would be directed toward securing
material gains, rather than political liberation.
Early Soviet optimism about African labor organizations led them to overlook this time-worn Leninist
injunction, leaving them unprepared for the extended African strikes and chaos that often ushered
in reactionary regimes.

Certain Soviet Africanists persisted in these
rather sanguine analyses of the progressiveness and
organizational strength of the African labor unions
as late as 1967. Thus, surprisingly enough in view
of his extensive studies of the effects of ethnicity
on African politics, Vladimir Iordanskii deemed the
unions relatively unaffected by reactionary tendencies and survivals. He explained that the high
level of class consciousness of the workers helps
them to sift out the damaging aspects of tribal association while retaining those helpful to the
labor movement:

> Thus, the ties with the villages aid
> the workers' movement in attaining
> union with certain peasant groups,
> the ties of many workers' families
> with land tilling allows the work-
> ers to conduct strikes with great
> persistence, the strength of the
> survivals of tribal solidarity fa-
> cilitates the attainment of class
> solidarity, helping the workers to
> see any attack by the entrepreneurs
> against their leaders and friends
> as an attack against the entire
> workers' collective.[18]

He maintains that these strikes will be directed
against exploiting forces, thus serving to harness
the hitherto spontaneous actions of the people to
a progressive goal.

However, Soviet Africanists of Iordanskii's
persuasion are now in a minority. The analysts
continue to extol the progressive potential of the

African workers and their organizational arm, the
trade unions, but the majority are aware of the existence of certain factors that hinder the realization of this capability. Liubimov inaugurated this
new evaluation of African trade unions in his 1965
textbook, <u>Africa in World Economics and Politics</u>.
He pointed to the partial success of the Western International Conference of Free Trade Unions (ICFTU)
and to the efforts of certain African leaders to
torpedo the formation of an All-African Trade Union
Federation (AATUF) as evidence that the trade union
movement was not as cohesively anti-imperialist as
some had predicted. Furthermore, he explained that
this was not surprising in view of the nature of
the African proletariat--a class that is "young,
divided among many small enterprises, strongly tied
to agriculture and handicrafts, and as yet has not
become the decisive and leading force of national
progress in the majority of African countries."[19]

Solodovnikov attempted to attribute these problems of the African labor movement to efforts of reactionary governments to hamper the unions in their
bid for political influence.[20] However, in 1969,
even Iordanskii amended his earlier views, declaring
that, although class consciousness was increasing
among the union membership, the fact that many
unions were actually based on "traditional forms of
association" meant that progress in this area would
be quite slow.[21] In other words, although the Russians had expected the unions to overcome tribal
and ethnic disunity, they had to acknowledge that
the influence of the base on the organization might
be greater than even a cohesive movement could withstand. As Fyodorov lamented in his analysis of the
Nigerian labor movement,

> In Nigeria, with a population of
> 56.6 million, there are less than
> half a million wage workers. Half
> of them are engaged in agriculture,
> building and various services.
> The working class is weak because
> of the general socioeconomic

> backwardness of the emerging coun-
> tries, their poorly developed pro-
> ductive forces, the long "coexis-
> tence" of different socioeconomic
> structures, extreme chronic over-
> population in the countryside and
> the dispersion of the proletariat
> in numerous small enterprises.[22]

It is obvious that, if Nigeria, the most developed
country in black Africa, is plagued by these problems, then the labor movement in the poorer nations
must be encountering extreme difficulties in functioning either as an integrative force or a united
forum of progressive ideas. Even if the ethnic hostility of the industrial workers could be overcome,
the fact would still remain that these men form
only a small percentage of Africa's labor army, for,
among most African wage-earners, ethnic fragmentation is amplified by the atomization that stems
from working in the service sector, migrant labor,
or in a small two- or three-man operation. This
hinders the formation of class consciousness--the
primary Soviet concern--but also impedes even rudimentary forms of collective bargaining, leaving the
more homogeneous employer class with almost free
rein to continue its exploitative policies. Thus,
the power of the bourgeois reactionaries remains
strong and relatively unchallenged as a result of
the persistence of precapitalist ideas and modes of
production among the African working class.[23]

The question arises as to which factors can
compensate for the backwardness and underdeveloped
political consciousness of the African proletariat.
During the Khrushchev era, the Soviets promised--
and at times threatened--to use the "power and might
of world socialism" to ensure that the workers' progressive potential was realized.[24] Brezhnev, however, has abjured any mention of power, preferring
instead to concentrate on more theoretical compen-
sations:

> There can be no doubt that the most
> far-reaching development of the

> working class struggle in the young
> national states against imperialism
> and its allies is yet to come. . . .
> The responsibility that rests with
> us Communists in this matter is
> large. What is required of the Com-
> munist movement is an <u>enormous amount</u>
> <u>of attention</u> to the peasant allies of
> the proletariat and the <u>additional</u>
> <u>elaboration</u> of certain aspects of
> strategy and tactics to conform to
> the specific conditions of the
> former colonial countries.[25]

The peasant allies have, of course, already been
examined closely--and have been found wanting.
Therefore Brezhnev's injunction to develop tactics
to accord with African realities has prompted Soviet Africanists to take a new look at the African
intelligentsia--a group described in one of Potekhin's last publications as a potentially progressive stratum. He explained that, although "the
workers and peasants of Africa may not yet understand" their historic mission to move their countries along the path to socialism and national
unity, "they are being helped to such understanding by their patriotically minded intellectuals."[26]

THE AFRICAN INTELLIGENTSIA

Intellectuals, as a group, are neither trusted
nor mistrusted by Soviet analysts; in fact, just as
the Bolsheviks alternatively railed against the Russian intellectuals or appraised them more positively when they could be of service to the regime, the
current Soviet leadership extends this same ambiva-
lence to the African elite. Thus, before assuming
power, Lenin made no effort to conceal his hostility toward the intellectuals, claiming that their
influence was even more insidious than that of the
landowners--a group whose exploitative designs, at
least, were overt.

But the influence of the <u>intelligen-
tsia</u>, who do not take a direct part
in exploitation, who are trained to
play with general phrases and concepts, who go in for every "good"
idea and who sometimes from sincere
stupidity elevate their mid-class
position to a <u>principle</u> of non-class
parties and non-class politics--the
influence of this bourgeois intelligentsia over the people is dangerous.
Here, and here alone, do we find an
infection of the masses which is
capable of doing real harm and which
demands the exertion of all forces
of socialism in an endeavor to counteract this poison.[27]

After the Bolsheviks assumed control, however, they
realized that, if the intellectuals were by-passed
or eliminated, it would be all but impossible to
fulfill their goals of the industrialization and
all-around development of the Soviet Union. Therefore, the decision was made to evaluate the intellectuals more objectively, retaining those who
wished "to work for the cause of the masses" and
who might eventually be "sovietized."[28] This pragmatism was evident in the Bolshevik attitude not
only toward the Soviet intellectuals, but also toward the intellectuals in the colonies--men described by the Sixth Comintern Congress as able to
assist local Communist Parties in both their organizational and propaganda work.[29]

However, just as the Bolsheviks believed that
the intellectuals could be trusted if they were
"sovietized," that is, brought under the control of
the ruling ideology and the ruling political institution, so they have faith in the progressive potential of the African elite only if they are committed to ideas and programs that will aid the working masses in their efforts to effect a noncapitalist system. This subordination of the task of the

intelletuals to that of the proletariat provides
Soviet analysts with a convenient yardstick for ap-
praising the role of the African intelligentsia.
Thus, if the ideas they propound are in the national
interest (as interpreted by Moscow), they are evaluated positively; if, however, their ideas might
strengthen the position of the reactionaries--that
is, provide them with a rationale for their choice
of the capitalist path or their emphasis on a
uniquely African road to development--then they
are condemned.

Marxist-Leninists do not underestimate the persuasive powers and capacity for influence of the intellectuals in an underdeveloped country. They are
aware that, in a country where the politicized people form such a small part of the total population,
the intellectuals would possess influence all out
of proportion to their numerical significance. It
is for this reason that Soviet commentators watch
the African intellectuals so closely and are con-
stantly prepared to produce an immediate analysis
of their beliefs and behavior. For, if the elite
is so powerful, it would be the height of folly to
allow its negative behavior to go unchallenged; it
must be criticized as soon as possible in order to
alert the forces who might be able to combat it.
Similarly, if the ideas it advances serve the cause
of progress, it must be praised--lest the intellectuals, as is their wont, turn their short attention
spans to the discussion of a new proposal or idea-
tional system.

The African intellectuals have been praised by
Soviet analysts for their role in popularizing several concepts, most notably, the idea that African
countries should form sovereign and unified nation-
states. They were among the leaders of the independence movement for two reasons. First, their
foreign educations had exposed them to the ferment
of new ideas in Europe about the right of every nation to self-determination. Second, and perhaps
equally important, their elite positions under the
colonial powers had given them a taste for power--
power that they knew would increase if they helped

govern an independent state, rather than one that
formed just another link in a vast colonial system.
Soviet analysts were aware of the self-interest involved in the intelligentsia's support of the independence movement, noting that, "in several African
countries, it is the _elite_ of the colonial period
and has close relations with the feudalists and with
local businessmen." However, in spite of this interest in "the bourgeois way of life," the intelligentsia was not slated to play a reactionary role.
For, "not owning the means of production, it does
not exploit labor, does not propagate traditional
capitalism, and does not oppose the state sector."[30]
This lack of a strong vested interest in the capitalist mode of development, coupled with the progressiveness of certain of its ideas, meant that
the intelligentsia could help advance the socialist
cause.

It could also make an indirect contribution by
promoting the concept of national unity. Soviet
nationality theory has traditionally accorded the
intelligentsia an important role in the nation-
building process, crediting it as joining the working class to form "the basic forces of the unity
of the nation and the development of national culture."[31] Soviet scholars have extended this distinction to the African intellectuals, crediting
them with engendering and promoting "the consciousness of national community" that is so essential a
spur to the integration process. As the Africanist
L. D. Iablochkov explained, "this kind of convic-
tion is usually born in the minds of people with a
broader social outlook who therefore understand the
inevitability and usefulness of consolidating on a
country-wide scale."[32] The African intellectuals
not only possessed this understanding, but their
self-interest ensured that they would strive to con-
vey it to other societal groups. Furthermore, the
extent of their influence meant that they might
succeed.

However, there are several factors peculiar to
the intellectual stratum that might vitiate--or
even negate--any positive contribution that it might

make to the socialist cause. The first is its lack
of organization or cohesiveness. Admittedly, the
group is fairly homogeneous in its social outlook,
to use the Soviet term, and in its life-style. By
contrast, however, the narrowness of each member's
area of expertise, coupled with a strong belief in
the right to self-expression, gives rise to "the
habit of individual patriotically minded intellectuals to act on the principle that everyone can be
a smart fellow in his own way."[33] According to
Ivanov, this led to the near fatal fragmentation
and paralysis of the Congolese anticolonialist movement; if the intellectuals could not cooperate with
each other and with other social forces in the face
of such a well-defined goal and such an obvious danger, the question arises whether they would close
ranks against the more subtle incursions of the neo-
imperialist era.

Soviet analysis of this problem has led to a
not altogether optimistic conclusion. For, in addition to the atomization caused by the personal
interests of the intellectuals, this group is also
fragmented by more systemic factors--factors that
directly affect its revolutionary character. These
elements are so strong that Iordanskii was impelled
to note that

> there is one characteristic law: the
> more distinct the class antagonism,
> the stronger and more evident is the
> demarcation of the intelligentsia
> along social lines. And, on the
> other hand, in those countries with
> strong tribal traditions, it is along
> ethnic lines.[34]

In the countries of black Africa, tribalism is def-
initely a problem; if Soviet theories about the
growing class stratification are accepted also,
then it is obvious that there are many antagonisms
within the intellectual stratum that prevent it
from adopting a unified stance. This means that,
while there may be some intellectuals actively

involved in progressive politics, there are also
many who will be drawn into the service of the reactionary camp.

They may advance the reactionary cause either
consciously or indirectly. They provide indirect
assistance by their fragmentation along professional,
ethnic, or class lines--a fragmentation that prevents them from constituting a serious opposition
to the maneuvers of the right. They also aid the
reactionaries, albeit unwittingly, by their espousal
of lofty theoretical concepts that can provide a
cloak of respectability to those forces bent on
frustrating the popular liberation movement. This
applies especially to the intellectuals' adherence
to African socialism--an ideology viewed by Soviet
analysts as an attempt to legitimize an essentially
elitist system and to convince the masses that there
is another model of development and true independence beyond that represented by the USSR. Soviet
Africanists recognize that the intellectuals may
support African socialism because it provides a useful integrative and developmental mechanism for
their societies.[35] However, they warn that this
goal might cause the intellectuals to lose sight of
their true role--alerting the masses to the real
meaning of socialism.

For a while, Potekhin believed that the intelligentsia would fulfill this mission of helping "a
large number of the masses to distinguish the true
supporters of socialism from all kinds of false Socialists."[36] However, it soon became apparent that,
regardless of their intellectual familiarity with
Marxism-Leninism, the African intellectuals were
too infected by the same "national egoism"[37] preva-
lent among other segments of the elite to point out
the theoretical invalidity of the concept of a
uniquely African path. Instead, they were busy
studying the evolution of African culture, elucidating the relevance of such survivals as the commune to current develpment efforts, and sifting the
various cultures for symbols that could be elevated
to the role of integrative mechanisms. Soviet

analysts viewed this as a useful endeavor, but also
a dangerous one--a wariness that most African intellectuals did not share.

Therefore, they continued--indirectly or unwit-
tingly--to conduct programs and research that, in
the final analysis, supported the elitist and supra-
class masquerade of the bourgeois reactionaries.
Also, because their expertise made them indispens-
able to the ruling elite, they tended to reinforce
the all-too-frequent tendency of this elite to neglect or by-pass the proletarian masses. As _Pravda_
noted in 1969,

> Lenin understood better than anyone
> else that the scientific and techni-
> cal revolution would exert an enor-
> mous influence on all aspects of
> social life. . . . Regarding the
> growth of the new popular intelli-
> gentsia and its increased role in
> the life of society to be a natural,
> law-governed process, he emphasized
> that this could not detract from the
> historic role of the working class
> . . . [which] continues today to re-
> main the leading revolutionary force,
> capable of uniting around itself all
> working people, leading them in an
> attack on imperialism, and directing
> their efforts in building socialism
> and communism.[38]

Thus, although Soviet ideologues would not deny the
intellectuals a prominent role in society--especial-
ly in underdeveloped countries where class formation was a slow process, they were wary lest this
temporary dominance become a permanent societal
feature. Mindful, perhaps, of the experience of
their own country, where the possibility exists
that the attitudes of the functional elites might
change the character of the party, they are particularly desirous that African regimes consider and expand the role of the more trustworthy proletariat.

The workers are deemed more dependable because this is a tenet of Marxism-Leninism and because the African intelligentsia has at times directly supported the reactionaries. Thus, in Ghana, for example, there is ample evidence that the intellectuals allied with the tribal chiefs to support the ouster of Nkrumah. Of course, the workers also can be faulted for their passivity in the face of the National Liberation Council's maneuvers, as Soviet analysts have acknowledged. However, theirs was an error of omission, rather than commission, and for this they can be pardoned; the intellectuals cannot. It is a tribute to the intellectuals that Moscow expected so much of them--to the point of assigning them a leading role in the nation-building process and in the establishment of vanguard parties, the ultimate symbols of socialism.[39] However, as a result of its high expectation level, Moscow's disappointment was acute.

THE BUREAUCRACY

The African bureaucracy or civil servant stratum is another segment of the elite that Soviet Africanists have studied and found wanting. To be sure, the appraisal has not always been negative. Initially, the Russians were so preoccupied with the role of the colonial administrators in perpetuating the spirit, if not the actuality, of imperialist rule that they were certain that the "Africanization" of the administrative system, that is, the replacement of the colonial civil servants by native personnel, would result in a significant liberalization. They recognized that many of the Africans had been trained by the colonialists; however, it was felt that their desire for independence had surely nullified the effects of the most reactionary foreign attitudes. If not, these men would soon be replaced by more progressive Africans as the newly activated national education systems produced their first graduates.

The Russians obviously did not anticipate the mushrooming of the African bureaucracy that the

first decade of independence entailed; consequently,
they were not prepared for the strain that this
growth would place on the African educational institutions and on the ability of the regime to screen
the bureaucracy thoroughly. Selectively applied,
the experience of the CPSU might have yielded certain clues to the African situation, for, within
five years of the revolution, the CPSU apparatus
numbered over 15,000 workers--4 percent of the total
membership.[40] However, in many black African countries, the party apparatus was not necessarily the
key governing unit; therefore, if the Russians were
to observe its rate of growth, they would not necessarily have found the situation too alarming. Meanwhile, though, the civil service membership was increasing rapidly--to the point where functionaries
actually outnumbered the industrial workers (a
frightening thought for a Marxist-Leninist) and administrative expenses accounted for over half the
total state budget.[41] Unfortunately, the preoccupation of Soviet analysts with the experience of the
USSR meant that their attention was focused on the
African parties, not on the civil administration,
where the greatest expansion was occurring.

When Soviet analysis caught up with African
reality, two contradictory reactions set in. The
first--and minority--response was a positive one,
expressed by such men as G. Mirskii, of the Institute of World Economy and International Relations.
He held that even the bureaucratic elite, although
politically conservative, would not oppose the expansion of the state sector--an expansion deemed
crucial to the noncapitalist path. Furthermore,
the medium and small civil servants--"younger and
more radical than the better off bureaucratic
elite"--could be trusted to "express the anti-
imperialist sentiments of the masses . . . and demand change." Both the elite and subordinate
strata of the bourgeoisie may be primarily "interested in developing the state sector because the
state sector in turn is what sustains it economically."[42] Nevertheless, regardless of their mo-
tives, their activity still served to promote the

development of socialism and the integration of the
nation.

The process by which Soviet analysts assigned
the bureaucracy a leading role in the nation-building
process is an interesting one. Their research convinced them that conditions peculiar to black Africa
had all but negated the dominant position usually
attributed to other societal sectors. Thus, the
working class was economically and politically un-
developed, and the party apparatus was "less effective" than that of the government, "impelling the
political leaders to try to lean on the bureaucracy."
This reliance could not be successfully resisted by
the national bourgeoisie--a stratum whose weakness
actually created "the objective conditions for the
active intrusion of the government into the economy
and the [further] growth of the state sector."[43]
In the final analysis, the weakness of other strata
combined to lend an all but autocephalous character
to the bureaucracy--an autonomy which, in turn,
served to restrict the power of these other groups.
As Iablochkov commented in 1967,

> It can be said with sufficient certain-
> ty that in Tropical Africa, the rela-
> tively predominant part of society
> consists now of the officials. . . .
> This is a very definite layer in
> Tropical Africa, and its political
> platform is etatism--which means
> conversion of the state apparatus
> from a function of the public will
> into an independent force. . . .
> It is precisely for this social
> layer that national unity within
> the framework of a single state has
> become a clearly realized necessity.
> That is why this very layer has as-
> sumed the functions of national con-
> solidation.[44]

The positive appraisals of Iablochkov et al.
have been challenged with increasing virulence by

the majority of Soviet Africanists, who question
not only the alleged effect or at least neutrality
of the bureaucracy in the struggle for socialist
development, but also the new effect of this group
on the national integration process. Skepticism
regarding the political progressivism of the bureaucracy was evident in the early 1960's, when critics
such as Kudriavtsev and Alexandrovskaia began to
warn that the self-interest that prompted the bureaucracy to support the state sector would also
impel it to divert the resources and energies of
this sector completely to its own needs. Not only
would the interests of the workers and peasants be
completely disregarded, but the bureaucracy would
engage in exploitation of these groups. In other
words, the bureaucratic elite would develop inevitably into the bureaucratic bourgeoisie.[45]

Early commentators such as Alexandrovskaia and
Kudriavtsev tended to exempt the bureaucracy of
states on the noncapitalist path from this inevitable bourgeoisification. However, further experience
with the functionaries of these states persuaded Soviet analysts that this exemption was not warranted.
Thus, in January, 1966, a <u>World Marxist Review</u> article referred to the problems of certain states
"accepting scientific socialism" with "bureaucracy
and bonapartism in the machinery of state."[46] It
is probable that the article was referring mainly
to Ghana, for, after Nkrumah's overthrow, the criticisms of Ghana's civil service stratum were multi-
fold. Furthermore, as W. Scott Thompson has elucidated, Soviet advisers in Ghana were frustrated con-
stantly by the bureaucracy in their efforts to "lib-
eralize" Ghanian politics. Thus, the civil servants
were opposed to the establishment of collective
farms in Ghana, complained bitterly about the economic inefficiency of Soviet development proposals,
and generally attempted to hinder Ghana's evolution
toward the Soviet model.[47] In this last effort, of
course, they were ultimately, if not consistently,
successful. Their support of the coup against
Nkrumah was so galling that even Mirskii was impelled to reformulate his earlier views. He now

noted their transformation into "a caste of state-
capitalist sharp dealers" and observed that it was
no wonder that military coups occurred "incessant-
ly" in black Africa.[48]

Not surprisingly, the role of the functionaries
in the ouster of Nkrumah--the first pro-Soviet leader in black Africa to be overthrown, prompted the
publication of a spate of critical analyses of the
bureaucratic bourgeoisie. Ul'ianovskii did venture
to imply that perhaps Nkrumah himself had been at
fault, in the sense that the "unrestrained curtailment of democracy may result in . . . concentrating
too much power in the hands of the executive government agencies."[49] However, most Soviet commentators by-passed any discussion of the regulative
role of the chief executive in their haste to criticize the reactionary bureaucracy. This criticism
was pointed and acerbic, as it was beginning to appear that the all-pervasive bureaucracy represented
a basic check to the expansion and consolidation of
the noncapitalist path in black Africa.[50]

Several shortcomings of the bureaucratic bourgeoisie were spotlighted by Soviet Africanists.
The first, of course, was its surrender to what
Brutents terms "imperialist seduction."[51] Driven
by an insatiable appetite for influence and material
possessions, the bureaucracy opened the door to foreign monopolies, providing them almost unlimited opportunities for expansion in return for a certain
monetary compensation. This collusion was a serious
obstacle to the national liberation struggle: Foreign dominance over the new states was intensified,
and, because of the vested interest of the administrators in perpetuating this system, it was doubtful
whether it could ever be overturned.

The national liberation struggle has also been
hampered by the corruption bred by this imperialist
collusion--corruption that "has expanded to the extent that it is a social danger."[52] The bureaucrats
often divert scarce government funds to their own
use or employ them to buy consumer goods that cannot

be purchased in their own country. This increases
the already high import-export ratio and necessi-
tates the use of funds that might otherwise be ear-
marked for internal development to pay the debts
incurred to the industrialized nations. (N.B.:
These debts are often owed to the Western countries,
as the Soviet bloc does not produce goods that comply with the high standards of the African bourgeoisie.) Thus, the situation of the average citi-
zen worsens--or, at best, does not improve--while
that of the bureaucrats approaches luxury. This
obvious contrast hardly serves to increase the respect of the masses for their leaders--or for the
socialist ideology that many leaders continue to
proclaim.

According to Soviet analysts, this polarity in
life-styles also does nothing to further the national integration process. First, it serves to
render suspect all the ideas--including the need
for a unified nation--propounded by the bourgeoisie.
Second, the corruption and associated nepotism acts
to intensify ethnic rivalries; in no way does it
fulfill certain Western analysts' claims of contributing to constructive political development,[53] for
example, by materially inducing large clans or
tribes to transfer their political loyalties and
demands to the central government. Third, the bourgeois emphasis on the nation as a springboard for
economic gain works, at times, to reinforce disintegrative tendencies. In other words, the bureaucrats of a certain wealthy region may decide that
their personal assets might be even greater if it
were not for the drain imposed on governmental resources by the subsidization of a poorer area.
Thus, they may opt out of the national union, as
Katanga did, or out of a federation, as did the
Ivory Coast.[54]

Soviet analysts have advanced a variety of
solutions to the problem of the bureaucratic bour-
geoisie--most of which can be faulted on the
grounds that they are vague, unrealizable, or unrealistic. The remarks of G. Starushenko, Deputy
Director of the African Institute, illustrate these

weaknesses very clearly: On one page, he advises
the national-democratic regimes simply to "scrap
the old and create a new governmental apparatus of
people dedicated to the cause of social progress,"
while his only concretization comes a few pages
later, when he reminds his readers that "democratization of the state apparatus is the real weapon
against bureaucratism. It consists of strictly observing the law, eliminating the institution of professional parliamentarians, letting the workers par-
ticipate in the direction of production, etc."[55]
It is apparent that replacing the old bureaucracy
with the new would only substitute one set of problems for another, and it is doubtful whether a sufficiently large personnel pool exists for this type
of wholesale reorganization. As for eliminating
the professionals or according the workers manage-
rial responsibilities, these steps would place a
tremendous administrative burden on the political
party. Because this task would overtax existing
party workers, additional ones would have to be
added--thereby making the party the very bureaucratic monster that now characterizes the state
machine.

Thus, it appears that there are no simple reme-
dies for the bureaucratization of African society--
a point that many Soviet Africanists have acknowledged. Political leaders can increase their vigi-
lance, establishing commissions and campaigns to
uncover abuses and ensure the appointment of individuals "who are really loyal to the people" and to
the cause of national development.[56] These measures, unfortunately, are not likely to produce
widespread immediate results. In the meantime,
officialism, nepotism, and corruption will continue,
and popular restiveness will rise, paving the way
for continued instability and the rising incidence
of military coups.

THE MILITARY

The approaches of Soviet and American analysts
to the problem of the role of the military in black

Africa have been strikingly similar, evolving from
relative scholarly neglect in the early 1960's to
the current position that, whereas a party system
would be preferable, the qualities of military regimes that accord with Great Power interests can
certainly be appreciated. Thus, the United States
tends to regard the military regimes in Ghana and
Mali favorably, as they effected the downfall of
"leftist" rulers; the Soviet Union, by contrast,
sees positive value in the coups effected against
such states as Upper Volta and the Central African
Republic, for here "reactionary" regimes were overthrown. However, the ideological predispositions
of both East and West have been strongly tempered
by pragmatic considerations, for in view of the
fact that twelve African states are currently ruled
by the military--and several others have only recently returned to civilian rule (among them, Ghana,
Dahomey, and Sierra Leone)--the gaps in one of the
Great Powers' diplomacy would be severe if restricted
only to parliamentary regimes. Furthermore, certain
countries struck by military coups have been the
scene of direct East-West involvement (for example,
Nigeria and Somalia); in these cases, it would be
folly to allow the dictates of ideology to outweigh
those of national interest. Finally, the dismay of
both Eastern and Western countries over the political and ethnic conflicts that plague black Africa
has prompted serious consideration of the possible
positive role of the military. When all other institutions and organizations have proved unequal to the
task, it is not surprising that the military--the
only organized and disciplined force--should be re-
appraised.

     Civilian control over the military has been a
strong tradition in the United States and the Soviet
Union--a fact that undoubtedly accounts, in large
part, for the unpreparedness of both Powers for the
autonomous position and extramilitary functions assumed by the army in black Africa. It must be admitted, of course, that Washington and Moscow had
had long experience in dealing with military regimes
in other parts of the world (for example, in Latin

America, the Middle East, and North Africa). However, it is apparent that the long colonial tutelage
in Africa by powers constitutionally dedicated to
civilian rule, the tight control over the military
by colonial administrations, and the presumed isolation of Africa from the pressures and prejudices of
other Third World areas evoked the hope that black
Africa would remain immune to military take-overs.
As a Soviet author acknowledged in 1966, the realization that "the coming to power of the army in many
African and Asian countries is not a chance episode,
but a definite phenomenon based on the laws of development [is] one that until recently escaped the
attention of scholars."[57]

The systemic causes of African military coups
were not examined by Soviet scholars for two reasons: (1) The attentions of CPSU officials and
ideologues were directed toward the role of political parties and the state administration; and (2)
this predisposition was amplified by the academics,
who directed their efforts toward illuminating the
bases for official optimism. Thus, as long as the
civilian institutions were allegedly performing
well, little impetus existed for the Africanists to
study the organizational aspects of the African military. Similarly, as long as the fiction of increased proletarianization of the population was
maintained, it was assumed that the people would
not be reconciled to any army regime that happened
to assume power.[58] They would recognize the army
as a tool of the imperialist reactionaries--reac-
tionaries who had stirred up the economic and ethnic difficulties in order to maneuver their agents
into power.

The awakening of Soviet Africanists to the
true significance of the coups was a two-staged
process. In the first stage, they realized that
most of the early coups were directed against pro-
Western regimes--for example, against Hubert Maga
of Dahomey in 1963, Moise Tshombe in Congo-Kinshasa
in 1965, and Maurice Yameogo, Premier of Upper
Volta, in 1966. It was apparent that a positive

role could be imputed to the military in certain
countries, as it was helping the population to
achieve its true goal and objective--embarkation on
the noncapitalist path. The second stage, however,
witnessed the defeat of certain progressive rulers
by the military and an increase in Soviet realism
about black Africa's potential for rapid development. Once the factors of African politics did not
have to be moulded to fit a preconceived ideological framework, the way was cleared for a thorough
investigation of the military: the factors paving
its rise to power, its class nature, and the achievements and difficulties that might be expected of a
noncivilian regime.

     The degree of Soviet consensus on these as-
pects varies from almost zero regarding the class
orientation to strong disagreement on the subject
of what the military can accomplish. The only topics that elicit even a semblance of unanimity are
the negative ones--that is, the weaknesses inherent
in the African political structure that served to
facilitate military take-overs, but that will also
impede the army's efforts to realize any genuine reforms. This negative emphasis is unfortunate, for
it has resulted in the devotion of the majority of
scholarly attention to synopsizing the ills of African society, rather than to analyzing those aspects
of military tradition and training that might produce an entirely new leadership ethos. In other
words, by analyzing the military according to the
time-bound Marxist criteria of class and political
affiliation, Soviet analysis has only rarely zeroed
in on the professionalism, respect for technology,
and international orientation that render of the
military a distinct sociopolitical unit.

     Thus, for the most part, Soviet writings on
the military have concentrated on the deficiencies
of African society rather than the strengths of the
African military. It must be acknowledged that
these weaknesses paved the way for the rise of the
military, but these external factors, although contributing, were not causal. This fact rarely

emerges from Soviet analysis. Thus, the following
factors are listed time and time again as explana-
tions for the rash of coups in modern Africa:
(1) the ethnic and religious diversity which have
fragmented key political institutions; (2) popular
dissatisfaction with the proimperialist policies of
civilian regimes; (3) the low level of mass politicization; (4) the inability of progressive regimes
to resolve urgent economic difficulties while maintaining the support of the people; (5) the corruption and venality of the bureaucracy; and (6) the
underdeveloped nature of class stratification,
which has impeded the workers, peasants, and national bourgeoisie from directing the revolutionary
process.[59]

It is significant that Soviet Africanists now
acknowledge that military coups may be the result
of something systemic, rather than simply the product of imperialist machinations.[60] However, the
problems of African politics have been analyzed in
detail and to summarize the studies contributes
little to an understanding of the African military.
Nevertheless, there are indications that Russian
scholars are attempting to redress this situation.
For example, in a 1967 _Izvestia_ article, A.
Iskenderov mentioned that the army's participation
in the independence struggle in many African countries may have given rise to its self-image as the
guardian of popular freedom and democracy, while
the training that many officers received abroad
made them feel "especially sharply the necessity of
political and social and economic changes."[61] They
often possess sufficient power to effect the change
in government that they deem so essential to these
goals for two reasons: (1) The esprit de corps
characteristic of military units instills a cohesion sufficient to counteract the centifugal forces
that plague other African organizations; and (2) the
army often looms larger in the African political
structure because it has been called upon many times
to effect governmental policies--for example, "to
repress national minorities or other insurgents."[62]
The enactment of these functions not only entails an

increase in the size and strength of the armed
forces but also often brings about contempt for the
civilian regime unable to cope with centrifugalism
by other than coercive means.

Soviet writers have investigated one other aspect of the African military: its class orientation. However, this has not achieved the intended
result of illuminating the goals or political direction of new military regimes, for the difficulties
in applying the concepts of class analysis to any
African stratum are magnified by the heterogeneity
of the military. As a result, Soviet analysis has
been caught up in a raging debate over the progressivism or reactionary character of the army--a debate that is so heated that the original motivation
for the research has been all but forgotten.

Thus, in one camp are aligned those authors
who believe that the military can contribute little
to the progress of the national liberation revolution. They claim that, in black Africa, coups are
usually effected by the commanding forces of the
army--officers who "in their way of life and political opinions side with the bureaucratic bourgeoisie."[63] Mirskii, in fact, speaks of a "military-
bureaucratic caste which is objectively conducive
to the development of capitalist relations." He
explains that, while the army may have played a progressive role in the independence struggle and in
the early period of social change, the nature of
the army is itself affected by the contradictions
that plague African society:

> in the development of the social revo-
> lution ever more conservative tenden-
> cies are developing in the army. The
> corporate interests of the army, its
> wish to preserve its privileged posi-
> tion, can make it an opponent of
> left-wing forces striving for radi-
> cal solutions. This suits the im-
> perialist circles which regard the
> army in the "Third World" as one of
> the major objects of their influence.[64]

Thus, Mirskii believes that, in the final analysis,
military regimes further the interests of the re-
actionaries--a view shared, revealingly, by V.
Kudriavtsev, _Izvestia_'s political commentator, and
by Colonel E. Dolgopolov, who writes in the Soviet
Army newspaper, _Red Star_.[65]

Expressions of the opposite view can be found
in the writings of a number of lesser-known Soviet
Africanists and, interestingly enough, in the tran-
scripts of Moscow Radio broadcasts to Africa. This
alliance provides ample evidence of Moscow's pragmatism regarding its relationship with Third World
military regimes. _Izvestia_ may question their progressivism, but the radio commentaries beamed to
Africa will tread softly lest they offend those
military leaders with whom the Kremlin must deal.
Thus, the Russian Peace and Progress network declared that "in Nigeria, Congo-Brazzaville, the
United Arab Republic and Algeria . . . the army
leaders have attained tangible successes. Facts
speak for themselves." Indeed, Moscow Radio's primary worry seems to be that the military leaders
will be so preoccupied with the need to effect sociopolitical transformations that they will be at-
tracted to radical solutions.

> Certain people want to take advan-
> tage of this, to subjugate the Afri-
> can country in which the coup has
> taken place to their influence. For
> example, the Chinese cultural revo-
> lutionaries are propagating the use
> of army methods in political life.
> But being subjugated only to orders
> from the top, suppressing the ini-
> tiative and activity of the masses,
> and removing them from participat-
> ing in the political life of the
> country has nothing in common with
> the ways of ending the difficul-
> ties which the country where the
> coup has taken place is living
> through.[66]

This statement illuminates not only official Soviet concern about Chinese Communist inroads in states such as the former French Congo, but also the belief that military leaders are capable of initiating policies compatible with Soviet--and Communist--interests.

This view is supported by the editors of the journal Azia i Afrika Segodnia, and by scholars such as Iu. Sumbatian, who strongly disputes Mirskii's claim that conservative tendencies must inevitably appear in the army. He contends, instead, that the army can play a prominent role in the struggle against the forces of reaction--both internal and external--as its cohesion and middle sector background render it a "base of national regeneration and social progress."[67] The AAS editors agree that the army can be progressive, as it stands above the tribal, religious, and ethnolinguistic survivals that plague other African institutions.[68]

Thus, the bifurcation that exists among Soviet authorities on the question of the class orientation of the African military is paralleled almost exactly by the division regarding the army's nation-building potential; that is to say, the proponents of the view that the army is linked to the progressive groups also hold that the army can function as both a factor and symbol of national consolidation. (Moscow Radio has commented on the desire of the Nigerian military, for example, to end tribal conflict and dissension as soon as possible.[69]) However, it must be acknowledged that this pattern is broken by Mirskii, who, while skeptical of the army's progressive role, still grants it an important position in the national integration process. In a manuscript published in a study of Classes and the Class Struggle, he declared that

> the army is the one organism in
> which mingle all segments of the
> population, the natives of the dif-
> ferent regions, the representatives
> of tribes and social groups not

> conscious of belonging to one nation.
> The illiterate peasant, whose hori-
> zon was extremely narrow in the
> little world of his village, meets
> with people from other regions and
> social sectors in the army, and be-
> gins to see himself as a member of
> one national family. . . .   There-
> fore, the army has become a symbol
> of national unity and the bearer of
> the idea of sovereignty.[70]

Although Mirskii is an exception, the pattern nevertheless reappears when the writings of other scholars who see the army as reactionary are examined. They deny the army any detribalizing function, claiming instead that the military organization only mirrors the centrifugalism characteristic of the society at large. Nor can the situation be otherwise, for men of one tribe are often dispatched to stem a rebellion in a rival region, thereby simply reinforcing traditional antipathies. Furthermore, recruitment often proceeds on a tribal basis-- a pattern inherited from the colonialists and perpetuated by the still ethnocentric officer class. These factors led Iordanskii to conclude, in an ill-disguised blast at his more sanguine colleagues, that African armies "represent the flesh and blood of the half-feudal, tribal and bourgeois leaders of African countries, traveling the capitalist path, permeated with its ideology, serving its interests."[71]

Of course, whichever class analysis is correct, the fact remains that the Soviet government must adjust to the existence of many military regimes in black Africa, hoping only to stem any further movement to the right by the so-called reactionary army leaderships and to prod the "progressive" ones further to the left. Both processes have been subsumed under the Soviet term "democratization"--ostensibly a plea that the military consider the aspirations of the masses in formulating its policies, but actually a hope that a return to civilian rule will eventually be effected. However, Soviet officials are aware

that this will be an extremely slow process (in the
past five years, only three countries have returned
to civilian rule: Dahomey, Sierra Leone, and Ghana),
that the civilian regimes might not be any more progressive than their military counterparts, and finally, that coups and military putsches will undoubtedly occur in countries previously unaffected.[72]

Nevertheless, Soviet analysts still display a
marked reluctance to conclude that military rule is
an inevitable stage in the development of black African states or an unavoidable result of their systemic weaknesses.[73] To do so would contradict the
basic ideological premise that the proletarianization and politicization of the masses--although
spotty and fraught with difficulties--is proceeding
at a noticeable pace. Furthermore, such an admission would completely destroy the façade of optimism characteristic of Soviet views on the development of Guinea--the sole state in sub-Saharan Africa
still avowedly committed to the national democratic
path. According to Soviet commentators, Toure's
regime has made great strides in emulating the Russian pattern of civilian control of the military--
for instance, the army has been placed under Parti
Democratique de Guinee (PDG) control, agitprop sections for the education of military personnel have
been established, and reactionary elements in the
officer corps have been purged. Gaps still exist,
of course, in the subjugation of the military to
the control of the progressive sectors. However,
if, as the Russians allege, "the new armies reflect
the profound social processes that take place in
the formation of liberated countries,"[74] then surely
a regime so dedicated to the noncapitalist path and
to such careful imitation of the Soviet model cannot
but possess an army dedicated to the continued liberalization of Guinea under the leadership of Sekou
Toure.

A final reason for the Soviet refusal to admit
the inevitability of military coups in Africa is
that it might aid the campaign of certain (reactionary) groups for the abolition of all African armies,

on the 'grounds that their instability potential is
far greater than any protective functions they might
fulfill. Soviet authorities counter that the African states

> need armies, and the need will exist
> until the entire continent is cleared
> of colonials and racialist [sic] re-
> gimes. Ian Smith would never have
> ventured to challenge the whole of
> Africa if neighboring states had
> strong and effective armies. . . .
>   Rhodesia is not the only prob-
> lem that makes it necessary for the
> African countries to maintain na-
> tional armies.[75]

The nature of the other problems is not mentioned,
but one suspects that the Soviet Union's concern
with its own national interests is among them. The
African armies may be small, ineffective, and factors in the aggravation of ethnic conflicts and
centrifugalism; furthermore, they may even be instrumental in toppling pro-Communist regimes. However, they at least represent an ample force for
the purposes of most African regimes: They can suppress insurgency, act in border conflicts, and ensure internal security. This relative sufficiency
helps to ensure that the black African states will
make few demands on the military aid and assistance
program of the USSR--a program already strained by
the financial and munitions demands of the Arab and
Southeast Asian countries. Furthermore, extensive
Soviet military aid to an African country would
greatly disturb the relative balance of power that
currently exists among the sub-Saharan states--a
balance that ensures that the political stability
desired by the Kremlin for strategic and economic
reasons will be maintained. Admittedly, military
coups inject instability into the African arena in
the sense that leaderships and ideological inclina-
tions may change; however, most African military regimes continue the trading and diplomatic patterns

of their civilian predecessors.* Thus, from the
perspective of Soviet national interests, if not
ideologically, the current rash of military coups
provides a peculiarly African interpretation of the
French dictum, "Plus ça change, plus ça la meme
chose."

NOTES

1. As Soviet analysts have undertaken increas-
ingly detailed studies of African integration, they
have shifted their attention from the amorphous "na-
tional bourgeoisie" to more specific subgroups.
However, for a comprehensive examination of their
views on the national bourgeoisie, see Ishwer C.
Ojha, "The Kremlin and Third World Leadership:
Closing the Circle?" in W. Raymond Duncan, ed.,
Soviet Policy in Developing Countries (Waltham,
Mass.: Ginn-Blaisdell, 1970), pp. 9-28.

2. See R. Avakov and G. Mirskii, "Class Structure in the Underdeveloped Countries," Mirovaia
ekonomika i mezhdunarodnye otnosheniia, 4 (April,
1962), 68-81; trans., in Thomas Thornton, ed., The
Third World in Soviet Perspective (Princeton, N.J.:
Princeton University Press, 1964), p. 285.

3. K. Ivanov, "The National and Colonial Question Today," International Affairs, 5 (May, 1963), 4.

4. R. N. Ismagilova, Narody Nigerii (The Peoples of Nigeria) (Moscow: Izd'vo Vostochnoi literatury, 1963), pp. 10-11.

5. E. V. Tadevosian, "Dal'neishee sblizhenie
sotsialisticheskikh natsii v SSSR" ("The Further
Drawing Together of Socialist Nations in the USSR"),
Voprosy filosofii, 6 (1963), 11.

---

*Ghana under the National Liberation Council
may be cited as an exception, but Somalia, Mali,
Nigeria, and Algeria confirm the statement.

6. V. Iordanskii, "Rassloenie afrikanskogo krestianstvo" ("Stratification of the African Peasantry"), Mirovaia ekonomika i mezhdunarodnye otnosheniia, 3 (March, 1969), 47.

7. L. I. Brezhnev, Speech at the International Conference of Communist and Workers' Parties in Moscow, July 7, 1969, Pravda and Izvestia, July 8, 1969, pp. 1-4; trans., CDSP, XXI, 23 (July 2, 1969), 9; cf. I. I. Potekhin, Africa: Ways of Develment (Moscow: Nauka, 1964), p. 53.

8. V. Solodovnikov, Antiimperialisticheskaia revoliutsiia v Afrike (The Anti-Imperialist Revolution in Africa) (Moscow: Nauka, 1967), p. 283; cf. W. K., "The Agrarian Question," Survey, 43 (August, 1962), 32.

9. A. Iskenderov, "Vliiatel'naia sila sovremennosti ("Influential Force of Modern Times"), Izvestia, April 28, 1968, p. 5.

10. P. M. Rogachev and M. A. Sverdlin, "On the Concept 'Nation,'" Vosprosy istorii, 1 (January, 1966), 36; trans., CDSP, XVIII, 21 (June 15, 1966), 14-21.

11. I. Iastrebova, ed. Rabochii klass Afriki (The Working Class of Africa) (Moscow: Nauka, 1966), pp. 235ff; A. M. Sivolobov, Natsional'no-osvoboditel' noe dvizhenie v Afrike (The National-Liberation Movement in Africa) (Moscow: Znanye, 1961), p. 5.

12. N. N. Liubimov, ed., Afrika v morovoi ekonomike i politike (Africa in World Economics and Politics (Moscow: Mezhdunarodnye Otnosheniia, 1965), p. 73.

13. Iskenderov, op. cit., p. 5.

14. Note the statement by Mamadou Dienne that the working class of Biafra had remained immune to the ethnicity that had enveloped the other classes. "Nigerian Patriots Want National Unity," World Marxist Review, X, 10 (October, 1967), 19.

15. Problemy vostokovedeniia, 1 (1960), 19; quoted in Kurt Muller, The Foreign Aid Programs of the Soviet Bloc and Communist China (New York: Walker, 1967), p. 103.

16. V. Balabushevich, "O nekotorikh osbenno-stiakh rabochego dvizheniia v stranakh vostoka na sovremennom etape" ("Certain Peculiarities of the Workers' Movement in Countries of the East in the Contemporary Epoch"), Problemy vostokovedeniia, 2 (1959), 59; on the migrant workers, see N. Gavrilov, "O migratsii rabochei sily v zapadnoi Afrike" ("Labor Migration in West Africa"), Problemy vos-tokovedeniia, 3 (1959), 82-90.

17. T. Amath, "Class Structure in Tropical Africa," World Marxist Review, IX, 2 (February, 1966), 26.

18. V. Iordanskii, "Sotsial'nye sdvigi v gorodakh Tropicheskoi Afriki" ("Social Shifts in the Towns of Tropical Africa"), Mirovaia ekonomika i mezhdunarodnye otnosheniia, 10 (October, 1967), 76. (Italics mine.)

19. Liubimov, ed., op. cit., pp. 84ff.

20. Solodovnikov, Antiimperialisticheskaia revoliutsiia v Afrike, pp. 295-96.

21. V. Iordanskii, "Tropicheskaia Afrika: cherty novogo goroda" ("Tropical Africa: Charac-teristics of the New Town"), Narody Azii i Afriki, 1 (1969), 23, 26.

22. V. Fyodorov, "The Driving Forces of the National-Liberation Revolution," International Af-fairs, 1 (January, 1968), 68.

23. K. Brutents, "Rastushchaia revoliutsionnaia sila" ("A Growing Revolutionary Force"), Pravda, Jan-uary 23, 1970, p. 4; B. Fitch and M. Oppenheimer, Ghana: End of an Illusion (New York: Monthly Re-view Press, 1966), p. 87. Also, note the surprising

conclusion of L. Gordon and L. Fridman that, in a
number of developing countries, the functionaries
outnumber the industrial workers: "Rabochii klass
osvobodivshchikhsia stran" ("The Working Class of
Liberated Countries"), Mirovaia ekonomika i mezhdunarodnye otnosheniia, 1 (January, 1966), 34.

24. N. Khrushchev, "Speech in Sofia," Pravda,
May 20, 1962, pp. 1-3; trans., CDSP, XIV, 20 (June
13, 1962), 7; N. I. Gavrilov, ed., Nezavisimye
strany Afriki (The Independent Countries of Africa)
(Moscow: Nauka, 1965), p. 288.

25. Brezhnev, op. cit., p. 9.   (Italics mine.)

26. Potekhin, Africa: Ways of Development,
pp. 53-54.

27. V. I. Lenin, "In Memory of Count Heyden,"
1907, Selected Works, XI, p. 694; excerpted in
Stefan Possony, ed., Lenin Reader (Chicago: Regnery,
1966), p. 66.

28. Joseph Stalin, "On the Mutual Dependence
of Central Russia and the Russian Borderlands,"
Sochineniia, IV (October, 1920), 360; excerpted in
Xenia Eudin and Robert North, Soviet Russia and the
East, 1920-1927 (Stanford, Calif.:   Stanford Univer-
sity Press, 1957), p. 52.

29.   "The Revolutionary Movement in the Colonies and Semicolonies"; cited in Xenia Eudin and
Robert Slusser, Soviet Foreign Policy, 1928-1934
(2 vols.; University Park: Pennsylvania State University Press, 1966-67), I, p. 143.

30.   "Sotsializm, Kapitalizm, slaborizvitye
strany" ("Socialism, Capitalism, Underdeveloped
Countries"), Mirovaia ekonomika i mezhdunarodnye
otnosheniia, 6 (June, 1964), 63; cited in "The USSR
and the Developing Countries. A Discussion in Moscow," Special Issue of Mizan, VI, 10 (November,
1964), 14.

31. Rogachev and Sverdlin, op. cit., p. 36.

32. L. D. Iablochkov, "Evolution of African Nationalism as a Political Ideology," Papers Presented by the USSR Delegation to the Second International Congress of Africanists, Dakar, 1967, p. 9; also G. B. Starushenko, Natsiia i gosudarstvo v osvobodaiushchikhsia stranakh (Nation and State in the Liberated Countries) (Moscow: Mezhdunarodnye Otnosheniia, 1967), p. 243.

33. K. Ivanov, "Kongo i Afrika" ("The Congo and Africa"), Pravda, March 30, 1961, p. 3.

34. V. Iordanskii, "Afrika: intelligentsiia na putiakh revoliutskii" ("Africa: Intelligentsia on the Path to Revolution"), Azia i Afrika Segodnia, 2 (February, 1966), 23.

35. Iablochkov, "Evolution of African Nationalism as a Political Ideology," pp. 13ff.

36. I. I. Potekhin, "On African Socialism," International Affairs, 1 (January, 1963), 75-76; cited in Arthur Klinghoffer, Soviet Perspectives on African Socialism (Rutherford, N.J.: Fairleigh Dickinson University Press, 1969), p. 87; see also K. Brutents, "Nekotorye osobennosti natsional'no-osvoboditel'nogo dvizheniia" ("Certain Peculiarities of the National-Liberation Movement"), Voprosy filosofii, 6 (1965), 32.

37. R. Ul'ianovskii, "O edinstve sil sotsializma i natsional'no-osvoboditel'nogo dvizheniia" ("On the Unity of the Forces of Socialism and of the National-Liberation Movement"), Pravda, October 14, 1968, p. 5.

38. V. Afanasiev, "Leninizm--Marksizm nashei epokhi" ("Leninism--The Marxism of Our Era"), Pravda, January 20, 1969, p. 3.

39. N. I. Gavrilov, "Africa: Classes, Parties and Politics," International Affairs, 7 (July, 1966), 44.

40. Merle Fainsod, How Russia Is Ruled (Cambridge, Mass.: Harvard University Press, 1963), pp. 180-81.

41. Gordon and Fridman, op. cit., p. 34; also B. G. Gafurov, G. F. Kim, et al., Natsional'no-osboboditel'noe dvizhenie v Azii i Afrike, Vol. III (Na Novom Puti) (The National-Liberation Movement in Asia and Africa, Vol. III [On a New Path]) (Moscow: Nauka, 1968), p. 208.

42. "The USSR and the Developing Countries," pp. 14-15.

43. M. Frenkel', "Plemena--partii--biurokratiia" ("Tribes--Parties--Bureaucracies"), Mirovaia ekonomika i mezhdunarodnye otnosheniia, 11 (November, 1968), 110-14.

44. Iablochkov, op. cit., p. 12.

45. "The USSR and the Developing Countries," p. 20; also V. Kudriavtsev, "Afrika: podzemnyi gul narastaet" ("Africa: The Rumbling Grows Louder"), Azia i Afrika Segodnia, 8 (August, 1964), 2-3; V. Kudriavtsev, "Neo-Colonialism and African Reality," International Affairs, 4 (April, 1965), 60.

46. A. Ramzi and A. Levkovsky, "The Petty-Bourgeois Masses in the Revolutionary Movements of the Third World," World Marxist Review, IX, 1 (January, 1966), 63.

47. W. Scott Thompson, "Parameters on Soviet Policy in Africa: Personal Diplomacy and Economic Interests in Ghana," in Duncan, ed., op. cit., pp. 83-106.

48. G. Mirskii, "Socialist Trends in Developing Countries," Izvestia, October 5, 1966, p. 2; trans., CDSP, XVIII, 40 (October 26, 1966), 22.

49. R. A. Ul'ianovskii, ed., Nekapitalisti-cheskii put' razvitiia stran Afriki (The Non-Capitalist Path of Development of the Countries of Africa) (Moscow: Nauka, 1967), p. 369.

50. A noted Sovietologist points out that in
the three cases where the Communists have seized
power (Yugoslavia, China, and Russia), they were
able to do so because the bureaucracy had previously been smashed by a foreign invading power. Hugh
Seton-Watson, Nationalism and Communism (London:
Methuen, 1964), p. 44.

51. Brutents, "Rastushchaia revoliutsionnaia
sila," p. 4.

52. R. A. Ul'ianovskii, "Na novikh rubezhakh:
o nekotorikh chertakh sovremennogo etapa natsional'
no-osvoboditel'nogo dvizheniia" ("At New Frontiers:
On Certain Characteristics of the Current Stage of
the National-Liberation Movement"), Pravda, January
3, 1968, p. 4.

53. Joseph Nye, "Corruption and Political De-
velopment: A Cost Benefit Analysis," American Po-
litical Science Review, LXI, 2 (June, 1967), 417-27;
cited in Ernest Lefever, "State-Building in Tropical
Africa," Orbis, XII, 4 (Winter, 1969), 994. Cf.
I. I. Potekhin, "Problemy bor"by c perezhitkami
proshlogo na Afrikanskom kontinente" ("Problems of
Struggling Against the Survivals of the Past on the
African Continent"), Sovetskaia etnografiia, 4
(July-August, 1964), 189-92.

54. V. Iordanskii, "Tropicheskaia Afrika: o
prirode mezhetnicheskikh konfliktov" ("Tropical
Africa: On the Nature of Interethnic Conflicts"),
Mirovaia ekonomika i mezhdunarodnye otnosheniia,
1 (January, 1967), 47.

55. Starushenko, op. cit., pp. 225, 228-29;
see also V. Iordanskii, "Protivorechiia nekapitalisticheskogo razvitiia v Afrike" ("Contradictions
of Non-Capitalist Development in Africa"), Narody
Azii i Afriki, 3 (1968), 47-56; John Keep, "The
Soviet Union and the Third World," Survey, 72
(Summer, 1969), 23.

56. F. Tarasov, "Otkuda iskhodit 'opasnost'"
("Whence the Danger?"), Pravda, December 18, 1967,

p. 5; also V. Solodovnikov and F. Tarasov, "On the Path of Progress--Results of the Eighth Congress of the Democratic Party of Guinea," Pravda, October 18, 1967, p. 4; trans., CDSP, XIX, 42 (November 7, 1967), 46.

57. V. Vasiliev, "Armiia i sotsial'nyi progress" ("The Army and Social Progress"), Azia i Afrika Segodnia, 9 (September, 1966), 5.

58. See, for example, Iu. Potomov, "Sudan in Turmoil," Pravda, October 28, 1964, p. 3; trans., CDSP, XVI, 43 (November 18, 1964), 24.

59. A. Iskenderov, "The Army, Politics, and the People," Izvestia, January 17, 1967, p. 2; trans., CDSP, XIX, 3 (February 18, 1967), 9; V. Kudriavtsev, "Afrikanskie gorizonty" ("African Horizons"), Izvestia (December 21, 1968), p. 4; "Intense Heat of Struggle in Africa," Izvestia, March 6, 1966, p. 3; trans., CDSP, XVIII, 10 (March 30, 1966), 23; V. Popov, "Bitva za umy" ("Battle for Minds"), Krasnaia zvezda, June 30, 1968, p. 3; G. Mirskii, "Ofitserstvo" ("The Offi-cers"), in V. L. Tiagunenko, et al., eds., Klassy i klassovaia bor'ba v razvivaiushchikhsia stranakh (Classes and the Class Struggle in the Developing Countries), Vol. I (Moscow: Mysl, 1967), p. 341; T. Kolesnichenko, "The Army and Politics," Pravda, November 2, 1966, p. 5; trans., CDSP, XVIII, 44 (November 23, 1969), 27.

60. Popov, op. cit., p. 3.

61. Iskenderov, "The Army, Politics, and the People," p. 9.

62. Mirskii, "Ofitserstvo," p. 342; see also V. Solodovnikov, Afrika Segodnia (Africa Today) (Moscow: Znanye, 1969), p. 49.

63. Gafurov, Kim, et al., op. cit., p. 313.

64. G. Mirskii, "Politcheskaia rol' armii v stranakh Azii i Afriki" ("The Political Role of the

Army in the Countries of Asia and Africa"), <u>Narody Azii i Afriki</u>, 6 (1968), 6; cf. his earlier views in "The USSR and the Developing Countries," p. 14.

65. Kudriavtsev, "Afrikanskie gorizonty," p. 4; E. Dolgopolov, "Vooruzhenye sily razvivaivshchikhsia stran" ("The Armed Forces of Developing Countries"), <u>Krasnaia zvezda</u>, May 31, 1969, p. 5.

66. Moscow Radio Peace and Progress in English to Africa, 1430 GMT, December 12, 1968.

67. Iu. Sumbatian, "Armiia v politicheskoi sisteme natsional'noi demokratii" ("The Army in the Political System of National Democracy"), <u>Narody Azii i Afriki</u>, 4 (1969), 35, 38.

68. "Armiia i osvoboditel'noe dvizhenie" ("The Army and the Liberation Movement"), <u>Azia i Afrika Segodnia</u>, 9 (September, 1966), 3.

69. Moscow Radio, February 11, 1966; quoted in "Nigeria," <u>Mizan</u>, VIII, 3 (May-June, 1966), 130; cf. the negative views of Ghana's military regime, Moscow Radio in Hausa to Africa, 1830 GMT, October 7, 1969.

70. Mirskii, "Ofitserstvo," pp. 336-37.

71. V. Iordanskii, "O kharaktere voennikh diktatur v tropicheskoi Afrike" ("On the Character of Military Dictatorships in Tropical Africa"), <u>Narody Azii i Afriki</u>, 4 (1967), 36; see also Dolgopolov, <u>op. cit.</u>, p. 3; L. Etinger, "Natsionalizm v Afrike" ("Nationalism in Africa"), <u>Azia i Afrika Segodnia</u>, 8 (July, 1968), 11; V. Kudriavtsev, "Afrika: Novoe rozhdaetsia v mukakh" ("Africa: The New Is Born in Pain"), <u>Azia i Afrika Segodnia</u>, 11 (November, 1966), 28.

72. Interview with M. Bourdakin; see also E. Dolgopolov, "Armii osvobodivshikhsia stran" ("The Armies of the Liberated Countries"), <u>Krasnaia zvezda</u>, May 19, 1968, p. 3; Vasiliev, <u>loc. cit.</u>; G. Mirskii, "Third World: Illusions and Realities," <u>New Times</u>, 1 (January 1, 1969), 12.

73. Dolgopolov, _ibid_.

74. E. Dolgopolov, "Vooruzhenye sily razvivaiushchikhsia stran," p. 5. Guinea's progress in incorporating the army into the noncapitalist revolution is also discussed in B. Paveltsev, "The Military
Coups in Africa," _New Times_, 4 (January 26, 1966),
12. Note, however, that Paveltsev also contended
that Keita was in full control of the Malian army.

75. Paveltsev, _op. cit_., pp. 11-12.

8

The preceding discussion has investigated the nature of Soviet theories on the nation-building process in sub-Saharan Africa. This topic has never been fully explored in Western literature, and the few studies that have been done have been, for the most part, inadequate. These previous analyses either have stressed the efforts of the Soviet Union to foist its own nation-building model on the African countries, or have claimed that, because the Soviet Union deemed national instability in Africa to be in its best interests, the problem of national integration was never closely evaluated.

In contrast to these studies, we have concluded that national integration in Africa is considered highly relevant to Soviet policy goals. The conception that Soviet policy has always been directed toward the promotion of instability is based on the premise that the objectives of the CPSU leadership do not stress the establishment of strong relations with existing governments, but rather the installation of Communist-oriented leaders in Africa and the accession to power of ruling Communist party systems. We have, in fact, shown that, although the extension of communism to Africa might well remain a long-term goal, the expansion of Soviet, not Communist, influence is the Kremlin's dominant concern.

In view of this emphasis, tribal conflicts and manifestations of national centrifugalism in black Africa would appear to be counterproductive because they (1) disrupt continental (and anti-imperialist) unity in Africa; (2) divert the attention of the African worker from ideological to ethnic concerns; (3) impede the progression from tribalism to nationalism to internationalism predicted by Marxism-Leninism; (4) might impel the Soviet government to take sides in a national dispute, reducing its ability to maintain friendly relations with a large number of African governments and peoples; and (5) could lead to an East-West confrontation in Africa.

Soviet leaders were not fully aware of the significance of these factors in the early period of their African involvement because their academic and political interest was not completely aroused, by their own admission, until 1960--Africa Independence Year. Furthermore, there had been no dangerous outbreaks of tribalism in the first countries to attain independence--an absence that persuaded Soviet analysts that the unity forged during the liberation struggle would persist throughout the fight for true political and economic independence. Thus, neither the government nor the scholars were in possession of information that would indicate the potential of ethnic rivalries for serious disruption.

However, in 1962-63, the long-smouldering Congo problem flared into an all-out crisis, and United Nations troops again entered the fray, supported strongly by the United States and other Western powers. The secession of Katanga was finally ended, but thoughts of the example that it might set for other ethnic groups, the long period of instability that the secession entailed, and the opportunity it provided for an expansion or consolidation of Western influence persisted in Soviet circles. The crisis indicated that African ethnic conflicts were

not only an intrastate, but also an interstate, matter. Therefore, Soviet analysts embarked on a program of investigating the causes of these conflicts
and possible solutions.

However, Khrushchev's renewed optimism (in the
face of certain successes) about the prospects for
the diffusion of socialism on the African continent
persuaded him that the states of national democracy
could solve any problem, including the national question. Therefore, although the national integration
issue at least was being examined, research remained
colored by the preconception that the socialist path
would provide the answers.

The death of Dr. Potekhin in September, 1964,
and the downfall of Nikita Khrushchev the next month
created the possibility for devising a new approach
to sub-Saharan Africa. Brezhnev and Kosygin recognized the need and instructed Soviet theoreticians
to fill it, motivated not only by their acknowledgment of the effects of "the cult of personality" on
Soviet African Studies but also by their assessment
of the Soviet Union's internal situation. The economic and industrial training of these new leaders
impelled them to examine the country's domestic
problems; the difficulties they saw convinced them
that Russia must turn its energies and financial resources inward. Because this meant that the foreign
aid drain on the Soviet Union should be minimal,
analysts were urged to investigate whether the Soviet developmental model--the tenets of which guided
Soviet aid allocations, was actually contributing to
the success of nation-building efforts in black Africa.

The features of the Soviet nation-building
model are, of course, numerous. Certain of them,
such as a dominant nationality group, were long
recognized by Soviet analysts as inapplicable to
Africa. However, the relevance of other aspects
was the subject of detailed discussion for many
years, as this study has shown. On almost all aspects, the progression of Soviet analysis was fairly

uniform: from a positive assessment to one characterized by the utmost pragmatism and flexibility.
In other words, whereas the dominant consideration
during the Khrushchev years was which solution was
predicated by Marxism-Leninism, the foremost thought
since the inauguration of the Brezhnev-Kosygin regime has been: Will it work?

Regarding most features of the Soviet national
integration pattern, Soviet scholars and officials
now hold that the answer is negative--at least for
the foreseeable future. Thus, the potential role
long ascribed to the single-party system, ideology,
the dominance of the party over the state, totalitarian control, and economic aid to backward regions,
will not be realized soon in black Africa.

Thus, we note that, in establishing a strong
single-party system, the Bolsheviks were aided by
the chaos and atomization of the Russian Revolution,
their control of the soviets, the powerful factory
labor organizations, and the discontent of most segments of the population with landlessness, hunger,
and war. Furthermore, they were helped by the presence of a dominant ethnic group, the Russians, who
comprised the majority of the population. By en-
listing the allegiance of this group through a
weighted system of job and resource allocation, the
Bolsheviks were able to consolidate their power.
By the time that certain national groups began to
realize that perhaps Bolshevik goals did not corre-
spond to their own, the dominance of the party over
the economy and state apparatus was complete--as
was its control of the instruments of coercion and
persuasion.

The dominance of the party over the state
meant that the Bolsheviks could use all the typical
governmental resources and prerogatives to realize
their objectives in the nationality sphere. For example, the CPSU could develop an extensive system
of local autonomy for the various nationality groups
because its political network permeated the entire
country and because it alone had control of the

military and paramilitary organizations. Thus, it
could rekindle national sentiments to unite the
people against an outside enemy, and use the police
to extirpate them when they were no longer useful;
it could forcibly settle the nomads and destroy the
religious hierarchy, knowing that the police would
suppress any dissent. Finally, if any of the autonomous units it created began to develop into a
focus of national pride and chauvinism, the CPSU
could arrange to supersede the national republic
with a new variant of regional administrative organization.

However, the absence of a small, tightly knit
controlling organization means that these political
aspects of the Soviet nation-building model are not
applicable to Africa. The sub-Saharan party-
governments depend on an uneasy coalition of all
the ethnic and religious groups in their countries
in order to continue in power. Most cannot move
against minority leaders, because these men are
part of the power network. Certain governments, in
fact, subscribe to a system that might almost be
called one of "indirect rule": They coopt the key
religious and ethnic leaders into the political system, depending on them to symbolize and uphold the
regime among their followers. The chain of loyalty
and support is thus a broken one of national gov-
ernment--local leaders--masses; the government is
therefore hesitant to move against the ethnoreligious hierarchy lest it alienate a citizenry still
enmeshed in the traditional systems.

Similarly, most African party-governments cannot maintain strict control over the bureaucracy
and the military. This lack of control interferes
with the political centralization deemed essential
by Soviet authorities to any resolution of the African national integration problems. For such centralization

> facilitates on a more favorable
> basis the economic and political
> concentration of the population

in socialist enterprises and farms,
keeping in mind the limits of territorial autonomy, involving the population in production, developing national culture and language, coordinating the interests of the whole
state with the national interests
of each people.[1]

However, this ideal is thwarted in black Africa by
the burgeoning growth of an increasingly amorphous
bureaucracy--an institution whose attraction for
the elite seems greater than that of the party and
whose diffuse nature seems to preclude any centralized solution of the political problems. The ideal
is further thwarted by the tenuous governmental authority over the military and paramilitary organi-
zations--a tenuousness amply illustrated by the
rising number of military coups.

The absence of civilian control over the military is both a contributing cause, and an effect,
of the national integration problems in sub-Saharan
Africa. It is an effect in that most of the enlisted men--and the officers--retain a strong religious and/or tribal orientation. It is a cause, in
that this weakens their loyalty to the national regime, spurring them to react strongly to any attempts at central suppression of their ethnic
groups (for example, the Ibo-directed coup in Nigeria in January, 1966). If African leaders attempted to follow the Soviet example of alternately
strengthening and negating the autonomy of nationality groups according to the political interests of
the regime, they would encounter more of the civil
insurrection that has greeted such efforts in the
Congo (Kinshasa) and Nigeria. Certain of these re-
bellions have been successfully subdued; however,
the regulative capability of an African regime is
too weak to withstand any frequent occurrence of
such incidents.

Thus, Soviet expectations regarding the role
of the state in sub-Saharan Africa have not been

fulfilled. Of course, the Soviet Communists often
relied on coercion to elicit the public support
that may not otherwise have been forthcoming. However, they are noticeably ambivalent in their recommendations to African leaders regarding the use of
force to speed up national amalgamation. This am-
bivalence stems from two sources: (1) their insistence on maintaining the myth of the voluntary unification of Soviet peoples; and (2) their uncertain-
ty about the sentiments and capabilities of African
governments regarding the coercion issue. Soviet
analysts continue to state in their writings that
nation-building in the USSR, even under Stalin, was
characterized by "natural" assimilation, produced
by the "direct contact of peoples and their cultures
and conditioned by the whole process of the socioeconomic development of society."[2] However, certain
Soviet Africanists will admit privately that mistakes were made in the nationality sphere, especially during the Stalinist era.

Thus, in view of the discrepancy between theory
and policy in the Soviet Union on the issue of coercion, the fact that Soviet authorities extol the
usefulness of the Soviet "experience" to the young
African states is rather confusing. At first
glance, it is questionable whether they are suggest-
ing that the Africans follow their formulas or their
example; in fact, even a thorough study of their
writings reveals a marked split between moderates
and assimilationists.

The moderates on the African integration question second the views of M. S. Dzhunusov, a frequent
contributor to discussions of Soviet nationality
policy. He cautions that

> in the development of relationships
> among nationalities, such factors
> as psychology and human sentiment
> play a role. Any use of compul-
> sion with respect to nationalities
> not only does not break down their
> structure, their social life, but,

on the contrary, promotes the
strengthening of their decision
to preserve their nationality and
all its attributes.[3]

Dzhunusov's counterparts in the field of African
Studies are such men as G. Starushenko, Deputy Director of the Africa Institute; E. Zhukov, a member
of the Academy of Sciences Presidium; Y. Semenov,
Chairman of the Philosophy Faculty at Riazan Medi-
cal Institute; and V. Kudriavtsev, the Izvestia
correspondent. Semenov, for example, writes,

The heterogeneity of the ethnic composition of a country's population
does not in itself condition the
emergence of several nations within
it, but only creates the possibility
of their emergence. To make this
possibility a reality, it is necessary to have such a factor as dis-
crimination along ethnic lines, suppression of the language and culture
of the small ethnic communities,
etc.--in short, everything that com-
prises national oppression. It is
precisely the latter that prevents
the people belonging to the suppressed
ethnic community from recognizing the
country as a whole as their motherland
and from becoming its patriots.[4]

G. Starushenko concretizes such admonitions against
the use of force as a spur to integration by citing
the example of the United Arab Republic. He claims
that any incipient loyalty that may have been developing among the Syrians toward the new amalga-
mated state was disrupted by Nasser's refusal to
grant them firm constitutional guarantees of their
national rights. His attempts to assimilate them
forcibly not only shattered the veneer of pan-Arab
feeling that had facilitated the union, but deep-
ened the Syrians' national consciousness.

The opposition to the moderates is headed by
B. G. Gafurov, Director of the Institute of Asian
Peoples; G. F. Kim, his collaborator; and R. A.
Ul'ianovskii, a frequent contributor to African
Studies journals in the Soviet Union. These scholars may be termed assimilationists, that is, they
feel that all energies and resources of the state
should be directed toward the fastest possible consolidation of disparate ethnic groups into a single
nation. They acknowledge that resistance to this
policy can be expected but counter that it would be
exhibited by reactionaries, the natural enemies of
the progressive state.

Gafurov and Kim concern themselves mainly with
the resistance that might meet any economic aspects
of integration policy, for example, the collectivization of agriculture. They note that it is unlikely that the peasants will voluntarily comply with
orders to relocate or to donate a specified share
of their production to the state. Incentives will
probably fail to motivate them; therefore, "extraeconomic methods" will be required.[5]

Ul'ianovskii writes of force to counter resistance to integration efforts in the social sphere,
for instance, language, education, religion, etc.
He introduces a typically post-Stalinist caveat regarding the use of governmental power, that is,
that the "unrestrained curtailment" of individual
rights may result in a dangerous cult of personality surrounding the governmental leader. However,
he then proceeds to state that, in the conditions
of acute class struggle that are plaguing the young
African states, "it is inevitable that certain aspects of political democracy are subject to restric-
tions." Furthermore,

> in case imperialism and domestic re-
> actionaries launch open counterattacks,
> the protective functions assume a lead-
> ing role in order that the dictator-
> ship of the proletariat might be

> strengthened. Should an emergency
> arise, the state has to resort to
> coercion to deal with its internal
> and external enemies.[6]

These enemies may be political, or more likely,
nationality groups.

It is tempting to conclude from a comparison
of Ul'ianovskii's policy suggestions with the policies actually adopted by the Soviet government toward the Ibo and Katanga secessions that the assimilationist position is shared by those charged with
decision-making in the arena of Soviet foreign policy. However, although Moscow did support efforts
to end the independent state existence proclaimed
by Biafra and Katanga Province, it also has not
overtly criticized the nonpunitive measures adopted
by the Nigerian Federal Government to reintegrate
the Ibo people into the national system. Furthermore, our analysis of Soviet writings on various
social, political, and economic integrating proposals reveals a marked reluctance--born of pessimism,
perhaps--to state that executing these programs
with the utmost haste would increase their effectiveness or their workability. Therefore, it is
possible to conclude that the Soviet government
favors the use of force to combat ethnicity and
centrifugalism in Africa only when the very existence of the unified state is threatened.

This hesitance on the part of the USSR is partly attributable to the realization that the power
resources of the sub-Saharan African state are limited and to the acknowledgment that the skillful
use of ideology is usually a more effective--and
lasting--integrative mechanism. The Bolsheviks
used Marxism-Leninism to rationalize their actions,
as a vehicle for educating the public and as a complex of ideas to which all nationality groups could
and would subscribe. The ideological message was
at first presented in various national forms, as it
was viewed more as a vehicle for the expansion of
Communist influence than for the unification of the

many nationality groups. Gradually, however, the
communists sought to substitute their ideology for
the various religious and national outlooks that
separated the Soviet peoples. Once all peoples
were Communist, that is, shared a common world view,
they would have no reason to cling to the religious-
ly and politically sanctioned national distinctions.

In black Africa, anti-imperialism as an idea-
tional spur to unity worked in the early days of
African statehood; however, this lofty goal has now
been superseded by more practical aims of securing
adequate food, clothing, and shelter. African leaders have developed different ideologies to explain
their programs for achieving these goals, and several of them are often present within the conceptual
arsenal of a single ruling group. Soviet recognition that the use of ideology to further national
integration may not be applicable to Africa is growing. In July, 1969, V. Maevskii filed a report with
the Moscow monthly Za rubezhom (Abroad), on his conversations on this topic with the Nigerian Commis-
sioner of Information:

> Mr. Enahoro spoke thus: "Our main
> problem is to create a unified coun-
> try. . . . But it seems to me that
> we cannot use your experience at the
> present time. You had a civil war
> on a class basis, we have a war on
> another basis. You established the
> community of your country over cen-
> turies, we have only existed for a
> half-century. Your association of
> nations was established historically,
> while ours was established by con-
> querors. You have the Communist
> Party--a united force. We have an-
> other system. Politics is based on
> a tribal and only on a tribal foun-
> dation. . . . You had an idea which
> all supported--the socialist idea.
> We have no such unifying idea.[7]

Maevskii had no comment.

The Soviet authorities have shown themselves
to be extremely pragmatic when the dictates of their
model would have contradicted their policy inter-
ests--interests that include reducing the economic
drain represented by Africa, promoting stability on
that continent, and establishing good government-to-
government relations with the various regimes. In
this study, we have demonstrated the dominance of
pragmatism over ideology in several cases: (1) Soviet willingness to set aside the Stalinist definition of a nation when the African states were striving for independence, when the union of French and
British Cameroon was proposed, and when the Nigerian
Federal Government was opposing the secession of the
Ibo--a people who met all the Stalinist criteria for
a nation; (2) the flexibility of Soviet analysts on
the role of religion in Africa, the question of a
national language, and the problem of cultural rela-
tivism; and (3) Soviet acknowledgment that the military and the intelligentsia play a more important
role than the workers or peasants in the construction of strong and united African states.

However, it must be admitted that the ideological tenets have been retained on several key issues,
including the right of a nation to self-determination,
the definition of a nation, and the Marxist prediction of an inverse relation between nationalism and
economic growth. It can be asserted with reasonable
certainty that these elements will remain part of
the Soviet ideological arsenal as a result of the
absence of official agreement on alternative formulations. Furthermore, these ideological tenets
touch directly upon issues of Soviet domestic national relations, and can always serve to legitimize
a particular policy decision.

This same dualism that characterizes the attitude of the Soviet leaders toward ideology is also
evident in their posture toward the findings and research conclusions of Soviet Africanists. Thus,
they will allow the scholars wide rein and may even
incorporate their conclusions into official programs
if these conclusions promote the policy interests of

the government--for example, if they will help to
reduce the need for aid commitments or facilitate
political stability by pinpointing the causes of
ethnic centrifugalism. Paradoxically, however, the
level of academic freedom for Soviet Africanists
also is increased if official interest is oriented
toward other areas of the world.

Thus, the years from about 1965 to 1971 have
witnessed a marked decrease in governmental concern
with Africa's problems as the Kremlin's preoccupations have shifted to Southeast Asia and the Middle
East. If the protracted conflicts that now engage
the Soviet government in other parts of the world
continue, it is likely that only a few incidents
will occur in black Africa (for example, in Somalia,
partly because of its strategic location vis-à-vis
the Middle East) in the next decade to cause a
flurry of Soviet official interest and activity
there.

In view of this situation, the attention of
the Kremlin's policy-makers will probably not be
focused on Africa. This may well have the fortunate
consequence of allowing scholarly objectivity to
flourish among Soviet Africanists. Perhaps their
more impartial research findings will be heeded by
the relatively few top-level officials now concerned
with black Africa. However, it is also possible
that this research will increase in quality and
quantity, remaining officially unexamined for the
most part until the eruption of the next serious
crisis of national integration.

NOTES

1. A. Agaev, "Narodnost' kak sotsial'naia
obshchnost" ("Nationality as a Social Community"),
<u>Voprosy filosofii</u>, 11 (1965), 33; also V. Kozlov,
"Nekotorye problemy teorii natsii" ("Certain Problems of the Theory of a Nation"), <u>Voprosy istorii</u>,
1 (January, 1967), 96-97.

2. V. Kozlov, "Tipy etnicheskikh protsessov i osobennosti ikh istoricheskogo razvitiia" ("Types of Ethnic Processes and Peculiarities of Their Historical Development"), Voprosy istorii, 9 (September, 1968), 98.

3. M. S. Dzhunusov, "Soviet Autonomy and the Vestiges of Nationalism," Istoriia SSR, 1, 1963; trans., Soviet Sociology, II, 1 (Summer, 1963), 22; see also Grey Hodnett, "What's In a Nation?" Problems of Communism, XIV, 5 (September-October, 1967), 7-8.

4. Iu. Semenov, "K opredeleniiu poniatiia 'natsiia'" ("Toward a Definition of the Concept 'Nation'"), Narody Azii i Afriki, 4 (1967), 99; see also G. B. Starushenko, Natsiia i gosudarstvo v osvobodaiushchikhsia stranakh (Nation and State in the Liberated Countries) (Moscow: Mezhdunarodnye Otnosheniia, 1967), pp. 142, 153; E. Zhukov, "Natsional'no-osvoboditel'noe dvizhenie narodov Azii i Afriki" ("The National-Liberation Movement of the Peoples of Asia and Africa"), Kommunist, 4 (March, 1969), 32; V. Kudriavtsev, "Unity and Separatism," Izvestia, November 17, 1967, p. 2; trans., CDSP, XIX, 46 (December 6, 1967), 17.

5. B. G. Gafurov, G. F. Kim, et al., Natsional'no-osboboditel'noe dvizhenie v Azii i Afrike, Vol. III (Na Novom Puti) (The National-Liberation Movement in Asia and Africa, Vol. III [On a New Path]) (Moscow: Nauka, 1968), pp. 227-28.

6. R. A. Ul'ianovskii, ed., Nekapitalisticheskii put' razvitiia stran Afriki (The Non-Capitalist Path of Development of the Countries of Africa) (Moscow: Nauka, 1967), pp. 368-69.

7. V. Maevskii, "Besedy v Nigerii" ("Conversations in Nigeria"), Za rubezhom, 7 (February 14-20, 1969), 18. According to Gafurov and Kim, African states lack a simple ideology because their leaders think of the future only "as the creation of the abstract ideals of justice and equality," op. cit., p. 165.

BIBLIOGRAPHY

NEWSPAPERS

Izvestia

Krasnaia zvezda

New York Times

Pravda

INTERVIEWS

Africa Institute, Moscow. Personal interviews with
     P. Kuprianov, V. Kaufman, I. Sledzevskii,
     A. Letnev, historians.

_____. Personal interviews with V. Vigant, M.
     Kuznetsova, S. Bessornov, economists.

Institute of State and Law, Moscow. Personal inter-
     views with Iu. Iudin, V. G. Grafskii, and
     B. A. Strashun.

Soviet Embassy, Accra, Ghana. Personal interviews
     with M. Bourdakin, First Secretary.

United States Embassy, Dakar, Senegal. Personal
     interview with R. Benneville, former Economic
     Officer, United States Embassy, Conakry,
     Guinea.

COMMUNIST SOURCES--BOOKS

Bagramov, E. A. Natsional'nyi vopros i burzhuaznaia
     ideologiia (The National Question and Bourgeois
     Ideology). Moscow: Mysl, 1966.

Cuba: A Giant School. Havana: Information Depart-
     ment of the Ministry of Foreign Affairs, 1969.

Efimov, A. V., ed. Sovremennaia Amerikanskaia etno-
     grafiia (Contemporary American Ethnography).
     Moscow: Izd'vo Akademii Nauk SSSR, 1963.

273

Egorov, Iu., ed. <u>Natsional'no-osvoboditel'noe</u>
    <u>dvizhenie</u> (<u>The National-Liberation Movement</u>).
    Moscow: Politizdat, 1967.

Etinger, Ia. Ia. <u>Afrikanskaia solidarnost' i</u>
    <u>proiski neokolonializma</u> (<u>African Solidarity</u>
    <u>and the Intrigues of Neocolonialism</u>). Moscow:
    Znanye, 1967.

_____. <u>Politicheskie problemy Afrikanskogo edinstva</u>
    (<u>Political Problems of African Unity</u>). Moscow:
    Nauka, 1967.

Gafurov, B. G., ed. <u>Lenin i Vostok</u> (<u>Lenin and the</u>
    <u>East</u>). Moscow: Izd'vo Vostochnoi literatury,
    1960.

_____, Kim, G. F., <u>et al</u>. <u>Natsional'no-osboboditel'</u>
    <u>noe dvizhenie v Azii i Afrike</u>, Vol. III (<u>Na</u>
    <u>Novom Puti</u>) (<u>The National-Liberation Movement</u>
    <u>in Asia and Africa</u>, Vol. III [<u>On a New Path</u>]).
    Moscow: Nauka, 1968.

Gavrilov, N. I. <u>The National-Liberation Movement</u>
    <u>in West Africa</u>. Moscow: Progress, 1965.

_____, ed. <u>Nezavisimye strany Afriki</u> (<u>The Indepen-</u>
    <u>dent Countries of Africa</u>). Moscow: Nauka,
    1965.

Goncharov, L. V., ed. <u>Ekonomika Afriki</u> (<u>The Eco-</u>
    <u>nomics of Africa</u>). Moscow: Nauka, 1965.

_____, ed. <u>Stroitel'stvo natsional'noi ekonomiki v</u>
    <u>stranakh Afriki</u> (<u>Building a National Economy</u>
    <u>in the Countries of Africa</u>). Moscow: Nauka,
    1968.

Grafskii, V. G., and Strashun, B. A. <u>Federalizm v</u>
    <u>razvivaiushchikhsia stranakh</u> (<u>Federalism in</u>
    <u>Developing Countries</u>). Moscow: Mezhdunarodnye
    Otnosheniia, 1968.

Grigorian, S. N., ed. Ideologiia sovremennogo
    natsional'no-osvoboditel'nogo dvizheniia (The
    Ideology of the Contemporary National-Liberation
    Movement). Moscow: Nauka, 1966.

Iastrebova, I., ed. Rabochii klass Afriki (The
    Working Class of Africa). Moscow: Nauka,
    1966.

Iordanskii, V. Ognennye ieroglify (Fiery Hiero-
    glyphics). Moscow: Nauka, 1968.

Ismagilova, R. N. Narody Nigerii (The Peoples of
    Nigeria). Moscow: Izd'vo Vostochnoi litera-
    tury, 1963.

Israelian, V., ed. Soviet Foreign Policy. Moscow:
    Progress, 1967.

Iureva, M., ed. Noveishaia istoriia stran Azii i
    Afriki. Uchebnik dlia vysshikh uchebnikh
    zavedenii (Recent History of the Countries of
    Asia and Africa. A Textbook for Institutions
    of Higher Education). Moscow: Moskovskaia
    universiteta, 1965.

Korostovtsev, M. A., ed. Essays on African Culture.
    Moscow: Nauka, 1966.

Krutogolov, M. A., et al. Stanovlenie natsional'noi
    gosudarstyennosti v nezavisimikh stranakh
    Afriki (The Establishment of National Statehood
    in the Independent Countries of Africa).
    Moscow: Mezhdunarodnye Otnosheniia, 1963.

Lenin, V. I. Sochineniia. 30 vols. 3d ed.
    Moscow: Gospolotizdat, 1928-37.

Levin, I. D., and Krylov, B. S., eds. Burzhuaznye
    konstitutsii v period obshchego krizisa kapi-
    talizma (Bourgeois Constitutions in the Period
    of the General Crisis of Capitalism). Moscow:
    Nauka, 1966.

Liubimov, N. N., ed. Afrika v mirovoi ekonomike i politike (Africa in World Economics and Politics). Moscow: Mezhdunarodnye Otnosheniia, 1965.

Maslennikov, V. A. Uglublenie krizisa kolonial'noi sistemy imperializma (The Deepening Crisis of the Colonial System of Imperialism). Moscow: Gospolitizdat, 1952.

Osipov, G. V., ed. Town, Country and People, Studies in Soviet Society, 2. London: Tavistock, 1969.

Potekhin, I. I. Africa: Ways of Development. Moscow: Nauka, 1964.

_____. African Problems. Moscow: Nauka, 1968.

_____. Africa's Future: The Soviet View, an abridgement of Afrika smotrit v budushchee. Moscow: Izd'zo Zostochnoi literatury, 1960. Supplement to Mizan, III, 4 (April, 1961).

_____. Gana segodnia (Ghana Today). Moscow: Izd'vo geograficheskoi literatury, 1959.

_____. Stanovlenie novoi Gany (The Establishment of the New Ghana). Moscow: Nauka, 1965.

_____, and Ol'derogge, D., eds. Narody Afriki (The Peoples of Africa). Moscow: Institut Etnografii AN SSSR, 1954.

Sharevskaia, B. I. Starye i novye religii tropicheskoi i iuzhnoi Afriki (Old and New Religions of Tropical and Southern Africa). Moscow: Nauka, 1964.

Sivolobov, A. M. Natsional'no-osvoboditel'noe dvizhenie v Afrike (The National-Liberation Movement in Africa). Moscow: Znanye, 1961.

Solodovnikov, V. G., ed. Africa in Soviet Studies, 1968. Moscow: Nauka, 1969.

_____, ed. Afrika segodnia (Africa Today). Moscow:
Znanye, 1969.

_____, ed. Antiimperialisticheskaia revoliutsiia v
Afrike (The Anti-Imperialist Revolution in Africa). Moscow: Nauka, 1967.

Stalin, Joseph. Marxism and the National and Colo-
nial Question. Marxist Library. Works of
Marxism-Leninism. Vol. XXXVIII. New York:
International Publishers, 1934.

_____. Works. 13 vols. Moscow: Foreign Language
Publishing House, 1953-55.

Starushenko, G. B. Natsiia i gosudarstvo v osvobodaiushchikhsia stranakh (Nation and State in
the Liberated Countries). Moscow: Mezhdunarodnye Otnosheniia, 1967.

Tiagunenko, V. L., et al., eds. Klassy i klassovaia
bor'ba v razvivaiushchikhsia stranakh (Classes
and the Class Struggle in the Developing Countries). Vol. I. Moscow: Mysl, 1967.

_____. Problemy sovremennikh natsional'no-
osvonoditel'nikh revoliutsii (Problems of
the Contemporary National-Liberation Revolution). Moscow: Nauka, 1966.

Tiulpanov, S. I. Ekonomicheskie i politicheskie
problemy novikh suverennikh gosudarstv (Economic and Political Problems of New Sovereign
States). Leningrad: Izd'vo Leningradskogo
universiteta, 1964.

_____, ed. Itogi i perspektivi sotsial'no-
ekonomicheskogo razvitiia molodikh suverennikh
gosudarstv (Conclusions and Perspectives on
the Socioeconomic Development of Young Sovereign States). Leningrad: Izd'vo Leningradskogo universiteta, 1965.

Tuzmukhamedov, R. A. Natsional'nyi suverenitet
(National Sovereignty). Moscow: Izd'vo
Mezhdunarodnikh Otnoshenii, 1963.

_____. Nezavisimaia Afrika v dokumentakh (Indepen-
     dent Africa in Documents) Moscow: Universitet
     Druzhby narodov imeni Patrisa Lumumby, 1965.

_____, ed. Organizatsiia Afrikanskogo edinstva
     (The Organization of African Unity). Moscow:
     Mezhdunarodnye Otnosheniia, 1965.

Ul'ianovskii, R. A., ed. Nekapitalisticheskii put'
     razvitiia stran Afriki (The Non-Capitalist
     Path of Development of the Countries of Africa).
     Moscow: Nauka, 1967.

Verin, V. P. Prezidentskie respubliki v Afrike
     (Presidential Republics in Africa). Moscow:
     Mezhdunarodnye Otnosheniia, 1963.

Volodin, L., and Orestov, O. Trudnye dni Kongo
     (Difficult Days for the Congo). Moscow:
     Gospolitizdat, 1961.

Woddis, Jack. Africa: The Way Ahead. New York:
     International Publishers, 1963.

Zhukov, E. M. Sovremennye teorii sotsializma
     "natsional'nogo tipa" (Modern Theories of
     Socialism of the "National Type"). Moscow:
     Mysl, 1967.

COMMUNIST SOURCES--ARTICLES

Afanasiev, V. "Leninizm-Marksizm nashei epokhi"
     ("Leninism-Marxism of Our Era"), Pravda,
     January 20, 1969, p. 30.

"Africa--Continent of the Future," World Marxist
     Review, IV, 2 (February, 1961), 44-49.

Agaev, A. G. "Narodnost' kak sotsial'naia
     obshchnost" ("Nationality as a Social Com-
     munity"), Voprosy filosofii, 11, 1965, 26-36.

_____. "The Nation, Its Essence and Self-Awareness," *Voprosy istorii*, 7 (July, 1967), 87-104; trans., *CDSD* (*Current Digest of the Soviet Press*), XIX, 46 (December 6, 1967), 29-30.

Ahmedi, M. "Peaceful Frontiers for Africa," *World Marxist Review*, VII, 5 (May, 1964), 84-85.

Akhmedzianov, A., and Li, V. "Dve tendentsii 'musul'manskogo natsionalizma'" ("Two Tendencies of Muslim Nationalism"), *Azia i Afrika Segodnia*, 1 (January, 1964), 58-59.

Aleksandrovskaia, L. "Kooperativnoe dvizhenie" ("The Cooperative Movement"), *Azia i Afrika Segodnia*, 10 (October, 1963), 16-17.

_____. "Kooperativnoe dvizhenie v Afrike: problemy i perspektivi" ("The Cooperative Movement in Africa: Problems and Perspectives"), *Mirovaia ekonomika i mezhdunarodnye otnosheniia*, 3 (May, 1963), 39-51.

Amath, Thierno. "Class Structure in Tropical Africa," *World Marxist Review*, IX, 2 (February, 1966), 25-29.

_____. "Some Problems of Tropical Africa," *World Marxist Review*, IX, 8 (August, 1966), 31-34.

Amidou, C., and Dienne, M. "Senegal Marches Forward," *World Marxist Review*, VIII, 6 (June, 1965), 52-55.

Andreasian, R. "Revoliutsionnye demokraty Azii i Afriki" ("The Revolutionary Democrats of Asia and Africa"), *Azia i Afrika Segodnia*, 10 (October, 1966), 2-5.

Andreev, I. "Novoe v obshchine Mali" ("The New in the Mali Commune"), *Azia i Afrika Segodnia*, 11 (November, 1965), 19-20.

_____. "Obshchee i osobennoe v sotsial'nom razvitii
Mali" ("The General and the Specific in the Social Development of Mali"), Narody Azii i Afriki, 2, 1967, 42-54.

_____. "Obshchina i sotsial'nye protsessy v osvo-
bodaiushcheisia Afrika" ("The Commune and Social Processes in Liberated Africa"), Voprosy
filosofii, 8, 1965, 56-67.

Andrianov, B. V. "Problemy formirovaniia narodnostei
i natsii v stranakh Afriki" ("Problems of Forming Nationalities and Nations in the Countries
of Africa"), Voprosy istorii, 9 (September,
1967), 101-14.

Annaklychev, Sh. "Rol' promyshlennykh tsentrov v
protesesse sblizheniia natsional'nostei" ("The
Role of Industrial Centers in the Process of
the Rapprochement of Nationalities"), Sovetskaia etnografiia, 6 (November-December, 1964),
25-36.

"Armiia i osvoboditel'noe dvizhenie" ("The Army and
the Liberation Movement"), Azia i Afrika
Segodnia, 9 (September, 1966), 2-4.

Arnoldov, A. "Sotsializm i kul'turnyi progress"
("Socialism and Cultural Progress"), Izvestia,
October 3, 1968, p. 4.

Avakov, P., and Mirskii, G. "O klassovoi strukture
v slaborazvitikh stranakh" ("The Class Structure in the Underdeveloped Countries"),
Mirovaia ekonomika i mezhdunarodnye otnosheniia,
4 (April, 1962), 68-81.

Balabushevich, V. "O nekotorikh osobennostiakh
rabochego dvizheniia v stranakh vostoka na
sovremennom etape" ("Certain Peculiarities of
the Workers' Movement in the Countries of the
East in the Contemporary Epoch"), Problemy
vostokovedniia, 2 (1959), 49-60.

Batalov, E. Ia.   "Osnovnye napravleniia razvitiia
    filosofskoi mysli v stranakh Azii i Afriki"
    ("The Basic Trends of the Development of Philo-
    sophical Thought in the Countries of Asia and
    Africa"), Voprosy filosofii, 12 (1964), 14-24.

Bellamy, J.   "Testing Time for Ghana," The African
    Communist, 27 (Fourth Quarter, 1966), 20-27.

Bochkarev, Iu.   "Kommunisty--samye stoikie bortsi
    za natsional'nuiu nezavisimost'" ("Communists--
    The Staunchest Fighters for National Indepen-
    dence"), Kommunist, 5 (March, 1963), 105-13.

Braginskii, M. I.   "Sotsial'nye sdvigi v Trop-
    icheskoi Afrike posle vtoroi mirovoi voiny"
    ("Social Trends in Tropical Africa After the
    Second World War"), Sovetskaia etnografiia,
    6 (November-December, 1960), 31-42.

Brezhnev, L. I.   "Fifty Years of Great Victories of
    Socialism," Pravda and Izvestia, November 4,
    1967, pp. 2-6; trans., CDSP, XIX, 44 (November
    22, 1967), 3-20.

_____.   "For Strengthening the Solidarity of Com-
    munists, For a New Upswing in the Anti-
    Imperialist Struggle," Speech at the Interna-
    tional Conference of Communist and Workers'
    Parties in Moscow, July 7, 1969, Pravda and
    Izvestia, July 8, 1969, pp. 1-4; trans., CDSP,
    XXI, 23 (July 2, 1969), 3-17.

Bromley, B.   "Osnovnye napravleniia etnograf-
    icheskikh issledovanii v SSSR" ("Basic Trends
    of Ethnographic Research in the USSR"),
    Voprosy istorii, 1 (January, 1968), 37-56.

Bruk, S., and Cheboksarov, N.   "Sovremennyi etap
    natsional'nogo razvitiia narodov Azii i Afriki"
    ("The Current Stage of National Development of
    the Peoples of Asia and Africa"), Sovetskaia
    etnografiia, 4 (July-August, 1961), 74-99.

Brutents, K. "Kolonializm pod maskoi i bez maski"
     ("Colonialism Masked and Unmasked"), Kommunist,
     17 (November, 1960), 111-23.

_____. "The National-Liberation Movement Today,"
     Pravda, February 1, 1967, pp. 4-5; trans.,
     CDSP, XIX, 5 (February 22, 1967), 24-25.

_____. "Nekotorye osobennosti natsional'no-
     osvoboditel'nogo dvizheniia" ("Certain Pecu-
     liarities of the National-Liberation Movement"),
     Voprosy filosofii, 6 (1965), 26-37.

_____. "Voprosy ideologii v natsional'no-
     osvoboditel'nom dvizhenii" ("Questions of
     Ideology in the National-Liberation Movement"),
     Kommunist, 18 (December, 1966), 37-50.

Cheboksarov, N. "Problemy tipologii etnicheskikh
     obshchnostei v trudakh sovetskikh uchenikhi"
     ("Problems of Typology of Ethnic Communities
     in the Works of Soviet Scientists"), Sovetskaia
     etnografiia, 4 (July-August, 1967), 94-109.

Chistiakov, O. "Formirovanie RSFSR kak federativnogo
     gosudarstvo" ("The Formation of the RSFSR as a
     Federated State"), Voprosy istorii, 8 (1968),
     3-17.

Dansoko, A., Naumov, P., and Shelepin, V.   "Guinea's
     Tenth Year of Independence," World Marxist Re-
     view, 12 (December, 1967), 31-36.

Demianchuk, S. A. "Vocational Guidance for Students
     in Rural Schools," Shkola i proizvodstvo, 1,
     1969; trans., Soviet Education, XII, 1 (Novem-
     ber, 1969), 31-42.

Desheryev, Iu., Kammari, M., and Melikian, M. "The
     Development and Mutual Enrichment of the Lan-
     guages of the Peoples of the USSR," Kommunist,
     13 (September, 1965), 55-66; trans., CDSP,
     XVII, 47 (December 15, 1965), 14-19.

Diarra, I.   "The Mass Party and Socialist Construc-
    tion," World Marxist Review, X, 1 (January,
    1967), 30-34.

Dienne, Mamadou.   "Nigerian Patriots Want National
    Unity," World Marxist Review, X, 10 (October,
    1967), 16-19.

Dolgopolov, E.   "Armii osvobodivshikhsia stran"
    ("The Armies of the Liberated Countries"),
    Krasnaia zvezda, May 19, 1968, p. 3.

_____.   "Vooruzhenye sily razvivaiushchikhsia
    stran" ("The Armed Forces of Developing Coun-
    tries"), Krasnaia zvezda, May 31, 1969, p. 5.

Drozdov, I. F.   "Iavliaiutsia li traditsii proznakom
    natsii?" ("Can Traditions Be Regarded as an In-
    dicator of a Nation?"), Voprosy istorii, 3
    (March, 1968), 83-91.

Dzhunusov, M. S.   "The Nation as a Social-Ethnic
    Community," Voprosy istorii, 4 (April, 1966),
    16-30; trans., CDSP, XVIII, 23 (June 29, 1966),
    24-30.

_____.   "The National Question: Two Ideologies,
    Two Policies," International Affairs, 10
    (October, 1966), 39-47.

Efimov, A. V.   "On the Tendencies in the Study of
    Nations," Novaia i Noveishaia istoriia, 4 (July-
    August, 1967), 31-42; trans., CDSP, XIX, 46
    (December 6, 1967), 30.

Erasov, B. S.   "The Ideological Challenge in Tropi-
    cal Africa and Cultural Traditions," Papers
    Presented by the USSR Delegation to the Second
    International Congress of Africanists, Dakar,
    1967.

_____. "Kontseptsii kul'tury v ideologii natsional-izma razvivaiushchikhsia stran" ("Concepts of Culture in the Ideology of Nationalism of Developing Countries"), Narody Azii i Afriki, 2 (1969), 114-24.

_____. "Leopol'd Sengor i ego kontseptsiia kul'tury" ("Leopold Senghor and His Conception of Culture"), Narody Azii i Afriki, 2 (1967), 87-99.

_____. "Marksizm i ideologiia natsionalizma v stranakh Afriki" ("Marxism and the Ideology of Nationalism in the African Countries"), Azia i Afrika Segodnia, 11 (November, 1968), 6-8.

_____. "'Mify i totemy'ili real'noe edinstvo" ("'Myths and Totems' or Real Unity"), Voprosy filosofii, 3 (1969), 82-92.

_____. "Tropicheskaia Afrika: dva podkhoda k kul'ture" ("Tropical Africa: Two Approaches to Culture"), Azia i Afrika Segodnia, 6 (June, 1969), 5-7.

Etinger, L. "Natsionalizm v Afrike" ("Nationalism in Africa"), Azia i Afrika Segodnia, 8 (July, 1968), 10-12.

Federov, L. "Nigeriia do perevorota i posle" ("Nigeria Before the Coup and After"), Azia i Afrika Segodnia, 6 (June, 1966), 48-50.

Frenkel', M. "Plemena--partii--biurokratiia," ("Tribes--Parties--Bureaucracies)", Mirovaia ekonomika i mezhdunarodnye otnosheniia, 11 (November, 1968), 109-13.

_____. "Rol' vozhdei v Sierra-Leone" ("The Role of the Chiefs in Sierra Leone"), Azia i Afrika Segodnia, 7 (July, 1968), 20-21.

Fyodorov, V. "The Driving Forces of the National-Liberation Revolution," International Affairs, 1 (January, 1968), 66-72.

Gadzhiev, N. "Kul'tury sotsialisticheskikh natsii,
    ikh nastoiashchee i budushchee" ("The Cultures
    of Socialist Nations, Their Present and Future"),
    Kommunist, 1 (January, 1962), 62-72.

Gadzhiev, S. M. "Popytki modernizatsii islama v
    sovremennikh usloviakh" ("Attempts to Modern-
    ize Islam in Contemporary Conditions"),
    Voprosy filosofii, 12 (1961), 113-21.

Gafurov, B. G. "Mezhdunarodnyi forum orientalistov
    (k itogam XXV mezhdunarodnogo kongressa vos-
    tokovedov)" ("The International Forum of Orien-
    talists [On the Results of the XXV Interna-
    tional Congress of Orientalists]"), Voprosy
    istorii, 11 (November, 1960), 3-18.

_____. "Reshenie natsional'nogo voprosa v SSSR"
    ("The Solution of the National Question in the
    USSR"), Azia i Afrika Segodnia, 1 (January,
    1962), 6-9.

Gavrilov, N. I. "Africa: Classes, Parties and
    Politics," International Affairs, 7 (July,
    1966), 39-44.

_____. "O migratsii rabochei sily v zapadnoi
    Afrike" ("Labor Migration in West Africa"),
    Problemy vostokovedeniia, 3 (1959), 82-90.

_____. "Peobrazovanye afrikanskoi derevni" ("Trans-
    formations of the African Village"), Azia i
    Afrika Segodnia, 12 (December, 1962), 13-15.

_____. "Za edinstvo Afriki" ("For the Unity of
    Africa"), Azia i Afrika Segodnia, 2 (February,
    1964), 5-7.

Glezerman, G. "V. I. Lenin on the Interrelation
    of Economics and Politics in the Construction
    of the New Society," Kommunist, 7 (May, 1963),
    30-40; trans., CDSP, XV, 22 (June 26, 1963),
    3-7.

Gordon, L., and Fridman, L.   "Rabochii klass osvo-
    bodivshchikhsia stran" ("The Working Class of
    Liberated Countries"), Mirovaia ekonomika i
    mezhdunarodnye otnosheniia, 1 (January, 1966),
    27-39.

Goriacheva, A. I.   "Is Psychological Makeup a Char-
    acteristic of a Nation?" Voprosy istorii, 8
    (August, 1967), 91-104; trans., CDSP, XIX, 46
    (December 6, 1967), 30-31.

Grafskii, V. G.   "Federalizm v Tropicheskoi Afrike"
    ("Federalism in Tropical Africa"), Sovetskoe
    gosudarstvo i pravo, 9 (September, 1967),
    116-21.

Guliev, V.   "Antikommunisticheskie 'kritiki'
    sovetskogo natsional'no-gosudarstvennogo
    stroitel'stba" ("Anti-Communist 'Critics' of
    Soviet Nation-State Construction"), Sovetskoe
    gosudarstvo i pravo, 4 (April, 1964), 124-33.

Iablochkov, L. D.   "Evolution of African Nationalism
    as a Political Ideology," Papers Presented by
    the USSR Delegation to the Second International
    Congress of Africanists, Dakar, 1967.

_____.   "Perevod i predpislovie statiu Maks Glukman
    'Plemennoi uklad v sovremennoi Tsentral'noi
    Afrike'" ("Translation and Introduction to the
    Article by Max Gluckman 'Tribal Structure in
    Modern Central Africa'"), Sovetskaia etno-
    grafiia, 6 (November-December, 1960), 57-69.

Iordanskii, V.   "Afrika: intelligentsiia na
    putiakh revoliutsii" ("Africa: Intelligentsia
    on the Path to Revolution"), Azia i Afrika
    Segodnia, 2 (February, 1966), 22-25.

_____.   "Ghana: Power Crisis," New Times, 25 (June
    21, 1967), 12-14.

_____.   "O kharaktere voennikh diktatur v trop-
    icheskoi Afrike" ("On the Character of Mili-
    tary Dictatorships in Tropical Africa"),
    Narody Azii i Afriki, 4 (1967), 22-37.

_____. "Problems of Rural Africa," New Times, 28 (July 14, 1965), 18-20.

_____. "Protivorechiia nekapitalisticheskogo razvitiia v Afrike" ("Contradictions of Non-Capitalist Development in Africa"), Narody Azii i Afriki, 3 (1968), 54.

_____. "Rassloenie afrikanskogo krestianstvo" ("Stratification of the African Peasantry"), Mirovaia ekonomika i mezhdunarodnye otnosheniia, 3 (March, 1969), 44-54.

_____. "Reading Africa's Contemporary History," International Affairs, 11 (November, 1965), 95-97.

_____. "Sotsial'nye sdvigi v gorodakh Tropi-cheskoi Afriki" ("Social Shifts in the Towns of Tropical Africa"), Mirovaia ekonomika i mezhdunarodnye otnosheniia, 10 (October, 1967), 68-83.

_____. "Tropicheskaia Afrika: cherty novogo goroda" ("Tropical Africa: Characteristics of the New Town"), Narody Azii i Afriki, 1 (1969), 16-27.

_____. "Tropicheskaia Afrika: o prirode mezhet-nicheskikh konfliktov" ("Tropical Africa: On the Nature of Interethnic Conflicts"), Mirovaia ekonomika i mezhdunarodnye otnosheniia, 1 (January, 1967), 47-56; 2 (February, 1967), 41-50.

_____. "Vozhdi i narod" ("The Chiefs and the People"), Azia i Afrika Segodnia, 1 (January, 1969), 8-10; 2 (February, 1969), 16-19.

Iskenderov, A. "The Army, Politics, and the People," Izvestia, January 17, 1969, p. 2; trans., CDSP, XIX, 3 (February 8, 1967), 9-10.

_____. "Vliiatel'naia sila sovremennosti" ("In-fluential Force of Modern Times"), Izvestia, April 28, 1968, p. 5.

_____, and Starushenko, G. "Intrigues of Im-
     perialism in Africa," Pravda, August 14, 1966,
     p. 4; trans., CDSP, XVIII, 33 (September 7,
     1966), 19-20.

Ismagilova, R. N. "Etnicheskii sostav naseleniia
     Tanganiki" ("The Ethnic Makeup of the Popula-
     tion of Tanganyika"), Sovetskaia etnografiia,
     3 (May-June, 1956), 97-103.

_____. "Zasedanie uchenogo soveta instituta
     Afriki AN SSSR posviashchennoe problemam Kongo"
     ("A Meeting of the Scientific Council of the
     Africa Institute of the USSR Academy of Sci-
     ences Concerning the Problems in the Congo"),
     Sovetskaia etnografiia, 3 (May-June, 1961),
     93-96.

Iudin, Iu. "Politicheskie partii i odnopartiinie
     sistemy v nezavisimikh stranakh Tropicheskoi
     Afriki" ("Political Parties and One-Party Sys-
     tems in the Independent Countries of Tropical
     Africa"), Sovetskoe gosudarstvo i pravo, 12
     (December, 1966), 49-58.

_____. "Stanovlenie natsional'noi gosudarst-
     vennosti v nezavisimikh stranakh Afriki" ("The
     Establishment of National Statehood in the In-
     dependent Countries of Africa"), Sovetskoe
     gosudarstvo i pravo, 2 (February, 1961), 35-47.

Ivanov, K. "Kongo i Afrika" ("The Congo and Afri-
     ca"), Pravda, March 30, 1961, p. 3.

_____. "The National and Colonial Question To-
     day," International Affairs, 5 (May, 1963),
     3-10.

_____. "National Liberation and Territorial
     Conflicts," International Affairs, 5 (May,
     1964), 8-14.

_____. "The National-Liberation Movement and
     the Non-Capitalist Path of Development," In-
     ternational Affairs, 9 (September, 1964),
     34-43; 12 (December, 1964), 7-16.

_____, and Dementiev, Iu. "O formirovanii natsii
    v razvivaiushchikhsia stranakh" ("On the For-
    mation of Nations in Developing Countries"),
    Azia i Afrika Segodnia, 2 (February, 1969),
    6-7; 3 (1969), 4-7.

Kaboshkin, V., and Kuznetsov, I. "Kongo perestaet
    byt' 'bel' giiskii" ("The Congo Ceases to be
    'Belgian'"), Sovremennyi vostok, 6 (1960),
    20-23.

Kaltakhchian, S. T. "K voprosu o poniatii 'na-
    tsiia'" ("On the Question of the Concept 'Na-
    tion'"), Voprosy istorii, 6 (June, 1966), 24-43.

_____. "On National Unity, Real and Imagined,"
    Pravda, November 26, 1968, pp. 3-4; trans.,
    CDSP, XX, 48 (December 18, 1968), 4-6.

Kashik, D. "The Implementation of the Leninist Na-
    tionalities Policy in Central Asia (1917-1937),"
    Tashkent, 1965; trans., Central Asian Review,
    XIII, 4 (1965), 323-29.

Katagoshchina, I. "Ideas of Socialism in Africa,"
    International Affairs, 7 (July, 1965), 92-93.

Katsman, V., and Kuprianov, P. "O meste i roli
    vozhdei v Afrikanskom obshchestve" ("On the
    Place and Role of Chiefs in African Society"),
    Sovetskaia etnografiia, 3 (June-July, 1962),
    149-59.

Kheifets, A. N. "Bor"ba V. I. Lenina protiv melko-
    burzhuaznonarodnicheskikh vzgliadov na nekapi-
    talisticheskogo razvitiia" ("The Struggle of
    V. I. Lenin against Petty Bourgeois-Populist
    Outlooks on Noncapitalist Development"),
    Narody Azii i Afriki, 1 (1969), 3-15.

Khrushchev, N. S. "Speech in Sofia," Pravda, May
    20, 1962, pp. 1-3; trans., CDSP, XIV, 20 (June
    13, 1962), 7.

Kim, G., and Kaufman, A. "Non-Capitalist Develop-
    ment: Achievements and Difficulties,"

<u>International Affairs</u>, 12 (December, 1967),
70-76.

Kim, L. "Pervyi god nezavisimosti Nigerii" ("Nigeria's First Year of Independence"), <u>Mirovaia
ekonomika i mezhdunarodnye otnosheniia</u>, 8
(August, 1961), 96-99.

Kirichenko, M. G. "Razvitie Kommunisticheskoi par-
tiei leninskikh idei o sovetskoi natsional'noi
gosudarstvennosti" ("The Development in the
Communist Party of the Leninist Ideas of Soviet National Statehood"), <u>Sovetskoe gosudarstvo
i pravo</u>, 2 (February, 1969), 12-22.

Kolesnichenko, T. "The Army and Politics," <u>Pravda</u>,
November 2, 1966, p. 5; trans., <u>CDSP</u>, XVIII,
44 (November 23, 1969), 27-28.

Kon, I. "The Psychology of Prejudice" ("On the
Roots of Ethnic Prejudice in Social Psycholo-
gy"), <u>Novyi Mir</u>, 9, 1966; trans., <u>The Soviet
Review</u>, IX, 1 (Spring, 1968), 3-22.

Konopikhin, F. "Guinea Looks Ahead," <u>New Times</u>, 40
(October, 1968), 9-10.

Konovalov, E. "Somalia in Quest of Her Future,"
<u>New Times</u>, 33 (August 21, 1968), 20-22.

Korovikov, V. "Nigeriiskii Krizis" ("Nigerian Crisis"), <u>Pravda</u>, June 16, 1967, p. 5.

Korshunov, E. "Ispitaniia Nigerii" ("The Experi-
ences of Nigeria"), <u>Azia i Afrika Segodnia</u>, 10
(October, 1968), 22-23; 11 (November, 1968),
10-11.

Kosukhin, N. "Sotsial'no-ekonomicheskoe preobrazovaniia v Tanzanii," ("Socioeconomic Transformations in Tanzania"), <u>Narody Azii i Afriki</u>, 3
(1967), 38-47.

Kozlov, V. I.   "Nekotorye problemy teorii natsii"
    ("Certain Problems of the Theory of a Nation"),
    Voprosy istorii, 1 (January, 1967), 88-99.

_____.   "O razrabotke teoreticheskikh osnov
    natsional'nogo voprosa" ("Elaboration of the
    Theoretical Foundations of the National Ques-
    tion"), Narody Azii i Afriki, 4 (1967), 75-85.

_____.   "Tipy etnicheskikh protsessov i osoben-
    nosti ikh istoricheskogo razvitiia" ("Types of
    Ethnic Processes and Peculiarities of Their
    Historical Development"), Voprosy istorii, 9
    (September, 1968), 95-109.

Kremnyov, M.   "Africa in Search of New Paths,"
    World Marxist Review, VI, 8 (August, 1963),
    72-76.

Krylov, V.   "Osnovnye tendentsii razvitiia agrarnikh
    otnoshenii v Tropicheskoi Afrike" ("Basic Ten-
    dencies of the Development of Agrarian Rela-
    tions in Tropical Africa"), Narody Azii i
    Afriki, 4 (1965), 3-23.

Kubbel', L.   "J. S. Trimingham, Islam in West Afri-
    ca (Oxford: Clarendon, 1959)," Sovetskaia
    etnografiia, 6 (November-December, 1960),
    163-65.

Kudriavtsev, V.   "African Tremors," Izvestia, Janu-
    ary 15, 1966; trans., CDSP, XVIII, 2 (February
    2, 1966), 30-31.

_____.   "Africa's Hopes and Anxieties," Interna-
    tional Affairs, 11 (November, 1963), 40-45.

_____.   "Afrika kak ona est" ("Africa As It Is"),
    Izvestia, August 30, 1966, p. 2.

_____.   "Afrika: Novoe rozhdaetsia v mukakh"
    ("Africa: The New Is Born in Pain"), Azia i
    Afrika Segodnia, 11 (November, 1966), 27-29.

_____. "Afrikanskie gorizonty" ("African Horizons"), _Izvestia_, December 21, 1968.

_____. "Afrikanskie isbergi" ("African Icebergs,", _Azia i Afrika Segodnia_, 5 (May, 1969), 9-11.

_____. "Afrika: podzemnyi gul narastaet" ("Africa: The Rumbling Grows Louder"), _Azia i Afrika Segodnia_, 8 (August, 1964), 2-5.

_____. "Fighting Africa's Daily Round," _International Affairs_, 10 (October, 1962), 51-57.

_____. "Intense Heat of Struggle in Africa," _Izvestia_, March 6, 1966, p. 3; trans., _CDSP_, XVIII, 10 (March 30, 1966), 22-23.

_____. "Kenya: African Problems in Sharp Focus," _International Affairs_, 2 (February, 1964), 64-67.

_____. "Neo-Colonialism and African Reality," _International Affairs_, 4 (April, 1965), 57-63.

_____. "Real and Fictitious Difficulties," _Izvestia_, November 2, 1968, p. 4; trans., _CDSP_, XX, 44 (November 20, 1968), 21-23.

_____. "Test of Africa's Maturity," _Izvestia_, October 11, 1968, p. 2; trans., _CDSP_, XX, 41 (October 30, 1968), 20-21.

_____. "Tricks of Neocolonialism," _Izvestia_, April 30, 1966, p. 2; trans., _CDSP_, XVIII, 17 (May 18, 1966), pp. 27-28.

_____. "Unity and Separatism," _Izvestia_, November 17, 1967, p. 2; trans., _CDSP_, XIX, 46 (December 6, 1967), 16-17.

Kurgantsev, M. "Kolonializm--vrag kul'tury" (Colonialism--Enemy of Culture"), _Sovremennyi vostok_, 1 (1961), 32-33.

Langa, A.   "Socialism and Rural Revolution," The
    African Communist, 34 (Third Quarter, 1968),
    68-75.

Laptev, V.   "From Katanga to Biafra," New Times, 52
    (December 27, 1967), 17-18.

Lashuk, L. P.   "O formakh donatsional'nikh etnich-
    eskikh sviaziei" ("On Forms of Prenational
    Ethnic Ties"), Voprosy istorii, 4 (April,
    1967), 77-92.

Lepioshkin, A.   "Nekotorye voprosy Leninskoi teorii
    sovetskogo federalizma v svete novoi programmy
    KPSS" ("Certain Questions of the Leninist The-
    ory of Soviet Federalism in Light of the New
    Program of the CPSU"), Sovetskoe gosudarstvo i
    pravo, 5 (May, 1963), 60-70.

Letnev, A. B.   "Estimation of Agricultural Product
    Marketing Systems in Connection with Agrarian
    Reforms (The Case of West Africa)," Papers
    Presented by the USSR Delegation to the Second
    International Congress of Africanists, Dakar,
    1967.

_____.   "Novoe v Maliiskoi derevne" ("New Devel-
    opments in the Malian Village"), Sovetskaia
    etnografiia, 1 (January-February, 1964), 81-88.

_____.   "Problema Afrikanskikh partii v bur-
    zhuaznoi Afrikanistike" ("The Problem of Afri-
    can Parties in Bourgeois African Studies"),
    Voprosy istorii, 8 (August, 1968), 63-79.

Lozinov, D.   "African Conundrums," International
    Affairs, 5 (May, 1969), 78-82.

Lutskii, V. B.   "Problema arabskogo edinstva" ("The
    Problem of Arab Unity"), Sovetskaia etnografiia,
    1 (January-February, 1957), 106-17.

Maevskii, V.   "Besedy v Nigerii" ("Conversations in
    Nigeria"), Za rubezhom, 7 (February 14-20,
    1969), 16-18.

Matiushkin, N. I.   "Razreshenie natsional'nogo
    voprosa v SSSR" ("The Resolution of the Na-
    tional Question in the USSR"), Voprosy istorii,
    12 (December, 1967), 3-20.

"Message from N. S. Khrushchev, Chairman of the
    USSR Council of Ministers, to Heads of State
    of Countries of the World," Pravda and Izvestia,
    January 4, 1964, p. 1; trans., CDSP, XVI, 1
    (January 29, 1964), 4.

Midtsev, V.   "Gvineaia na novom puti" ("Guinea On
    A New Path"), Kommunist, 12 (December, 1965),
    85-93.

Mirskii, G.   "Politicheskaia rol' armii v stranakh
    Azii i Afriki" ("The Political Role of the
    Army in the Countries of Asia and Africa"),
    Narody Azii i Afriki, 6 (1968), 1-14.

_____.   "Socialist Trends in Developing Coun-
    tries," Izvestia, October 5, 1966, p. 2;
    trans., CDSP, XVIII, 40 (October 26, 1966),
    22-23.

_____.   "Third World: Illusions and Realities,"
    New Times, 1 (January 1, 1969), 10-12.

_____, and Pokataeva, T.   "Klassy i klassovaia
    bor"ba v razvivaiushchikhsia stranakh"
    ("Classes and Class Struggle in Developing
    Countries"), Mirovaia ekonomika i mezhduna-
    rodnye otnosheniia, 2 (February, 1966), 38-49.

Mitrofanov, N.   "Edinstvo v mnogoobrazii ("Unity in
    Versatility"), Azia i Afrika Segodnia, 6 (June,
    1963), 13-15.

Mnatsakanian, M. O.   "Natsiia i natsional'naia
    gosudarstvennost'" ("The Nation and National
    Statehood"), Voprosy istorii, 9 (September,
    1966), 27-36.

Morozov, M. A.   "Otvety na voprosy: O nekotorikh
    voprosakh razvitiia sovetskikh sotsialistich-

eskikh natsii" ("Answers to Questions: On
Certain Questions Regarding the Development of
the Soviet Socialist Nations"), Voprosy istorii KPSS, 10 (October, 1968), 104-11.

Nabokov, G. A. "Bol'she vnimaniia voprosam istorii
Afriki" ("Greater Attention to Questions of
African History"), Voprosy istorii, 11 (Novem-
ber, 1961), 137-40.

"Nekapitalisticheskii put' razvitiia i problemy
gosudarstvennosti" ("The Noncapitalist Path of
Development and Problems of Statehood"),
Sovetskoe gosudarstvo i pravo, 11 (November,
1967), 129-39.

Nikanovov, A. "Kamerun: u vulkana preobrazovanii"
("Cameroon: On the Volcano of Change"), Azia
i Afrika Segodnia, 8 (August, 1968), 7-9.

Nikoforov, A. V. "Zasedanie uchenogo soveta instituta Afriki AN SSSR" ("A Meeting of the Scientific Council of the Africa Institute of the
USSR Academy of Sciences"), Sovetskaia etnografiia, 6 (November-December, 1961), 124-26.

"Opyt stroitel'stva Sovetskogo gosudarstva kak
istochnik teoreticheskikh obobshchenii o
gosudarstve sotsialisticheskogo tipa" ("The
Experience of Building the Soviet State as a
Source of Theoretical Generalizations Regarding the State of the Socialist Type"), Sovetskoe gosudarstvo i pravo, 3 (March, 1967),
82-91.

Orestov, O. "Vseobshchie vybory v Nigerii" ("General Elections in Nigeria"), Sovremennyi
vostok, 4 (1960), 49-54.

Parnov, E. "Traditsii i sovremennosti" ("Traditions
and Modernity"), Azia i Afrika Segodnia, 4
(April, 1967), 6-9.

Paveltsev, B. "The Military Coups in Africa," New
Times, 4 (January 26, 1966), 11-13.

Peredentsev, V. I. "The Influence of Ethnic Factors on the Territorial Redistribution of Population," Izvestia Akademii Nauk SSSR, seriia geograficheskaia, 4 (1965); trans., Central Asian Review, XIV, 1 (1966), 45-54.

Polonskaia, L., and Litman, A. "Vlianie religii na obshchestvennuiu mysl' narodov Vostoka" ("The Influence of Religion on the Social Thought of the Peoples of the East"), Narody Azii i Afriki, 4 (1966), 3-15.

Ponomarev, B. "Concerning the National-Democratic State," Kommunist, 8 (May, 1961), 33-48; trans., CDSP, XIII, 22 (June 28, 1961), 3-7.

Popov, V. "Bitva za umy" ("Battle for Minds"), Krasnaia zvezda, June 30, 1968, p. 3.

Potekhin, I. I. "Afrika: itogi i perspektivy antiimperialisticheskoi revoliutsii" ("Africa: Results and Perspectives on the Anti-Imperialist Revolution"), Azia i Afrika Segodnia, 9 (September, 1961), 11-13; 10 (October, 1961), 14-15.

_____. "Bor"ba za vossoedinenie Kameruna" ("The Struggle for the Unification of the Cameroon"), Sovetskaia etnografiia, 5 (September-October, 1959), 62-68.

_____. "Etnograficheskie nabliudeniia v Gane" ("Ethnic Observations in Ghana"), Sovetskaia etnografiia, 3 (May-June, 1958), 125-35.

_____. "Legacy of Colonialism in Africa," International Affairs, 3 (March, 1964), 15-20.

_____. "Nekotorye problemy Afrikanistiki v svete reshenii XXII s"ezda KPSS" ("Certain Problems of African Studies in Light of the Resolutions of the 22d Party Congress of the CPSU"), Narody Azii i Afriki, 1 (1962), 6-16.

_____. "On 'African Socialism,'" International Affairs, 1 (January, 1963), 75-85.

_____. "O nekotorikh zadachakh afrikanisitiki v sviazi c konferentsiei narodov Afriki" ("On Certain Tasks of African Studies in Connection with the Conference of the Peoples of Africa"), Sovetskaia etnografiia, 2 (March-April, 1959), 10-17.

_____. "Novoe Afrikanskoe gosudarstvo--Gana" ("A New African State--Ghana"), Sovetskaia etnografiia, 2 (March-April, 1959), 106-15.

_____. "Pozemel'nye otnosheniia v stranakh Afriki" ("Agrarian Relations in the Countries of Africa"), Narody Azii i Afriki, 3 (1962), 16-31.

_____. "Problemy bor"by c perezhitkami proshlogo na Afrikanskom kontinente" ("Problems of Struggling Against the Survivals of the Past on the African Continent"), Sovetskaia etnografiia, 4 (July-August, 1964), 186-95.

_____. "Some Aspects of the National Question in Africa," World Marxist Review, IV, 11 (November, 1961), 41-46.

_____. "XXI S"ezd KPSS i zadachi vostokovedeniia" ("The 21st CPSU Congress and the Tasks of Oriental Studies"), Problemy vostokovedeniia, 1 (1959), 18-25.

_____. "Zadachi izucheniia etnicheskogo sostava Afriki v sviazi s raspadom kolonial'noi sistemy" ("Tasks of Studying the Ethnic Makeup of Africa in Connection with the Fall of the Colonial System"), Sovetskaia etnografiia, 4 (July-August, 1957), 103-10.

Potomov, Iu. "Sudan in Turmoil," Pravda, October 28, 1964, p. 3; trans., CDSP, XVI, 43 (November 18, 1964), 23-24.

Rakhimov, K. "The Great Power Policy of Mao tse-Tung and His Group on the Nationalities Question," Kommunist, 7 (May, 1967), 114-19; trans., CDSP, XIX, 20 (June 7, 1967), 3-4.

Rogachev, P. M., and Sverdlin, M. A. "On the Con-
    cept 'Nation,'" Voprosy istorii, 1 (January,
    1966), 33-48; trans., CDSP, XVIII, 21 (June 15,
    1966), 14-21.

_____. "The Soviet People Is a New Historical
    Community," Kommunist, 9 (June, 1963), 11-20;
    trans., CDSP, XV, 32 (September 4, 1963), 12-16.

Rosenko, M. "The Present Epoch and Some Questions
    of the Theory of Nations," Voprosy istorii, 7
    (July, 1968), 85-100; trans., Current Abstracts
    of the Soviet Press, I, 5 (October, 1968), 11.

Savelev, N. "Natsional'naia burzhuaziia Tropicheskoi
    Afriki" ("The National Bourgeoisie of Tropical
    Africa"), Azia i Afrika Segodnia, 12 (December,
    1966), 2-5; 1 (January, 1967), 18-19.

Semenov, Iu. "Iz istorii teoreticheskoi razrabotki
    V. I. Leninym natsional'nogo voprosa" ("From
    the History of the Theoretical Work of V. I.
    Lenin on the National Question"), Narody Azii
    i Afriki, 4 (1966), 106-29.

_____. "K opredeleniiu poniatiia 'natsiia'"
    ("Toward a Definition of the Concept 'Nation'"),
    Narody Azii i Afriki, 4 (1967), 85-102.

Shamrai, Y. F. "Problemy sovershenstvovaniia
    ekonomicheskogo sotrudnichestva sotsialist-
    icheskikh i razvivaiushchikh stran" ("Problems
    of Realizing Economic Cooperation Between the
    Socialist and Developing Countries"), Narody
    Azii i Afriki, 4 (1968), 3-14.

Shatalov, I. "International Symposium in Alma Ata,"
    International Affairs, 11 (November, 1969),
    53-55.

Shelepin, V. "Africa: Why the Instability?" New
    Times, 52 (December 30, 1968), 21-24.

"The Single Party Panacea," The African Communist,
    16 (First Quarter, 1964), 12-14.

Sinitsyna, I. E.   "Novoe i traditsionnoe v prave
    Tanzanii" ("The New and Traditional in Tanza-
    nian Law"), Sovetskaia etnografiia, 6 (November-
    December, 1968), 58-69.

Smirnov, V. V.   "Theoretical Problems Pertaining to
    the Management of the Economy of Developing
    Countries," Vestnik Leningradskogo universiteta,
    seriia ekonomiki, No. 4; trans., Problems of
    Economics, XII, 3 (July, 1969), 83-94.

Sobolev, A.   "National Democracy--The Way to Social
    Progress," World Marxist Review, VI, 2 (Feb-
    ruary, 1963), 39-48.

_____.   "Some Problems of Social Progress,"
    World Marxist Review, X, 1 (January, 1967),
    21-29.

Solodovnikov, V. G.   "Some Problems of Economic and
    Social Development of Independent African Na-
    tions," Papers Presented by the USSR Delegation
    to the Second International Congress of Afri-
    canists, Dakar, 1967.

_____.   "The Soviet Union and Africa," The Afri-
    can Communist, 36 (Fourth Quarter, 1968), 74-86.

_____.   "Zadachi sovetskoi afrikanistiki" ("The
    Tasks of Soviet African Studies"), Narody Azii
    i Afriki, 3 (1968), 1-12.

_____, and Tarasov, F.   "On the Path of Progress
    --Results of the Eight Congress of the Demo-
    cratic Party of Guinea," Pravda, October 18,
    1967, p. 4; trans., CDSP, XIX, 42 (November 7,
    1967), 46.

Starushenko, G.   "Cherez obshchedomokratisheskie
    preobrazovaniia k sotsialisticheskim" ("Through
    All-Democratic Transformations to the Social-
    ist"), Kommunist, 13 (September, 1962), 104-9.

Stepaniants, M. T.   "Islamskaia etika' i ee so-
    tsial'naia smysl" ("The 'Islamic Ethic' and

Its Social Purport"), *Voprosy filosofii*, 2
(February, 1966); trans., *Central Asian Review*,
XIV, 4 (1966), 294-305.

Stepanov, Lev. "The Future of Afro-Asia," *New
Times*, 51 (December 22, 1965), 5-8.

_____. "Troubled Year in the Third World," *New
Times*, 1 (January 4, 1967), 12-14.

Sumbatian, Iu. "Armiia v politicheskoi sisteme
natsional'noi demokratii" ("The Army in the
Political System of National Democracy"),
Narody Azii i Afriki, 4 (1969), 34-38.

Svanidze, I. A. "Problems of Raising the Productivity of Agriculture in Africa," Papers Presented by the USSR Delegation to the Second
International Congress of Africanists, Dakar,
1967.

Tabeliev, V. "Osobennosti planirovaniia v Afrike"
("Peculiarities of Planning in Africa"), *Azia
i Afrika Segodnia*, 7 (July, 1969), 4-5.

Tadevosian, E. V. "Dal'neishee sblizhenie sotsial-
isticheskikh natsii v SSSR" ("The Further
Drawing Together of Socialist Nations in the
USSR"), *Voprosy filosofii*, 6 (1963), 3-12.

Tarasov, F. "Otkuda iskhodit 'opasnost'" ("Whence
the Danger?"), *Pravda*, December 18, 1967, p. 5.

"The Tasks of the Struggle Against Imperialism at
the Present Stage and the Unity of Action of
the Communist and Workers' Parties and All
Anti-Imperialist Forces," Basic Document
Adopted by the International Conference of
Communist and Workers' Parties in Moscow on
June 17, 1969, *Pravda* and *Izvestia*, June 18,
1969, pp. 1-4; trans., *CDSP*, XXI, 28 (August 6,
1969), 14-24.

Teosyan, E. "One-Party System in Africa," *International Affairs*, 1 (January, 1967), 125-26.

Tigranova, M. "Splochenie natsii v Pakistane"
     ("The Consolidation of the Nation in Pakistan"),
     <u>Azia i Afrika Segodnia</u>, 8 (August, 1965), 30-31.

Tomilin, Y. "East Africa Chooses the Way," <u>Inter-</u>
     <u>national Affairs</u>, 1 (January, 1964), 41-47.

Tryanusov, A. "War or Peace?" <u>International Af-</u>
     <u>fairs</u>, 7 (July, 1968), 89-90.

Tsamerian, I. P. "Aktual'nye voprosy marksistko-
     leninskoi teorii natsii" ("Actual Questions
     Regarding the Marxist-Leninist Theory of the
     Nation"), <u>Voprosy istorii</u>, 6 (June, 1967),
     107-22.

_____. "The International Significance of the
     Experience of the CPSU in Solving the National
     Question in the USSR," <u>Voprosy istorii KPSS</u>, 9
     (September, 1968), 41-55; trans., <u>Current Ab-</u>
     <u>stracts of the Soviet Press</u>, I, 5 (October,
     1968), 11.

_____. "Leninskaia natsional'naia politika v
     deistvii" ("Leninist Nationality Policy in Ac-
     tion"), <u>Kommunist</u>, 9 (June, 1968), 18-28.

_____. "Pertinent Questions of the Marxist-
     Leninist Theory of the Nation," <u>Voprosy istorii</u>,
     6 (June, 1967), 107-22; trans., <u>CDSP</u>, XIX, 46
     (December 6, 1967), 29.

Ul'ianovskii, R. A. "Agrarnye reformy v stranakh
     blizhnego i srednego Vostoka, Indii, i ivgo-
     vostochnoi Azii" ("Agrarian Reforms in the
     Countries of the Near and Middle East, India,"
     and Southeast Asia"), <u>Narody Azii i Afriki</u>, 2
     (1961), 14-30.

_____. "Aktual'nye problemy natsional'no-
     osvoboditel'nogo dvizheniia (po itogovomu
     dokumentu mezhdunarodnogo soveshchania kom-
     munisticheskikh i rabochikh partii, 1969)"
     ("Actual Problems of the National-Liberation
     Movement [According to the Final Document of

the International Conference of Communist and
Workers' Parties, 1969]"), _Narody Azii i
Afriki_, 4 (1969), 1-14.

_____. "Nekotorye voprosy nekapitalisticheskogo
razvitiia" ("Certain Questions Regarding Noncapitalist Development"), _Kommunist_, 1 (June,
1966), 109-19.

_____. "O edinstve sil sotsializma i natsion-
al'no-osvoboditel'nogo dvizheniia" ("On the
Unity of the Forces of Socialism and of the
National-Liberation Movement"), _Pravda_, October 14, 1968, p. 5.

_____. "On Some Features of the Present Stage
of the National-Liberation Movement," _Pravda_,
January 3, 1968, pp. 4-5; trans., _CDSP_, XX, 1
(January 24, 1968), 9-11.

Ulrikh, O. "Industrialization Problems in Develop-
in Countries," _International Affairs_, 11 (November, 1968), 75-79.

Vasiliev, V. "Armiia i sotsial'nyi progress" ("The
Army and Social Progress"), _Azia i Afrika
Segodnia_, 9 (September, 1966), 5-7.

Zak, L. M., and Isaev, M. I. "Problemy pis'mennosti
narodov SSSR v kul'turnoi revoliutsii" ("Problems of the Written Languages of the Peoples
of the USSR in the Cultural Revolution"),
Voprosy istorii, 2 (February, 1966), 3-20.

Zanzolo, Albert. "Crisis in Africa," _The African
Communist_, 26 (Third Quarter, 1966), 15-27.

_____. "The National Question and Nigeria," _The
African Communist_, 36 (First Quarter, 1969),
18-24.

Zarine, D. "Classes and Class Struggle in Develop-
in Countries," _International Affairs_, 4 (April,
1968), 47-52.

_____. "Nekotorye cherty natsional'no-osvobo-
ditel'nogo dvizheniia narodov kolonial'nikh i
zavisimikh stran" ("Certain Characteristics of
the National-Liberation Movement of the Peoples
of the Colonial and Dependent Countries"),
Voprosy filosofii, 1 (1961), 16-25.

Zhagvaral, N. "From a Nomadic to a Settled Life in
Mongolia," World Marxist Review, IV, 8 (August,
1961), 50-53.

Zhukov, E. "Natsional'no-osvoboditel'noe dvizhenie
narodov Azii i Afriki" ("The National-
Liberation Movement of the Peoples of Asia and
Africa"), Kommunist, 4 (March, 1969), 31-42.

Zotov, V. D. "Sotsialisticheskie preobrazovaniia v
Srednei Azii i religioznyi vopros" ("Socialist
Transformations in Central Asia and the Religious Question"), Voprosy filosofii, 11 (1967),
60-68.

NON-COMMUNIST SOURCES--BOOKS

Almond, Gabriel, and Powell, C. Bingham, Jr. Comparative Politics: A Developmental Approach.
Boston: Little, Brown, 1966.

Austin, Dennis, and Weiler, Hans, eds. Inter-State
Relations in Africa. Frieburg im Bresgau, 1965.

Banton, Michael. West African City. London: Oxford University Press, 1957.

Becker, Seymour. Russia's Protectorates in Central
Asia. Cambridge, Mass.: Harvard University
Press, 1968.

Bennigsen, A., and Lemercier-Quelquejay, C. Islam
in the Soviet Union. New York: Praeger, 1967.

Black, Cyril, and Thornton, Thomas, eds. Communism
and Revolution. Princeton, N.J.: Princeton
University Press, 1964.

Braham, Randolph, ed. Soviet Politics and Government. New York: Knopf, 1965.

Conolly, Violet. Beyond the Urals. London: Oxford University Press, 1967.

Cowan, L. Gray, et al., eds. Education and Nation-Building in Africa. New York: Praeger, 1965.

Degras, Jane, ed. The Communist International, 1919-1943, Documents. 3 vols. London: Oxford University Press, 1956-65.

_____. Soviet Documents on Foreign Policy. 3 vols. London: Oxford University Press, 1951-53.

Dowse, Robert. Modernization in Ghana and the USSR. London: Routledge and Kegan Paul, 1969.

Duncan, W. Raymond, ed. Soviet Policy in Developing Countries. Waltham, Mass.: Ginn-Blaisdell, 1970.

Eudin, Xenia, and North, Robert, eds. Soviet Russia and the East, 1920-1927. Stanford, Calif: Stanford University Press, 1957.

Eudin, Xenia, and Slusser, Robert. Soviet Foreign Policy, 1928-1934. 2 vols. University Park: Pennsylvania State University Press, 1966-67.

Fainsod, Merle. How Russia Is Ruled. Cambridge, Mass.: Harvard University Press, 1963.

Fitch, B., and Oppenheimer, M. Ghana: End of An Illusion. New York: Monthly Review Press, 1966.

Friedland, William, and Rosberg, Carl, Jr., eds. African Socialism. Stanford: Stanford University Press, 1964.

Gehlen, Michael. The Communist Party of the Soviet Union. Bloomington: Indiana University Press, 1969.

Goldhagen, Erich, ed. <u>Ethnic Minorities in the So-</u>
    <u>viet Union</u>. New York: Praeger, 1968.

Gruliow, Leo, ed. <u>Current Soviet Policies: The</u>
    <u>Documentary Record of the Nineteenth Communist</u>
    <u>Party Congress and the Reorganization After</u>
    <u>Stalin's Death</u>. New York: Praeger, 1953.

_____. <u>Current Soviet Policies II: The Docu-</u>
    <u>mentary Record of the Twentieth Communist Par-</u>
    <u>ty Congress and Its Aftermath</u>. New York:
    Praeger, 1957.

_____. <u>Current Soviet Policies III: The Docu-</u>
    <u>mentary Record of the Extraordinary Twenty-</u>
    <u>first Communist Party Congress</u>. New York:
    Columbia University Press, 1960.

Hazlewood, Arthur, ed. <u>African Integration and</u>
    <u>Disintegration</u>. New York: Oxford University
    Press, 1967.

Hicks, Ursula, ed. <u>Federalism and Economic Growth</u>
    <u>in Underdeveloped Countries</u>. London: George
    Allen and Unwin, 1961.

Hoselitz, Berthold, ed. <u>The Progress of Underde-</u>
    <u>veloped Areas</u>. Chicago: University of Chicago
    Press, 1952.

Kirkwood, Kenneth, ed., <u>African Affairs</u>, No. 3.
    London: Oxford University Press, 1969.

Klinghoffer, Arthur. <u>Soviet Perspectives on Afri-</u>
    <u>can Socialism</u>. Rutherford, N.J.: Fairleigh
    Dickinson University Press, 1969.

Kohn, Hans, and Sokolsky, W. <u>African Nationalism</u>
    <u>in the Twentieth Century</u>. New York: Van
    Nostrand, 1965.

Kolarz, Walter. <u>Religion in the Soviet Union</u>. New
    York: St. Martin's Press, 1961.

_____. <u>Russia and Her Colonies</u>. U.S. (no city):
    Archon Books, 1967.

Laqueur, Walter. The Soviet Union in the Mediter-
    ranean 1958-1968. New York: Macmillan, 1969.

_____, and Labedz, Leopold, eds. Polycentrism.
    New York: Praeger, 1962.

Lederer, Ivo, ed. Russian Foreign Policy. New
    Haven, Conn.: Yale University Press, 1962.

Legvold, Robert. Soviet Policy in West Africa:
    1957-1968. Cambridge, Mass.: Harvard Univer-
    sity Press, 1970.

Little, Kenneth. The Mende of Sierra Leone: People
    in Transition. London: Routledge and Kegan
    Paul, 1951.

London, Kurt. New Nations in a Divided World. New
    York: Praeger, 1963.

McEwan, Peter, and Sutcliffe, Robert, eds. Modern
    Africa. New York: Crowell, 1967.

Mckay, Vernon. Africa in World Politics. New York:
    Harper and Row, 1963.

McKenzie, Kermit. Comintern and World Revolution.
    New York: Columbia University Press, 1964.

MacKintosh, J. M. Strategy and Tactics of Soviet
    Foreign Policy. London: Oxford University
    Press, 1962.

McLane, Charles. Soviet Strategies in Southeast
    Asia. Princeton, N.J.: Princeton University
    Press, 1966.

Meyer, Alfred. Leninism. Cambridge, Mass.: Har-
    vard University Press, 1957.

Middleton, John. Black Africa: Its Peoples and
    Their Cultures Today. New York: Macmillan,
    1970.

Muller, Kurt. The Foreign Aid Programs of the Soviet Bloc and Communist China. New York: Walker, 1967.

Nove, Alec, and Newth, J. A. The Soviet Middle East. New York: Praeger, 1967.

Paolozzi, Ursula. Communism in Sub-Saharan Africa: An Essay with Bibliographical Supplement. Washington, D.C.: American University Center for Research in Social Systems, 1969.

Pipes, Richard. The Formation of the Soviet Union. Cambridge, Mass.: Harvard University Press, 1964.

Possony, Stefan, ed. Lenin Reader. Chicago: Regnery, 1966.

Rivkin, Arnold, ed. Nations by Design. New York: Anchor, 1967.

Rubinstein, Alvin. Communist Political Systems. Englewood Cliffs, N.J.: Prentice-Hall, 1966.

_____. The Foreign Policy of the Soviet Union. New York: Random House, 1960.

_____. The Soviets in International Organizations. Princeton, N.J.: Princeton University Press, 1964.

Russia Looks at Africa. London: Central Asian Research Centre, 1960.

Sawyer, Carole. Communist Trade with Developing Countries: 1955-1965. New York: Praeger, 1966.

Schatten, Fritz. Communism in Africa. London: George Allen and Unwin, 1966.

Seton-Watson, Hugh. Nationalism and Communism. London: Methuen, 1964.

Spiro, Herbert, ed. Africa: The Primacy of Politics. New York: Random House, 1966.

Stokke, Baard. Soviet and East European Trade in Africa. New York: Praeger, 1967.

Tatu, Michel. Power in the Kremlin. (Trans., Helen Katel.) New York: Viking, 1969.

Thornton, Thomas, ed. The Third World in Soviet Perspective. Princeton, N.J.: Princeton University Press, 1964.

Tillett, Lowell. The Great Friendship: Soviet Historians on the Non-Russian Nationalities. Chapel Hill: University of North Carolina Press, 1969.

Ulam, Adam. The Unfinished Revolution. New York: Random House, 1960.

Wallerstein, Immanuel. Africa: The Politics of Unity. New York: Random House, 1967.

Watts, R. L. New Federations: Experiments in the Commonwealth. Oxford: The Clarendon Press, 1966.

Wilber, Charles. The Soviet Model and Underdeveloped Countries. Chapel Hill: The University of North Carolina Press, 1969.

Wolfe, Bertram D. Marxism: One Hundred Years in the Life of a Doctrine. London: Chapman and Hall, 1967.

Wolfe, Thomas. Soviet Strategy at the Crossroads. Cambridge, Mass.: Harvard University Press, 1964.

Zimmerman, William. Soviet Perspectives on International Relations 1957-1967. Princeton, N.J.: Princeton University Press, 1969.

NON-COMMUNIST SOURCES--ARTICLES

"Africa--Soviet Aims," *Mizan* (*The Mizan Newsletter*),
    V, 7 (July-August, 1963), 1-18.

"The Background of Soviet Decisions," *Mizan*, VI, 11
    (December, 1964), 1-9.

Baker, Ross K. "The Emergence of Biafra: Balkan-
    ization or Nation-Building," *Orbis*, XII, 2
    (Summer, 1968), 518-33.

Bienen, Henry. "An Ideology for Africa," *Foreign
    Affairs*, XLVII, 2 (January, 1969), 545-59.

Bilinsky, Yaroslav. "The Rulers and the Ruled,"
    Problems of Communism, XVI, 5 (September-
    October, 1967), 16-26.

Bird, Christopher. "Africa's Peoples--A Geograph-
    ical and Human Challenge for Soviet Research
    and Political Action," Paper Delivered at a
    Conference on Political Geography, Harvard
    University, 1957.

Bloembergen, Samuel. "The Union Republics: How
    Much Autonomy?," *Problems of Communism*, XVI, 5
    (September-October, 1967), 27-35.

Bowles, W. Donald. "Soviet Russia as a Model for
    Underdeveloped Areas," *World Politics*, XIV, 3
    (April, 1962), 483-504.

Clemens, Walter C., Jr., "Soviet Policy in the
    Third World: Five Alternative Futures," *Orbis*,
    XIII, 2 (Summer, 1969), 476-501.

Connor, Walker. "Ethnic Nationalism as a Political
    Force," *World Affairs*, CXXXIII, 2 (September,
    1970), 91-97.

_____. "Minorities in Marxist Theory and Prac-
    tice," paper delivered at the Sixty-fifth

Annual Meeting of the American Political Science Association, New York, September, 1969.

Demaitre, E. "The Origins of National Communism," Studies in Comparative Communism, II, 1 (January, 1969), 1-20.

"The Ebb Tide?," Mizan, VIII, 5 (September-October, 1966), 189-201.

"Editorial," Mizan, VIII, 1 (January-February, 1966), 1.

Emerson, Rupert. "African States and the Burdens They Bear," African Studies Bulletin, X, 1 (April, 1967), 1-15.

Feit, Edward. "Military Coups and Political Development: Some Lessons From Ghana and Nigeria," World Politics, XX, 2 (January, 1968), 179-93.

Friedrich, Carl. "Federalism and Nationalism," Orbis, X, 4 (Winter, 1967), 1009-21.

"Frontiers and Nations in Africa," Mizan, II, 7 (July-August, 1960), 10-13.

Gasteyger, Curt. "The Soviet Union and the Tiers Monde," Survey, 43 (August, 1962), 10-22.

Gregor, James. "African Socialism, Socialism and Fascism: An Appraisal," The Review of Politics, XXIX, 3 (July, 1967), 324-53.

Griffith, William. "Africa," Survey, 54 (January, 1965), 168-89.

Gungwu, Wang. "With Time Comes Understanding," Problems of Communism, XIII, 1 (January-February, 1964), 20-22.

Hodnett, Grey. "What's in a Nation?," Problems of Communism, XVI, 5 (September-October, 1967), 2-15.

Holdsworth, Mary. "African Studies in the USSR," _African Affairs, No. 1_. London: Chatto and Windus, 1961.

Howard, Peter. "The Definition of a Nation: A Discussion in 'Voprosy Istorii,'" _Central Asian Review_, XV, 1 (1967), 26-36.

Howe, Russell. "Africa: A Decade Back, A Decade Hence," _Survey_, 71 (Winter-Spring, 1969), 68-74.

Idenburg, P. J. "Political Structural Development in Tropical Africa," _Orbis_, XI, 1 (Spring, 1967), 256-70.

"Ideological Acrobatics," _Mizan_, VII, 3 (March, 1965), 1-6.

W. K. "The Agrarian Question," _Survey_, 43 (August, 1962), 31-43.

Kapil, Ravi. "On the Conflict Potential of Inherited Boundaries in Africa," _World Politics_, XVIII, 4 (July, 1966), 656-73.

Keep, John. "The Soviet Union and the Third World," _Survey_, 72 (Summer, 1969), 19-38.

Klinghoffer, Arthur. "The USSR and Nigeria: The Secession Question," reprinted from _Africa Report_ (February, 1968), in _Mizan_, X, 2 (March-April, 1968), 64-70.

Kolarz, Walter. "The Fate of Soviet Nationalities," _Problems of Communism_, X, 1 (January-February, 1961), 48-51.

_____. "The West African Scene," _Problems of Communism_, X, 6 (November-December, 1961), 15-23.

Lang, Nicolas. "Nouveaux aspects de la politique sovietique en Afrique noire," _Est et Ouest_, December 1-15, 1967, pp. 1-4.

Lefever, Ernest. "State-Building in Tropical Afri-
    ca," Orbis, XII, 4 (Winter, 1969), 984-1003.

Legum, Colin. "What Kind of Radicalism for Afri-
    ca?," Foreign Affairs, LXIII, 2 (January,
    1965), 237-50.

Legvold, Robert. "The Soviet Union and Senegal,"
    Mizan, VIII, 4 (July-August, 1966), 161-70.

"Mali," Mizan, VIII, 3 (May-June, 1966), 127-29.

"More Soviet Thoughts on African Nationalism,"
    Mizan, III, 6 (June, 1961), 15-17.

Morison, David. "Soviet Views on Customary Law in
    Tropical Africa," Mizan, XI, 2 (March-April,
    1969), 100-104.

Mosely, Philip E. "Soviet Policy in the Developing
    Countries," Foreign Affairs, XLIII, 1 (October,
    1964), 87-98.

"Nationalism: A New Soviet Appraisal," Mizan, IV,
    3 (March, 1962), 5-12.

"Nigeria," Mizan, VIII, 3 (May-June, 1966), 130-31.

"The Peasants and the Working Class," Mizan, IV, 11
    (December, 1962), 2-9.

Pennar, Jaan. "The Arabs, Marxism and Moscow: An
    Historical Survey," Bulletin of the Institute
    for the Study of the USSR, XVI, 10 (October,
    1969), 16-30.

Pipes, Richard. "Bolshevik National Theory Before
    1917," Problems of Communism, II, 5 (1953),
    22-27.

_____. "The Forces of Nationalism," Problems of
    Communism, XIII, 1 (January-February, 1964),
    1-6.

_____. "'Solving' the Nationality Problem,"
Problems of Communism, XVI, 5 (September-
October, 1967), 125-31.

Pistrak, L. "Soviet Views on Africa," Problems of
Communism, XI, 2 (March-April, 1962), 24-31.

"Pointers from the 23rd CPSU Congress," Mizan,
VIII, 3 (May-June, 1966), 95-100.

"Policy and Ideology," Mizan, IV, 7 (July-August,
1962), 13-18.

Possony, Stefan. "Nationalism and the Ethnic Factor," Orbis, X, 4 (Winter, 1967), 1214-32.

"Potekhin on African Frontiers," Mizan, VI, 4
(April, 1964), 10-12.

Pye, Lucian. "Soviet and American Styles in Foreign Aid," Orbis, IV, 2 (Summer, 1960), 159-73.

Ra'anan, Uri. "Moscow and the Third World," Problems of Communism, XIV, 1 (January-February,
1965), 22-31.

_____. "Soviet Tactics in the Third World,"
Survey, 57 (October, 1965), 26-37.

"Regimes of French-Speaking African Countries,"
Mizan, VI, 7 (July-August, 1964), 1-10.

Rywkin, Michael. "Central Asia and the Price of
Sovietization," Problems of Communism, XIII,
1 (January-February, 1964), 7-15.

Schwartz, J., and Keech, W. "Group Influence and
the Policy Process in the Soviet Union," American Political Science Review, LXII, 3 (September, 1968), 840-85.

Schwarz, Solomon. "Self-Determination Under the
Communist Regime," Problems of Communism, II
5 (1953), 18-24.

_____. "The Soviet Concept and Conquest of National Cultures," Problems of Communism, II, 6 (1953), 41-45.

"Second International Congress of Africanists, Dakar 1967," Mizan, X, 1 (January-February, 1968), 1-13.

"Some Features of Soviet African Studies," Mizan, IV, 9 (October, 1962), 2-12.

"The Soviet Approach to Islam," Mizan, II, 8 (September, 1960), 2-9.

"The Soviet Dilemma," Mizan, VIII, 2 (March-April, 1966), 49-52.

"Soviet Notions about the Peasant Commune in Africa," Mizan, VI, 2 (February, 1964), 7-20.

"Soviet Thoughts on Nigeria's Crisis," Mizan, IX, 4 (July-August, 1967), 174-77.

"Soviet Views on Nigeria," Mizan, IX, 2 (March-April, 1967), 70-74.

"Soviet Views on 'the Religious Factor,'" Mizan, VIII, 4 (July-August, 1966), 174-81.

"Soviet Writing on Ghana: An Introduction," Mizan, II, 11 (December, 1960), 17-23.

Stein, Michael. "Federal Political Systems and Federal Societies," World Politics, XX, 4 (July, 1968), 721-47.

"Sudan," Mizan, VIII, 3 (May-June, 1966), 134-35.

Taborsky, Edward. "The Communist Parties of the Third World in Soviet Strategy," Orbis, XII, 2 (Summer, 1968), 128-48.

"Thoughts on Peasant Unrest in Africa," Mizan, VII, 8 (September, 1965), 8-9.

Tillett, Lowell. "Nationalism and History," Prob-
    lems of Communism, XVI, 5 (September-October,
    1967), 36-45.

Urban, Peter. "A Soviet Discussion on the Concept
    of Nationhood," Bulletin of the Institute for
    the Study of the USSR, XIV, 5 (May, 1967),
    37-48.

_____. "The Twentieth Party Congress and the
    National Question," Belorussian Review (Munich),
    4 (1957), 83-95.

"The USSR and Africa in 1965," Mizan, VII, 5 (May,
    1965), 1-10.

"The USSR and Africa in 1966," Mizan, VIII, 1
    (January-February, 1966), 38-44.

"The USSR and the Developing Countries. A Discus-
    sion in Moscow," Special Issue of Mizan, VI,
    10 (November, 1964), 33 pages.

"The USSR and the War in Nigeria," Mizan, XI, 1
    (January-February, 1969), 31-38.

Valkenier, Elizabeth Kridl. "New Trends in Soviet
    Economic Relations with the Third World,"
    World Politics, XXII, 3 (April, 1970), 415-32.

_____. "Recent Trends in Soviet Research on the
    Developing Countries," World Politics, XX, 4
    (July, 1968), 644-59.

Vardys, V. Stanley, "Communism and Nationalities:
    Soviet Nation Building," Paper Delivered at
    the Sixty-fifth Annual Meeting of the American
    Political Science Association, New York, Sep-
    tember, 1969.

_____. "How the Baltic Republics Fare in the
    Soviet Union," Foreign Affairs, LXIV, 3 (April,
    1966), 512-17.

von Stackelberg, George. "Soviet African Studies
     as a Weapon of Soviet Policy," Bulletin of the
     Institute for the Study of the USSR, VII, 9
     (September, 1960), 3-14.

Wheeler, Geoffrey. "Asian Studies in the Soviet
     Union," Central Asian Review, XIV, 3 (1966),
     232-40.

_____. "The Muslims of Central Asia," Problems
     of Communism, XVI, 5 (September-October, 1967),
     72-81.

_____. "National and Religious Consciousness in
     Soviet Islam," Survey, 66 (January, 1968),
     67-76.

_____. "Nationalities Policy: A New Phase?,"
     Survey, 57 (October, 1965), 38-46.

Wilhelm, W. "Soviet Central Asia: Development of
     a Backward Area," Foreign Policy Reports, Feb-
     ruary 1, 1950, pp. 218-28.

Williams, David. "How Deep the Split in West Afri-
     ca?," Foreign Affairs, XL, 1 (October, 1961),
     118-27.

Yellon, R. A. "The Winds of Change," Mizan, IX, 2
     (March-April, 1967), 51-57.

Yurchenko, A. "The New Party Program and Current
     Soviet Views on the Nationality Question,"
     Studies on the Soviet Union, IV, 4 (1965),
     211-24.